SPECIAL COUNSEL

The Life of DeVier Pierson

BY
BOB BURKE

SERIES EDITOR: GINI MOORE CAMPBELL

ASSOCIATE EDITOR: ERIC DABNEY

OKLAHOMA *TRACKMAKER* SERIES

OKLAHOMA HERITAGE ASSOCIATION

CONTENTS

ACKNOWLEDGMENTS

It was a massive project to correctly and adequately tell the story of DeVier Pierson and his many contributions to Oklahoma and the law.

My editors, Gini Moore Campbell and Eric Dabney, guided the project with precision. I am thankful to Steve Rice at the University of Oklahoma College of Law and Linda Lynn, Melissa Hayer, Mary Phillips, Robin Davison, and Billie Harry at the Oklahoma Publishing Company for help in locating photographs. William Welge, Michael Dean, and Rodger Harris at the Oklahoma Historical Society gave research assistance.

Most of all, I am indebted to DeVier and Shirley Pierson for opening their lives to me. It was a great deal of fun to select photographs and review with them their long life together. This is a story of a great Oklahoman that needed to be told.

—*Bob Burke* 2009

PUBLICATION MADE POSSIBLE BY:

Mr. & Mrs. G. T. Blankenship
David L. & Molly Shi Boren
Thomas R. Brett
David Busby
Donald & Nancy de Brier
Nancy & Ed de Cordova
John W. Drake
Faith & Randy Everest
Dan & Sarah Hogan
Joel Jankowsky
Lynda & Dale Laurance

J. Larry Nichols
University of Oklahoma College of Law
Barbara & William G. Paul
H. E. Rainbolt
Jan & Bill Robinson
Hugh & Ann Roff
DeAnn & Lee Allan Smith
Judge & Mrs. Ralph G. Thompson
Bob & Nancy Torray
Jean Marie Warren
Gordon D. Williams

PREFACE

I was flattered when Bob Burke told me that he wanted to write my biography as part of the Oklahoma Trackmaker Series of the Oklahoma Heritage Association. Mindful of the Shakespearean admonition that the recollections of old men are often "remembered with advantage," this project has nonetheless caused me to take a look back at my life in some organized fashion for the use of my eminent biographer. While I believe that every life is interesting and that each of us has a story to tell, the reader will have to decide whether my story adds very much to Oklahoma lore.

It is certainly the story of a loyal Oklahoman by both birth and choice. I am a product of the public schools of Oklahoma City and my study at the University of Oklahoma, scattered over almost eight years, as both an undergraduate and at the College of Law. My educational experience at OU, both inside and outside the classroom, was one of the great formative experiences of my life. I have often said through the years that, while I may have been out-lawyered, I never thought that I had been out-educated. Oklahoma always has been home to me; my longtime Oklahoma friends have been among the most important friendships of my life. It has been a source of joy to maintain so many of these Oklahoma ties.

I do believe that my professional life has been eventful. I am a lawyer by training and inclination. Most of my adult life has been spent in providing legal and policy advice to those with actual or perceived needs. For over half a century, I have been counsel to an interesting and highly diverse group of clients, including one President of the United States, the United States Congress, a high government official facing charges of criminal activity, a substantial number of large public companies with problems with the federal government, other companies who were feeling the impact of major economic issues on corporate America, and two sovereign foreign nations. I have some interesting tales to tell.

There is an old Chinese saying—not clear whether it is intended as a blessing or a curse—that "may you live in interesting times." I have certainly done so. My boyhood and adolescence were marked by the Great Depression and World War II. I remember the attack on Pearl Harbor, the death of Franklin D. Roosevelt and the dropping of the atomic bomb on Hiroshima and Nagasaki. As a young man, I spent a year in Korea, including visits to the newly-established truce line, seeing first-hand the effects of that conflict. I met John F. Kennedy in 1958, became involved in his 1960 presidential campaign, and, by happenstance, was in Dallas when he was assassinated in 1963.

During the next five years, I had the opportunity to participate more directly in public affairs. I moved to Washington, D.C., as chief counsel to a special Senate-House committee on Congressional reorganization. I was President Lyndon B. Johnson's counsel during the last two years of his presidency, participating in the final implementation of the Great Society, helping to respond to the social unrest of the 1960s, witnessing the destructive force of the Vietnam War on the Johnson presidency, playing a small part in an effort to find a new path to ending that war, watching portions of Washington burn in the aftermath of the assassination of Dr. Martin Luther King, Jr., helping to deal with the protection of presidential candidates in the aftermath of Robert Kennedy's assassination, and telling President Johnson good-bye as he was greeting Richard Nixon on the morning of the Nixon inaugural.

Since leaving government service, I have spent the past 40 years in the nation's capital in the practice of law. During this time, I have witnessed and, from time to time, participated in a small way, in the events that shaped the remainder of the twentieth century and its aftermath—the first man on the moon, the trauma of Watergate, the resignation of President Nixon, the defeat in Vietnam, the Iran-Contra affair, the end of the Cold War, the rise of China, the horror of September 11th, and our two wars in the Middle East. These cosmic events had a profound effect on our country and on each of us. I have vivid memories of each of them and strong views as to the wisdom of our actions on some of them.

I owe any successes in my life to many others. They include my parents, my public speaking and debate teachers, professors at the University of Oklahoma who taught me about the world and the rule of law, my professional mentors, and my colleagues and team-mates in both government and private practice who shared in the triumphs. I take sole responsibility for the failures.

As I look back on this life, I am acutely aware that, when all is said and done, the most enduring blessing for each of us is family and friends. I am indebted most of all to Shirley, my wife of more than 50 years and a woman of great love and patience, for making so many of these good things possible. I take great pride in our three very adult children and our six beloved grandchildren, all of whom have many exciting chapters ahead in their own lives. My wonderful friends through the years have enriched my life in every important way.

If you have some time on your hands, I invite you to come along on this life journey.

—*W. DeVier Pierson*

CHAPTER ONE

A STRONG HERITAGE

I am an Oklahoman by birth and choice.

—DeVier Pierson

When a new baby boy was born to the Pierson family at the local hospital in Pawhuska, Oklahoma, on August 12, 1931, he was, with no prior consultation, given the name Welcome DeVier Pierson, Jr.

For more than three quarters of a century DeVier has been trying to live down—or least modify—this mouthful of a name. He was able to discard "Junior" before "it became a major embarrassment." In college, he was called DeVier or Drew, in honor of the best known columnist of the day, Drew Pearson. As a lawyer, he is known as W. DeVier Pierson, surely a more distinguished name for a distinguished calling.

Only the United States military and the Social Security Administration, with their fetish for first names, have proved to be an insurmountable problem. For his entire life, DeVier has searched in vain to determine the origin of his name. He has no better explanation than assuming his grandparents were so happy to see his father, they named him Welcome, and then found the name DeVier in a Sears Roebuck catalog.[1]

Welcome DeVier Pierson, Sr., and his wife, Frances Ratliff Pierson, were proud Sooners. Most members of the family lived out their lives in Oklahoma. DeVier and his wife, Shirley, are among the few Piersons who have strayed very far from home.

DeVier's pioneer roots run deep. His paternal great grandparents were George and Mary Pierson. George was a carpenter, cabinet maker, and cider mill operator in New York. In 1880, he moved his family west to Kansas with $500 cash and high hopes. He farmed the Kansas prairie and struggled with his neighbors to support his family. DeVier's grandfather, Frank Pierson, was born in 1868 in Watertown, New York, three years after the end of the Civil War. He was of Scotch-Irish and English ancestry. In a letter he wrote to his family at the age of 70, he bragged that he had "lots of Irish blood and it's proud I am of it."[2]

Frank was the oldest of four boys. He had to grow up quickly the year he turned eight years old because his mother died on Christmas Eve. Not only did he assume responsibility for his younger brothers, he became the man of the house when his father and youngest brother died of pneumonia during the winter of 1891. To support the family, Frank worked for $10 to $20 a month as a cowboy. As a result, his schooling was limited and ended in the eighth grade. However, before his mother died, she had taught him to read and write and he became a surprisingly literate person.[3]

Frank's first contact with the future state of Oklahoma was when he herded ponies for his ranch boss from Mexico to Kansas. On the trip in 1883 he camped near where Oklahoma City would become an overnight town six years later in the Land Run of 1889.

Frank liked what he saw in Oklahoma. In 1893, he participated in the Cherokee Outlet or Cherokee Strip opening. The September 16, 1893 opening was Oklahoma's fourth and largest land run. The land had been ceded to the Cherokees when the tribe was relocated from the southeastern United States along the Trail of Tears in the 1830s. After cattle ranchers began coveting the land, the Cherokees agreed to sell the land to the United States government at a price ranging from $1.40 to $2.50 per acre.[4]

On the day of the land run, tens of thousands gathered at makeshift booths constructed by cavalry troops. Historian Alvin Turner wrote, "Dry weather, choking dust, and smoke from nearby prairie fires afflicted the shuffling crowds. At least ten people died of heat stroke."[5]

Frank and three friends called the Cherokee Outlet opening "the greatest horserace of all time." They began the run near Honeywell, Kansas. Frank and his friends lined up with thousands of other pioneers looking for free land. He later wrote about the adventure:

When the shot was fired to start, and that line broke, it was almost like the roll of distant thunder. The whole earth seemed to tremble, and the black off the burned prairie rolled up and nearly blinded the sun. Men and horses all went wild. Some were shooting in the air, some were singing, others were yelling. Horses were stepping into holes, breaking their legs. Wagons and carts turned over and men were hollering for help. Cooking utensils and saddles were thrown from wagons and were scattered on the prairie. No one could stop to recover their property, for they would have been killed.[6]

Frank and his friends rode 25 miles in less than 90 minutes to stake their 160-acre claims. Then they traveled by horseback to the government land office in Perry, Oklahoma, and recorded their claims. Frank called Perry a town "no place for a minister's son." After dutifully proving to the government he owned his new parcel of land, Frank built a sod house and banded with his neighbors to guard against claim jumpers.

Ranching in the Cherokee Outlet was hard work. Because of chaotic conditions surrounding the opening of the land, towns were over-built and farmers went broke on land that was unsuitable for farming. By 1895, Frank gave up on the land, sold his claim, and returned to Kansas.

In 1896, Frank married Rose McBride and planted corn and wheat on rented land. When farming waned, he worked in a hardware store and saw mill. He was working in Medicine Lodge, Kansas, when DeVier's father, known as Welcome or W.D. Pierson, was born in 1899. Frank worked as a section foreman on the railroad. In 1906, he was working for the Kingman Milling Company in Kingman, Kansas, when he lost his right leg in an accident. After an eight-month recovery, he returned for a period of time as a warehouse foreman, but eventually was laid off. He sued his employer, but lost the case. It was before Kansas had a system in place to compensate injured workers.[7]

When Welcome was a teenager, his family moved to Oklahoma. He graduated from Nowata High School where he was a classmate of Ralph and Lee Thompson, Jr.—later distinguished Oklahoma attorneys. The bond of friendship between the Pierson and Thompson families has endured for two generations. DeVier has maintained special friendships with Lee—one of his closest friends in high school—and Ralph, a member of the Oklahoma legislature and longtime federal judge in Oklahoma City who lived next door to DeVier's parents in their later years.

Welcome enlisted in the United States Army in 1918 in the closing months of World War I. After discharge, he entered the University of Oklahoma (OU) in Norman—OU would become "the holy grail for Pierson education." Taking advantage of an accelerated college studies program available to returning veterans, Welcome completed his undergraduate degree and graduated from the OU College of Law with the class of 1922, a distinguished class that included Judge John Brett, legendary OU Law professor Maurice Merrill, and others.[8]

Frances Ratliff Pierson, DeVier's mother, was born in Hennessey, Oklahoma, in 1903 and lived there until her parents, Frank and Martha "Mattie" Viola Brown Ratliff, moved to Oklahoma City. Frank had moved to Hennessey, Oklahoma Territory, as a boy and moved back there to enter the local Ford agency business with his father. Mattie was born in Illinois in 1877, the daughter of a family that started in Pennsylvania and moved in the Western migration.

Frank and Mattie were married in Hennessey in 1900. The local newspaper called the marriage a significant event of the new century. *The Hennessey Clipper* said, "The bride and groom are among those of our best respected young people, the bride having formed a large circle of friends by her services as clerk in Ehler's and Crider's stores the past two years, and the groom is…well-known as an energetic and rustling businessman." Frank and Mattie rustled up DeVier's mother three years later.

DeVier's maternal grandfather, Frank Leon Ratliff, moved to Oklahoma Territory as a young boy.

Mattie Brown Ratliff, DeVier's maternal grandmother, was born in Illinois and moved west with her family.

Frances enrolled at OU in 1920 and graduated with a bachelor's degree in fine arts in 1924. Frances was a leader in everything she attempted. At OU she was president of Alpha Chi Omega sorority, president of the women's Pan-Hellenic Association, and a member of the honorary music and literary societies. *The Sooner* yearbook also listed her as a member of the Women's Chorus, the Oratorical Council, and the Young Women's Christian Association (YWCA). Frances was a fine pianist and later in life taught piano to a wide range of young people, including her granddaughter.[9]

Welcome and Frances were married on June 27, 1925, in the home of her parents at 1435 Northwest 40th Street in Oklahoma City. *The Daily Oklahoman* called the wedding "one of much interest" because of "the wide acquaintance of the young folk" and the fact that "both the bride and bridegroom are well-known over the state, having graduated from the University of Oklahoma." [10]

The newspaper story also cited Frances' many honors and leadership positions at OU. After the wedding, Welcome and Frances left for a honeymoon at a resort on Lake Michigan near Chicago before returning to their new home in the Virginia Apartments in Pawhuska.

Pawhuska was born in 1872 when the Osage Indian Agency was established on Bird Creek. The settlement was named for Paw-Hiu-Skah, chief of the Thorny-Valley People, one of the Osage tribe's five physical divisions that lived nearby. America's first Boy Scout troop was organized at Pawhuska in 1909. [11]

By the 1920s, Pawhuska had been booming for more than a decade after the discovery of oil in Osage County, making the Osage tribe the richest per capita people on earth. In 1920, at the peak of oil production attended by famous oilmen such as Frank Phillips, William G. Skelly, and E.W. Marland, Pawhuska had a population of more than 6,000. Unfortunately, the Piersons had no Osage blood.

By 1925, Pawhuska was the Pierson family home and it made sense for Welcome to establish his law practice there. Welcome's sister, Lola, had married a Pawhuska man, Greer Streetman, who ran a sporting goods store on Main Street. Frank's other sister, Muriel, and her husband, John Riley, split their time between Pawhuska and Oklahoma City, running a successful oil field machinery business.

Welcome and Frances enjoyed the closeness of family in

DeVier's mother, Frances Ratliff Pierson, as a young woman. She had an outstanding record at the University of Oklahoma and was an accomplished pianist.

DeVier's parents, Welcome D. and Frances Pierson were married in 1925 in Oklahoma City.

Pawhuska. Frances' family was scattered. Her brother, Jack, had moved to California, brother Bob was living in Bartlesville, and her third brother, Gordon, became a career officer in the United States Army and was stationed all over the world. When Frances was about to give birth to her new baby in 1931, the Great Depression was in full swing in Oklahoma. It began with the stock market crash in 1929 and worsened as banks failed, stores and factories closed, and millions of Americans were left jobless and homeless. Oklahoma's economy suffered mightily. Farmers had little or no income— foreclosures were daily events.[12]

The weather made the Great Depression, the worst and longest period of high unemployment and low business activity in modern history, even more unbearable. Oklahoma was wracked with dust storms. Sand blew in such quantities that travelers lost their way, airports closed, trains stopped, and chickens went to roost at noon in the dusty darkness. Many Oklahomans left, headed west for job opportunities, a tragedy chronicled in John Steinbeck's *The Grapes of Wrath*.

However, the Piersons stayed put in Oklahoma. That is where they were when DeVier entered the world in Pawhuska on August 12, 1931.

CHAPTER TWO

A HAPPY BOYHOOD

I was a Depression baby, although I never realized it.
—DeVier Pierson

DeVier's first recollection was of a moving van in the driveway of the family home on Leahy Street in Pawhuska when he was two years old. A worker was loading his hobby horse onto the van for a move to Oklahoma's capital city, Oklahoma City. DeVier's father was leaving his small town law practice to take a job as assistant attorney general in the office of Oklahoma Attorney General J. Berry King who had been elected in 1930 as a Democrat. In the same election, William H. "Alfalfa Bill" Murray was elected governor of Oklahoma.

DeVier was born in Pawhuska but his family moved to Oklahoma City when he was two years old.

Welcome D. Pierson in his Oklahoma City law office in the 1930s. After serving as an assistant state attorney general, he began private practice with the firm of Short & Pierson.

The Piersons moved to a house just four blocks from the State Capitol at 923 Northeast 20th Street. It would be DeVier's legal residence until he married nearly 25 years later. The house was more than adequate for the family. There was a living room, dining room, and kitchen, three small bedrooms, and a small bathroom at the end of the hall. There was no air conditioning, but large fans kept the hot Oklahoma summer air moving. There was a detached single-car garage and a large back yard.

The obvious good fortunes of the Pierson family in Oklahoma City contrasted with a simpler life DeVier saw on trips back to Pawhuska to see his grandparents and other relatives. His grandparents had no indoor plumbing—the outhouse was a respectful distance in the back. Water was pumped from a well near the back door and heated on a wood stove for bathing, cooking, and doing dishes.[1]

Even in Oklahoma City, many modern conveniences had not yet arrived. There were no refrigerators so DeVier often accompanied his father in their 1935 Oldsmobile sedan to the ice plant to pick up blocks of ice for the icebox at home. Groceries were purchased at a tiny market three blocks away. Milk was delivered each morning by a milkman in a horse-driven carriage. DeVier's normal mode of transportation to any destination beyond a block or two was by bicycle or trolley. The nearest trolley stop was only two blocks away at Northeast 22nd Street and Kelley Avenue.[2]

It was easy for anyone to see that the primary economic activity around the State Capitol, besides the running of government, was oil and gas. A string of producing wells on

Lincoln Boulevard from the Capitol to Northeast 13th Street was unique. There was an oil well on a vacant lot immediately behind the Pierson home—the light from the flared natural gas lit up DeVier's bedroom at night.

One of DeVier's parents' first acts after moving to Oklahoma City was to have their son baptized at the First Methodist Church in downtown Oklahoma City. From an early age, he attended Sunday School at the church and found the Bible stories interesting. He occasionally was so intrigued by a story that he read from the family Bible when he arrived home. Later, he wrote a piece at school on the meaning of Easter, "which showed some spiritual sensitivity." DeVier's only negative recollection of church was the inclination of his parents to suggest that some portion of his allowance be placed in the offering plate.[3]

When he was five years old, DeVier began grade school at Lincoln Elementary School at Northeast 11th Street and Lincoln Boulevard. The building still stands, housing a part of the Oklahoma School of Science and Mathematics. If the weather was nice, he and several children from the neighborhood walked the mile to school—first accompanied by one or more parents—then alone.

Grade school provided happy memories. In particular, he remembers his first grade teacher, Miss Mary Monfort, affectionately called "Miss Mary" by her students. She was only about 20 years old and DeVier thought her to be surely one of the most beautiful women in the world.[4]

DeVier made a number of neighborhood friends on the long walks to and from Lincoln Elementary. Roger Bob Clay, who died too early in life from multiple sclerosis; Roger McDuffey, who was later killed in an automobile accident while an OU student; and Pat Wallace, considered by DeVier to be the prettiest girl in the neighborhood, were regulars on the walks.

Outside the classroom, the normal games of grade school kids were played. DeVier received his first taste of current events by trading bubble gum "current events" cards that contained photographs and explanation of important events of the day. The card that still sticks in DeVier's memory is a card describing the massacre of hundreds of thousands of people in Nanjing, China, by the Japanese in 1937, a military action that many historians believe initiated the march toward World War II.[5]

Although DeVier had many friends, he was firmly "a loner." When he came home from school he usually retreated to his bedroom to listen to his radio. Sometimes he took his radio into the darkness of his closet to create the proper mood to be transported to other times and places by Captain Midnight, Terry and the Pirates, the Lone Ranger, the Shadow, and the Green Hornet. He faithfully ate cereals with the Lone Ranger on the box and ordered the Jack Armstrong Hike-a-Meter and any other gadget that was offered by one of his superheroes. He bought comic books to learn more about Superman, Batman, and the Green Lantern. For his entire life, the fantasy world has intrigued him, and one of his favorite parts of the newspaper is still the comic pages.[6]

DeVier has always been an avid reader of fiction and nonfiction. From the time he could read, he loved Greek and Roman mythology and purchased every book he could find on the gods. That hobby became extreme. He cut the books into pieces and made an enormous binder filled with information on each Roman god and his Greek counterpart. The destruction of the books did not always please DeVier's parents.

At a tender age, DeVier became acquainted with Charles Dickens and Louisa May Alcott at the Lincoln School library. However, he reached beyond his understanding when he checked out *Moby Dick*. Thinking it was an adventure story about a man and a whale, he struggled. After he heard the librarian say, "Can you imagine little DeVier reading Moby Dick," he tried again to no avail to decipher Melville and his allegory.[7]

Writing came naturally to DeVier. At age eight, thinking no small thoughts, he decided to write a series of children's books which he modestly identified as "The Conner Boys Series." He wrote a short story called "The Hidden Treasure" starring Jim and Bill Conner on a trip to Africa where they encountered the villain, Boris Kaldof, aka "The Hawk," who, in DeVier's words was, "Chief of the Underworld, the King of Evil, and was wanted for serious crimes in the Scotland Yard." In the short tale, the Conner boys triumphed over The Hawk as a result of the courage of their faithful dog Ginger.

Even though the Conner boys series was good reading for eight-year-old boys, there was no commercial success to DeVier's early literary efforts. However, he continued to write short pieces on a variety of subjects. When he was ten, he "ground out a series of one-pagers" on the meaning of Easter, the beauty of spring, and an "Ode to My Dad as My

Best Friend." Mr. Pierson may have looked at the tribute with mixed views. DeVier wrote, "He isn't so handsome, but I don't want a movie star for a father," and "He has faults but he is my dad and I'm satisfied."[8]

DeVier's greatest childhood hero was author and adventurer Richard Halliburton. After graduating from Princeton University in the early 1920s, Halliburton "bummed his way" around the world on a freighter and lived a life of high adventure which he recorded in five books. DeVier read all the books before he was ten. Halliburton told of swimming the Panama Canal, jumping from the sacrificial ledge of the Incas at Chichen Itza, climbing in the Alps, discovering the pink city of Petra in Jordan, being arrested in the reflecting pool in front of the Taj Mahal, flying a rickety bi-plane across Russia, and much more. He died while trying to sail a junk from Shanghai to San Francisco. Halliburton brought the wonders of the world to a young Oklahoma boy who had never been outside the boundaries of the state.

DeVier was an only child for his first years, until his sister, Carol, was born in 1940. Once Carol outgrew her crib, she was moved into DeVier's room, causing him to reluctantly share his valuable territory. Throughout his childhood, DeVier treasured the privacy of his room for reading and listening to the radio.

DeVier did well in school. Lincoln teachers, long before the days of no-fault grading, used narratives rather than letter grades. He received good marks in reading, social science, and speaking, although one teacher noted in her evaluation, "He talks too much." In the category of "keeping hands off others," he drew an unsatisfactory mark one semester.[9]

One of DeVier's earliest adventures involved a runaway milk wagon. One afternoon while walking home from school, he saw a milk wagon speeding by, pulled by a runaway horse and with no driver. He chased the wagon, hopped aboard, and tugged on the reins to slowly bring it to a stop. A few minutes later, the "huffing and puffing" driver arrived. DeVier was rewarded for his "exceptional bravery" with three free bottles of milk and a carton of ice cream. The story took on gargantuan proportions in future decades as DeVier told it to his friends.

DeVier, at age 10, already had begun taking public speaking lessons from Mary Gray Thompson.

DeVier and his friends enjoyed riding their bicycles to the Ritz Theater at Northeast 13th and Kelly Avenue on Saturday afternoons. On a good day, they could see a double feature, newsreel, cartoon, short subject, and a serial—all for a dime. His favorite serials were the Green Hornet and the Lone Ranger. "Life was good," DeVier remembered, "the hero was always in dire straits at the end of the serial, but miraculously was found to have survived the following Saturday."[10]

DeVier's mother was relentless in her search for his self improvement, "an act of love" for which he will always be grateful. She sent him for speech lessons with Mary Gray Thompson, one of the nation's finest private speech teachers of the day. DeVier had a slight lisp—the rhyme Lucy Lockett came out Wucy Wockett—until he was rehabilitated during speech sessions at the Municipal Auditorium where Mrs. Thompson's studio was located.

Mary Gray Thompson was one of the handful of people DeVier believes molded his life. She taught him everything about speech, from preparation to technique. He learned how to organize and write an oration, how to speak extemporaneously, and how to stand and gesture. Her genius allowed DeVier to become a skilled speaker.

The speech lessons were not all work—a lot of fun was involved. He enjoyed his friendship with fellow student Mary James, who later married Judge Tom Brett, although Mary called DeVier's hand gesture while speaking "the claw." The association with Mrs. Thompson gave DeVier a short career in radio. He received a Social Security card so he could be paid as a regular member of the cast who read the comic strips on WKY Radio each Sunday. DeVier was delighted to see sound effects created in the studio, from rain to doors opening and sirens. Sometimes he burst into laughter while he was reading his lines.[11]

DeVier formed a special friendship with fellow eight-year-old Terry Diacon. "It was the two of us against the world," DeVier remembered. They formed the Sports Club, later named the Aviation Sports Club, because of the popularity of airplanes during World War II. The club operated from a small clubhouse built by DeVier's father behind the family garage.

"The most unique feature of the club was that DeVier and I were the only members," Diacon remembered.[12] The two boys alternated the positions of president and secretary. The club had bylaws, an official color, red, and an official hobby, stamp collecting. There was even a demerit system with fines for neglect of courtesy, vulgar actions, and failing to have required reports on schedule. Minutes were kept at regular club meetings. Among the rules were "no chewing candy while meetings are going on" and "no whispering unless you ask permission and tell what it is about." [13]

Each meeting began with the pledge of allegiance to the flag, the reading of selected Bible verses, singing, and an occasional joke. The handwritten minutes of one meeting in August, 1943, report that "DeVier read Psalms 1. We sang 'Carry Me Back to Old Virginia.'" [14] As the winds of war were discussed by their parents and teachers, the songs grew more patriotic. Campfire favorites gave way to the "Marine Hymn" and "You're in the Army Now." The club endured until 1944, giving way to a more broad-based social schedule for the boys. [15]

In the summer of 1941, when DeVier was ten, he began attending Camp Classen, the YMCA summer camp near Turner Falls in southern Oklahoma. He was an enthusiastic, but mediocre, athlete as the youth participated in softball, volleyball, table tennis, boating, and swimming. A big hit for DeVier were the evening camp fires with jokes and ghost stories. There was no homesickness for him—his letters to home begged for permission to stay longer.

DeVier and his fellow campers were housed in cabins financed by and named for leading Oklahoma businessmen such as C.R. Anthony, Frank Buttram, and Virgil Browne.

One year DeVier stayed in a cabin which had been donated by ten persons of lesser means—it was called the "Poor boys' Cabin."

While at Camp Classen, DeVier met the teenage crafts director who helped him make a belt for his father. The teenager was Bill Crowe of Oklahoma City. William J. Crowe became one of Oklahoma's most prominent people. After a distinguished career in the United States Navy he served as Chairman of the Joint Chiefs of Staff in the administration of Presidents Ronald Reagan and George H.W. Bush and as President Bill Clinton's Ambassador to the Court of St. James. Crowe and DeVier became lifetime friends.[16]

When Admiral Crowe presented DeVier for induction into the Oklahoma Hall of Fame in 2002, he recalled their first meeting at Camp Classen. Admiral Crowe said, "DeVier's work on his father's belt convinced me that his talents must surely lie in a different direction."[17]

Scouting was another important part of DeVier's young life. He joined a Cub Scout pack at age nine with his mother as den mother. DeVier was selected to serve in a Cub Scout honor guard during the Oklahoma City visit of child actor Johnny Sheffield, who played Boy in the Tarzan movies. DeVier remembered, "He was my idol, a strapping young fellow who could swim alongside Johnny Weismuller, swing on vines through the trees, and basically do everything I could not do. I thought it would be the biggest day of my life."[18]

On the day of Boy's visit, DeVier was elated to sit next to the star in front of the Municipal Auditorium at a booth selling war stamps. However, Sheffield did not have a good disposition and used very foul language in asking for more stamps. DeVier was shattered, finding that his idol "had feet of clay." [19]

DeVier was ten years old when the Japanese bombed Pearl Harbor on December 7, 1941, and America entered World War II. Soon he and his friends were collecting scrap metal, tin cans, waste paper, and other important materials to take to the local fire station for the war effort. His mother grew a victory garden and DeVier sometimes helped her can fruits and vegetables. The family bought war bonds and DeVier collected pennies for war stamps. He was also part of the patriotic propaganda effort. He appeared in a series of plays at Lincoln School where President Franklin Roosevelt, British Prime Minister Winston Churchill, and other Allied leaders were lauded as heroes while the students hissed at the appearance of Adolph Hitler, Benito Mussolini, and Tojo. [20]

The Pierson family showed its patriotism and love for country in various ways. At Thanksgiving and Christmas, DeVier and his father drove to the downtown YMCA and selected two or three soldiers to come home with them for a holiday dinner. Frances always had presents for the boys. DeVier remembers the day he was delivering newspapers when a woman greeted him in tears to say that President Roosevelt had died.

DeVier's Uncle Bob Ratliff was in the military and his wife, Joyce, stayed with DeVier and his family for much of the war. On an awful day in 1943, a man in uniform brought a telegram to the Pierson home. DeVier was whisked away to a neighbor's house across the street. When he returned, he was told that that the telegram carried news that Uncle Bob had been killed when he stepped on a landmine while on patrol to get water for his camp in Bougainville in the South Pacific. The sadness in the Pierson household was unfortunately one that was repeated a half-million times in large cities and small villages around the country during the four years of World War II.[21]

CHAPTER THREE

GROWING UP

*Some of the girls were very friendly, particularly at movies
and on walks home, but they mostly seemed to be
just beyond our grasp.*

—DeVier Pierson

The rite of passage between boyhood and adolescence
for DeVier was marked primarily by completing elementary
school, which he did in May, 1943, and entering the very different environment of junior high school.

Before he started junior high, he became a full-fledged
Boy Scout at the age of 12. He was a member of Troop 29
that met on the top floor of the State Capitol just four blocks
from DeVier's home. He could not get enough of Scouting. He
earned merit badges at record pace, learning about everything
from insects to lifesaving. In May, 1945, at age 13, he became
an Eagle Scout in the Franklin Delano Roosevelt class.[1]

DeVier was active in his Boy Scout Troop 29. He is fourth from right in the second row.

DeVier's greatest love for Scouting was based on camping. Often scouts from Troop 29 camped overnight in Lincoln Park. In the summer, Boy Scout camps competed with Camp Classen for DeVier's attention. One summer he attended Camp Kickapoo, Camp Little Wolf, the Quartz Mountain Camp, and went on the Illinois River Float Trip, a trifecta of all available Boy Scout locations in Oklahoma.

In the fall of 1943, DeVier and his parents had a choice of which junior high school he would attend. He chose Webster Junior High School on Northeast 11th Street two blocks east of Lincoln. Most of DeVier's friends in the neighborhood—Roger Bob Clay, Roger McDuffey, Pat Wallace, and others—also attended Webster.[2]

DeVier still took private speech lessons from Mary Gray Thompson. Mary James, now Brett, remembered attending Mrs. Thompson's classes at the old Municipal Auditorium and the teacher's attempts at stopping DeVier from gesturing with his left hand.[3] Another member of Mrs. Thompson's class was William J. "Bill" Ross. "In our group," Ross recalled, "DeVier's eloquence outshined the rest of us. It was obvious to me that the brilliant Mrs. Thompson knew that in DeVier she had a rare jewel under her wing."[4]

As a seventh grader, DeVier won the Buttram Oratorical Contest, the premier speech competition at Webster. In a speech titled "What Does Your Government Mean to You?," DeVier waxed eloquent about American ideals:

There is no one within sound of my voice who doubts the superiority of our constitutional form of government. All of us are aware that it has permitted a more rapid and sat-

isfactory development than any form yet known to man.
But are we as conscious of the fragile fabric of which it
is woven? Do we stop to consider that it may slide through
our hands as easily and noiselessly as a delicate piece of
silk might slither through fingers and fall unnoticed on the
floor.[5]

Rules did not allow DeVier to defend his title in oratory, so he turned his attention to school plays, although his only success was a bit part in the forgettable drama "Don't Ever Grow Up."

DeVier became a member of the staff of the school newspaper, the *Webster Echo*. He was officially the sports editor, although he wrote about any subject from student dress to public affairs. He enjoyed writing so much, he often considers that he could have been happy with a life in journalism, rather than pursuing the law.[6]

After he read the book *Navy Blue and Gold*, DeVier became infatuated with the Naval Academy. He read everything on the subject and even contacted the office of Oklahoma Congressman Mike Monroney for information about applying for an appointment to Annapolis. He was jerked back to reality when he discovered that the Naval Academy was a fine engineering school with a premium on prowess in math. Because math was his weakest subject, he concluded he should stick to law or journalism.

Physically, DeVier was small, in his own words, "a little shrimp." His size took him "out of the running" with some of the more attractive girls at school and limited his athletic ability. He was too small to play football, could not hit well in baseball, and played only well enough in basketball to participate in pickup games. So, he learned to play golf.[7]

His father gave him a set of cut-down clubs and paid for lessons from a pro at the driving range at Northwest 36th Street and Broadway Avenue. On the way home from lessons, DeVier often stopped at the old Lincoln Boulevard golf course and played a few holes before dinner. Webster friend Leighton McIntire and DeVier often rode their bicycles to the Green Hills Course, a nine-hole layout with sand greens near Lincoln Park, where they played for 50 cents a round. Sometimes he accompanied his father to the public course in Capitol Hill. By the time DeVier was 15, he had a fairly decent golf game.[8]

His male social life was built around a pep club called "The Bulldogs." Members of the club often acted as cheerleaders at school sporting events and the Bulldogs sat as a group at school assemblies. For three years, other Bulldogs were his best friends, although that was not entirely a good thing.

The Bulldogs had a number of questionable virtues of adolescent fraternities such as hazing seventh grade pledges, occasional smoking, and jerking trolley lines from the rear of trolley cars in the neighborhood. If caught, the latter infraction would have earned the boys a trip downtown to the police station. In many ways, DeVier's ninth grade year was his year of living dangerously.[9]

As DeVier began looking at girls in an entirely different manner, his parents intervened. They and the parents of some of DeVier's friends formed an organization called the Holiday

Club which had as its members the "right" young boys and girls. DeVier learned ballroom dancing at the infamous Gertrude Cox Sims School of Dance so he would not be embarrassed at the Holiday Club's annual Christmas dance. The club had a number of well-chaperoned parties and picnics held throughout the year. Looking back, DeVier said, "Our parents were smart. The Holiday Club served two purposes. It put us with the young women of their choice, not always ours, and it kept us off the streets and away from the dreaded Bulldogs." [10]

By making the Webster Honor Society "by the skin of my teeth," DeVier and fellow Honor Society members were rewarded with a bus trip to Carlsbad Caverns, New Mexico. It was only the second time DeVier had traveled beyond the boundaries of Oklahoma.

DeVier graduated from Webster Junior High School in May, 1946. A review of the yearbook, the *Webster Echo*, shows how DeVier's life was progressing. In the prophecy section, Pat Wallace designated him as her "third husband." DeVier's resolution was "to be twice as good as I was bad last year." In his speech at the graduation ceremony, DeVier spoke on the subject of youth wanting a democratic community. [11]

CHAPTER FOUR

CROSSING TOWN TO CLASSEN

*I knew very few of my classmates at Classen and was at first
on the outside, looking in.*

—DeVier Pierson

DeVier was ready for high school. He was, by his own
estimates, a little undersized, a gifted speaker, fairly good
student, mediocre athlete, socially gregarious, and a bundle
of adolescent insecurities. In addition to that confusion, he
had several choices of where to attend high school. His home
was on the boundary between Northeast and Central High
Schools. He also could apply for a transfer to another school.
His parents looked at a number of issues.

It was not a racial question at all. All public schools under
consideration were white only—segregation under Jim Crow
Laws was still the law of the land. African American students
were in a separate system and went to Douglass High School.
It was eight years before the United States Supreme Court,
in *Brown v. Board of Education*, would strike down laws that
allowed such "separate but equal" schools.

The Piersons lived in an entirely white neighborhood
and DeVier admits that he had not given much thought to
the racial divide in the country. He had been puzzled as a
child that African Americans were relegated to sit in the back
of streetcars. Those seats were open and comfortable, and
DeVier often sat there as a matter of comfort.[1]

DeVier's mother was heavily influenced by many of

her friends who lived on the west side of Oklahoma City. She was convinced that DeVier should transfer to Classen High School so he could be "part of the right Oklahoma City environment." DeVier wanted to go to Classen for a different reason—he knew of the school's strong public speaking program. Classen had had a state championship debate team and the debate coach, C.E. "Pop" Grady, was nationally known. DeVier's public speaking mentor, Mrs. Thompson, also thought Classen was a good idea.

Classen it was. DeVier enrolled in the fall of 1946, hoping that someone else he knew might also opt for Classen. To his happy surprise, Pat Wallace, Roger Clay, and Roger McDuffey, three of his closest neighborhood friends, also chose Classen. Of utmost importance, Clay was the proud owner of a motor scooter that carried DeVier and him across town to Classen High School.

DeVier not only was pleased that these neighborhood friends were at Classen, he also discovered that his special friend from boyhood days, Terry Diacon, was there. Another Webster classmate, Chet Bynum, was in his class. But most of the students were strangers—not an ideal position for a 15-year-old with all of the classic adolescent social insecurities. These students had grown up together and tended to "travel in packs." The high school fraternities, the Phi Lams, Alpha Omegas, and Auvergne Demolays, were keys to the social kingdom, and, initially, DeVier was not part of that world.[2]

A telephone call changed DeVier's fortunes at Classen. He received a call from Mrs. John Brett, a good friend of DeVier's mother, who, after what sounded like a good

deal of arm-twisting, put young John on the line. John asked
DeVier if he would like to attend a meeting of the Auvergne
Demolays. Clearly, this was a mother-to-mother set-up. With
John as his big brother and Tom Brett as a new friend, DeVier
became a member of the Auvergnes that subsequently joined
the national high school fraternity of Kappa Alpha Pi. He was
no longer just looking in, but was now part of a social group.

It is hard to overstate how important membership in a
group was to DeVier. Many of the friends he made at Classen
have been friends for life. Fellow members of his Kappa Alpha Pi class included John Drake, Tom Brett, Lee Thompson,
Paul Lindsey, and many others. Brett became a distinguished
federal judge, Lindsey was a federal bankruptcy judge. The
class a year older than DeVier included future Oklahoma
Governor David Hall, John Brock, and John Shawver. DeVier
also developed friendships with young classmates from rival
fraternities, most notably Bill Robinson and Dougal Jeppe.[3]

Not forgetting his principal reason for attending Classen, DeVier launched his public speaking efforts. He caught
an early break when he was asked to speak at the inaugural
dinner of the YMCA Memorial Building Fund Campaign.
After he was introduced by Governor Robert S. Kerr, DeVier
challenged citizens to give to the building program. Under a
headline, "YMCA Keynote Sounded by Boy," DeVier's entire
speech was printed in The Daily Oklahoman. In part, DeVier
said:

> *We are unknown Americans, unknown because our lives
> lie in the unexplored future. But we boys of today are
> America's hope for a glorious tomorrow. Are we worth*

enough to you, so that you are willing to safeguard our
lives in every possible chance to grow up to be strong,
manly men? Will you protect we unknown Americans for
the promise of the future which we hold in our hands?[4]

DeVier was on cloud nine after the speech. However, a
letter from a farmer in Calumet who read the address in the
newspaper brought DeVier back to Earth. The farmer meticu-
lously and correctly found grammatical errors and lectured
DeVier on the need to "master the use of good English" if he
wanted to amount to anything.[5]

DeVier presented himself to Pop Grady to learn the art of
debate. Grady had taken Classen High School debate teams
to many victories at the state and national levels. DeVier said,
"He was the best, a wonderful man, kind, but demanding. I
could not have asked for a better debate mentor."[6]

DeVier, right, and John Cox prepare for a debate tournament at Classen High School in 1947.

Debate became the central preoccupation of DeVier's young life. It was public speaking with a purpose. It required the development of research and analytical skills on a national debate topic chosen each year. The major issues had to be identified and organized to "separate the wheat from the chaff." Debate, requiring both prepared oratory and extemporaneous speaking, gave DeVier the opportunity he had been waiting for.

Classen had two very good senior debate teams, so landing a spot on a tournament team was a challenge. DeVier had to have a partner and eventually settled into a partnership with junior John Cox. Cox was a gifted orator with a deep voice and imposing presence. As they trained together, the best course of presentation seemed to be for John to speak first to set their position on either side of an issue and for DeVier to answer the contentions of their opponents. It was a perfect fit.[7]

DeVier and John won almost every tournament they entered on campuses of state colleges who supported debate competition. They won 30 consecutive debates without a loss—a national record. It was an unforgettable year that included winning an invitational tournament at Sunset High School in Dallas, Texas. But when it came time to represent Classen in the state tournament, Pop Grady sent his senior team. DeVier and Cox could hardly wait for next year.[8]

A problem arose when DeVier's grades in classes other than debate suffered. He spent most of his time during his sophomore year with research, organization of materials, and practice for debate tournaments. Combined with his new-found social life as a member of a fraternity, there was little time left for study, and his grades showed it. His parents were happy with his success in debate, but they hoped he could improve in other areas of study.

DeVier's worst performance was in geometry. Tom Brett and DeVier were classmates in the subject and both were lost. They finally adopted a practice that when they were called upon for an answer, the response would automatically be "two sides and the included angle." Their young minds reasoned that the Pythagorean Theorem would be the correct answer more times than any other answer. Through the kindness of his geometry teacher, Mrs. Gordon, DeVier somehow managed to scrape through the course with a C.[9]

DeVier turned 16 in the summer of 1947. He was elected vice president of the Junior Red Cross High School Council and attended a week-long training camp outside Hot Springs, Arkansas—a rare trip outside Oklahoma. When he returned, he prepared to take the test to obtain an Oklahoma state drivers license. Believing in good planning, he had made a date for the evening of his driver's test and successfully requested use of the family car to go to a drive-in movie. He passed the written test "with flying colors," but failed the driving test. To his surprise, his parents were merciful and allowed him to drive illegally that night. The following day, DeVier took the driving test again and became a legal driver.[10]

CHAPTER FIVE

SIGNS OF LEADERSHIP

I wore Pop Grady's reference to me as "his last boy"
as a badge of honor.

—DeVier Pierson

When DeVier returned to Classen in the fall for his junior year, he hoped he could do something in sports. Football was out of the question—his driver's license correctly listed his height as five foot six and his weight at 120 pounds. He went out for basketball but was humiliated when he was cut from the B-team to make way for new students who might eventually play for the varsity. All was not lost. He landed a spot on the First Methodist Church basketball team in a church league, but otherwise was a spectator at sporting events.

Debate season finally rolled around. John Cox was a senior and he and DeVier formed Classen's first team. They picked up where they had left their success the previous year. They won tournaments around Oklahoma and invitationals at Baylor University in Waco, Texas, and at Byrd High School in Shreveport, Louisiana. At Baylor, they competed against 81 other teams from 39 schools in three states. For their win, they were awarded scholarships to Baylor. In the Shreveport competition, DeVier debated against Bennett Johnston, later a United States Senator from Louisiana.

By the end of the regular debating season, DeVier and Cox had won seven consecutive tournaments and 49 of 52 debates. It was a record, and Classen was ranked number one in the nation. The two debate partners represented Classen in the state tournament. In winning the championship, they defeated the defending state champions from Seminole High School. In two years, DeVier and Cox won 73 of 77 debates and 10 of 11 tournaments. Although there was no national tournament at the time, it was reported, at least by the Pawhuska newspaper, to be a national record.[1]

In the spring of his junior year, DeVier made his first, and last, foray into elective politics. He ran for president of the Student Council, a contest among friends because the other candidates were his old friend, Terry Diacon, his good friend, Bill Robinson, his fraternity brother, John Drake, and Peggy Parrott, "a very pretty girl" who DeVier definitely considered to be the most attractive candidate.

DeVier put together a coalition. He asked Pat Williams, a star on the Classen basketball team, to be his campaign manager. The move was popular with both the sports and the forensic crowd. In an open letter to Classen students, Williams wrote, "We...have a responsibility in selecting the best president for next year. When voting Friday morning, remember the election goes further than posters and assemblies. We are choosing the person to lead us."[2]

Opponent Diacon was president of the school's pep club, the Blue Jackets, and surely would have wide support among independents. DeVier believed he would split the fraternity-sorority vote with the other three candidates but pick up valuable support from other students because of his success in debate. The election unfolded according to plan. DeVier defeated Diacon in the runoff. Diacon was elected vice president, Parrott, secretary, and Robinson, treasurer.[3]

DeVier made lifelong friends in high school. He signed Bill Robinson's yearbook, "Inseparably yours," and has maintained that friendship through college and throughout their lives. DeVier is a Democrat and Robinson a conservative Republican, causing the annual exchange of a Christmas turkey with DeVier's "right-wing turkey" coming in the mail with greetings of "To Bill and his trophy wife, Jan." Robinson said, "DeVier has always had more 'will' than anyone I knew. If he set his mind to anything, he did it."[4]

DeVier was called "clever and lots of fun" by high school friend John Brock,[5] "one of the funniest and most brilliant guys I have known in life," by Lee Thompson, Jr.,[6] "energetic and super smart," by Judge Tom Brett,[7] and "a delight to be around, then and now," by Mary Brett.[8]

At the end of his junior year, DeVier attended Oklahoma Boys' State, a perennial training ground for youngsters aspiring to elective office. DeVier reports that he apparently did not impress many of his fellow students because he was chosen county commissioner after many of the other would-be politicians took the governor and state senate seats. He believed the Boys' State election was "a tip-off as to his future in elective office."

In the fall of 1948, DeVier began his senior year at Classen. The most significant improvement in his social status was that he had been given the family's vintage 1935 Oldsmobile and proudly arrived in style at the Kappa Alpha Pi parking area. He immediately noticed a measurable

The Classen yearbook photograph of DeVier as president of the student body at Classen High School.

increase in popularity as he was able to take his friends out to lunch and provide transportation at night to the local drive-ins. He had what he called "a four-wheel personality."[9]

As president of Classen, DeVier exercised his vast patronage powers to appoint John Drake as Chief Justice of the Supreme Court. DeVier presided over student council meetings and represented Classen at school events.

Debate was far different from the past two years. His partner, John Cox, had graduated and was attending OU. Pop Grady had retired and was County Superintendent of Schools in Oklahoma County. At first, DeVier decided not to compete in debate his senior year, but instead concentrate on individual speech events, especially extemporaneous speaking. However, after the debate teams were formed, he realized his decision was selfish. Debate had been very good to him and he believed he owed the school any help he could provide.[10]

He approached Paul Pennington, the new debate coach, and offered his help. Because teams had been formed for the initial tournaments from veteran debaters, DeVier settled on a sophomore, Tracy "Pody" Poe, who would become one of Oklahoma's most colorful characters.[11]

Poe was a first-time debater, but DeVier noticed he seldom lost an argument. He was better known as a golfer and card player than a public speaker, but promised DeVier he would try his best. For two weeks, the two worked around the clock to "harness" Poe's raw talent for the first tournament at Enid, Oklahoma. Surprisingly, they won, and kept winning. However, when it came time for the state tournament, the debate coach paired DeVier with Milton Laird, another senior and solid debater. It was the right choice and the twosome successfully defended Classen's state championship. DeVier retired from high school debate with a final record of 102 wins and eight losses.[12]

Poe became famous in other ways. While in college at OU, he began taking bets on sporting events. He was first arrested for gambling in 1967 and became Oklahoma's best known bookmaker. He was in and out of trouble with the law for decades. He worked in Las Vegas and was called "a king of organized crime" by federal authorities. Poe was released from prison in 2003 and died in 2005. In his autobiography, Poe mentioned his debate partnership with DeVier, saying of him, "Where did he go wrong?"[13]

After his senior year debate season, DeVier entered a national speech tournament sponsored by the National Forensic League. It was a competition among state winners in various fields. DeVier had won the state title in extemporaneous speaking and joined a group of Oklahoma students on a train to Longmont, Colorado, for the national competition.

After several days of preliminaries, the field was narrowed to six finalists in each category. DeVier struck up a casual friendship with a young man his age from Fairmount, Indiana. James Dean, after losing his mother to cancer, grew up on his aunt's farm outside Fairmount and studied forensics and drama. In the Longmont competition, he was a finalist in dramatic declamation.[14]

DeVier and Dean had dinner the night before the finals, wished each other luck, and went on their separate ways. The next day, DeVier won the national championship in extemporaneous speaking and Dean placed sixth in dramatic reading. Surely, the judges did not give him proper credit. Two years later, Dean dropped out of college, went to Hollywood, and starred in films *Rebel Without a Cause, East of Eden*, and *Giant* before being killed in an automobile crash in 1955. His death, at age 24, guaranteed his legendary status. He was the first actor to receive a posthumous Academy Award.[15]

When DeVier arrived home in Oklahoma City after his national win, he received letters from newly elected United States Senator Robert S. Kerr and other leaders. However, the letter he treasured most was to his parents from his old debate coach, Pop Grady, who wrote, "All year long I have had a feeling that DeVier was my last 'boy' and I sincerely hoped that he would win. Of course, I am in the background, but I shall remember him as one of 'my boys' as long as I may live." [16]

DeVier won the national championship in extemporaneous speaking the day after he had dinner with actor James Dean.

With debate season gone, DeVier had some long overdue, albeit short-lived, success in the sports world. He was fifth man on the Classen golf team, a substitute position because there were only four slots for competition with other high schools. On the week of a match against Northeast High School, one of the members of the Classen team grew ill and DeVier was forced into action. He birdied the 18th hole to win his match, one-up, and provide the points for a Classen victory. In his words, "I was in heaven!" [17]

DeVier would not stay in heaven very long. The next week, Classen played Central High School, the worst team in the competition, that had not won a single point in a match that season. The Classen coach, Carroll Smelser, decided to start DeVier and the other substitutes. DeVier played miserably and lost all three points to his opponent. In a span of just a few days, DeVier had experienced "the thrill of victory and the agony of defeat." [18]

Despite his checkered record in sports, DeVier was awarded a letter in golf. He remembered, "I finally had reached the goal that had eluded me for so long. I was a letterman in a high school sport and consequentially a certified jock!" [19]

DeVier's friends at Classen were primarily his classmates. He regularly dated, but formed no "ongoing entanglement," which he thought was an ideal way to move on to college. He paid little attention to the sophomores, although Kappa Alpha Pi pledge Dan Hogan showed some early promise. There was a "crop of sophomore girls" that was a especially attractive, including Sarah Maddox, Bibba Putney,

Kelsey Browne, and a particularly cute Shirley Frost. All these sophomores, especially Shirley, would become important in DeVier's life.[20]

DeVier graduated from Classen High School on June 4, 1949. His three years at Classen had been marvelous, but it was time to move on.

CHAPTER SIX

BOOMER SOONER

*DeVier, the real trick is to learn how to make good grades
<u>and</u> have a good social life.*

—William G. Paul

DeVier always had assumed he would attend the University of Oklahoma, in Norman, a short 20-mile drive from his home. A handful of his classmates at Classen were going away to Ivy League schools, but his close friends were headed for OU, and tuition for a private school education was not an option for the Pierson family.

DeVier was enthralled with the fraternity world and college rush that took him to Grand Lake and Lake Murray for boating and water skiing and to the Oklahoma City Golf and Country Club for golf. He was even taken to a major league baseball game in St. Louis, Missouri, and had dinner with Les Moss, catcher for the old St. Louis Browns. It was a new life for him, and he reveled in it.[1]

Pledging Phi Gamma Delta was an easy choice for DeVier. Two of his closest friends, John Drake and Bill Robinson, were headed for the Phi Gam house. He was being rushed by another group of Classen friends from the class ahead of him, including John Cox, his former debate partner, Dougal Jeppe, who would become a lifelong friend both in Oklahoma and Washington, D.C., David Hall, Frank Robinson, Earl Amundsen, and Bill Lockard, who would become DeVier's dentist and "periodic torturer."

The class two years older than DeVier had several Oklahoma City residents who would remain good friends. They included Jack Catlett, Lee Allan Smith, and Dick Van Cleef. The "old boys," returning veterans who ran the fraternity house, included Louie Trost, Joe Holmes, and Bill Dozier. Recent graduates Ben Head, Sidney Upsher, Dick Clements, Bill Whiteman, Ed Moler, and others supported the fraternity and urged DeVier to become a Fiji. To DeVier's barely 18-year-old eyes, it was an "extremely impressive" group. In September, 1949, he proudly wore his pledge ribbon on the lawn in front of the Phi Gam house at 119 West Boyd.[2]

It was a strong pledge class. In addition to DeVier's close Classen friends, Oklahoma Citians Dick Ellis, Bill Rucks, and Dick Dial were pledge brothers. DeVier became friends with Eddie Crowder of Muskogee, who would become one of OU's greatest quarterbacks, Lew Ground of Midland, Texas, who DeVier would see in Korea and who would be in DeVier's wedding, Bob Roop of Tulsa, who flew combat missions in Korea before being killed in an automobile accident on his way home after being discharged, and Ed Keegan of Chandler, Oklahoma.[3]

Keegan had lost a leg in a freak accident in a high school football game when he suffered a compound fracture and lime from the yardage marker entered the wound and caused gangrene. He was outgoing and popular. His artificial leg became something of a house trophy. DeVier and others frequently stole the leg while Keegan was sleeping and placed it on the living room mantle. It was a familiar scene for Keegan to hop down the stairs on one foot yelling, "Okay, which one of you [expletive deleted] have taken my leg this time?" DeVier later was a groomsman in Keegan's wedding when he married his long-time sweetheart, Martha Sue.[4]

DeVier "simply loved" his life as a college fraternity boy. He engaged in the highly intellectual pursuits of boys away from home for the first time—wine, women, and song, fast cars, kidnapping sophomores and dumping them off naked in the country, and other character-building activities. He was introduced to such cultural events as the Fiji Island party with its unlimited supplies of purple passion. Somehow, in his words, "by the grace of God," he survived.[5]

DeVier and John Cox, his high school debate partner and OU fraternity brother, welcome co-ed Peggy Weiss to a party at the Phi Gamma Delta house.

Not everyone DeVier knew survived. The highways between Norman and Oklahoma City, either US-77 or the old football road, were very dangerous passages for drivers under the influence. DeVier's boyhood friend, Roger McDuffey, was killed in a car crash. A number of other OU students died in the same manner during DeVier's years in Norman.

Despite the frivolity in the fraternity house, DeVier and his fraternity brothers were forced to mature. They had to learn to accommodate the schedules of others in the bedroom, bathroom, and dining hall. They were given a crash course in group table manners by their wonderful house mother, Jewel Hale, affectionately known as "Aunt Jewel." DeVier learned a lot about bridge and poker, but primarily enjoyed the "bull sessions" at all hours with his brothers. He said, "It was growing up and being part of a group of guys and maturing."[6]

DeVier also made friends outside the fraternity. On an early trip to Campus Corner with Eddie Crowder to pick up supplies, they ran into a young man in tattered blue jeans and a ragged tee shirt. His name was Billy Vessels. After their conversation, Crowder, a fellow freshman football player at OU, predicted Vessels would be the greatest running back in OU history. He was right. Vessels was OU's first Heisman Trophy winner. After he became a successful businessman in Florida, DeVier played many rounds of golf with him over the years.

The assignment of a roommate was a life-changing event for DeVier. He was paired with William "Willie" Paul of Pauls Valley, Oklahoma. Paul became DeVier's mentor. He taught DeVier that he could have academic success and a robust social life if he worked at it. DeVier had been indifferent at best as a student in high school and it would have been easy to continue that pattern. At Paul's urging, DeVier set his sights higher academically and made a serious effort for good grades. Had it not been for Paul's example, DeVier might not have reached this balance between fun and study.

Paul's first attempt at mentoring DeVier was a little embarrassing. When their first graded papers were returned by the professor in a class they were taking together, Paul had earned a grade of 99 and "wanted to show DeVier how it's done." Paul was shocked when he looked at DeVier's paper and saw that the professor had written, "Mr. Pierson, your paper was more than perfect, so I have given you a grade of 101."[7]

Paul later became an extremely successful lawyer, managing partner of the state's largest law firm, lead counsel for Kerr-McGee Corporation in the Karen Silkwood trial, general counsel of Phillips Petroleum Company, and one of only two Oklahomans to serve as president of the American Bar Association.[8]

DeVier's first academic success came when he was selected, along with John Drake, for induction into Phi Eta Sigma, the honorary freshman scholastic fraternity. DeVier was chosen to give the initiation response on behalf of the new members.

During the summer following his freshman year, DeVier worked in the Oklahoma oil fields as a roustabout on a Van-Grisso Oil Company lease near Velma. He spent the hot days painting tanks, digging ditches, and building fences—de-

manding manual labor for a "spoiled city boy." He did not
have a car and spent his nights in a small "dog house" on the
lease. He slept on a cot and his only furnishings were a clock,
an electric fan, and a radio. At night, he listened to New York
Yankees games. He was excited about the exploits of a young
Oklahoma boy from Commerce, Mickey Mantle, who was
DeVier's age and had taken New York City by storm.

DeVier boarded that summer with a farmer who lived
about a half mile down the road from the oil well lease. The
farmer's wife cooked him breakfast at dawn and prepared a
brown bag lunch. The family ate dinner at precisely 6:00 p.m.
and the radio was always tuned to the preaching of evangelist
Oral Roberts. On occasion, the farmer would allow DeVier to
drive his pickup into Velma to see a movie with the farmer's
daughter. She commented during one of those trips that a
movie with DeVier at least beat staying home and listening to
Oral Roberts.[9]

DeVier was getting along fine with his fellow roustabouts
until they discovered the only reason he had the job was
because he was dating Liz Grisso, an Oklahoma City girl and
the daughter of the oil company owner. While that fact offended their views of merit hiring, it was a small price to pay.
In August, DeVier hitchhiked to Santa Fe, New Mexico, and
spent the month with Liz and her family at their ranch outside
Santa Fe.

As a veteran at the Phi Gam house for his second year at
OU, DeVier saw more potential great citizens come into the
house, including Hardy Summers of Muskogee, later Chief
Justice of the Oklahoma Supreme Court, and Jim Davis, a

leading Oklahoma City attorney. DeVier also established friendships outside the fraternity with Randy Everest, Bill Bevers, and many others.[10]

OU football games were important social events. DeVier was a student at OU during part of the 47-game winning streak, a college football record that may never be broken, and for a national championship in his sophomore year. Eddie Crowder was the magical quarterback, Billy Vessels an incredible running back, and Bud Wilkinson was king as head coach.

Students dressed up for games. Despite the hot Oklahoma weather at the start of the fall season, young ladies wore skirts and often, high heels. For fraternity men, the dress included gray flannel pants, button-down shirt and tie, with a tweed blazer and hat. Appearance was importance.[11]

DeVier attended many OU football games, usually sitting in the student section with the fall heat beating down. He thought the most exciting game of all time was the OU-Texas A & M game in 1950 when, with the Sooners one point behind, Claude Arnold led the team the length of the field in the last two minutes with six consecutive completed passes and OU scored the winning touchdown as time expired. DeVier threw his expensive grey fedora high into the air and it was never seen again. Arnold later became a friend and the two of them have relived that moment in some exotic locations.

Phi Gams had a campus reputation as "party boys," although DeVier has long thought the reputation was overstated. Through the years, Judge Ralph Thompson, a Beta at OU, had kidded Phi Gam Bill Paul about what would have happened if they had traded roles. Thompson said to Paul, "You were the quintessential Beta-type, an overachieving small town boy. I was a city kid from Oklahoma City and most of my friends were Phi Gams. Just think, Willie, if you had been a Beta, you would probably be President of the United States—and I would have died of cirrhosis of the liver."[12]

During the summer following his sophomore year, DeVier roughnecked on a Van-Grisso exploratory well being drilled near Duncan. He lived in a Duncan rooming house and worked the swing shift from 4:00 p.m. to midnight. He had a car and took turns with other members of the crew driving to the rig. There was a crisis the first day on the job. DeVier did not know to bring a clean set of clothing to change into after getting miserably dirty on the drilling platform. At the end of the shift, he was about to get into the driller's car for the trip home in his dirty clothes. The driller ordered him to leave the dirty clothing behind and ride home in his skivvies. Fortunately, it was 1:00 a.m. when they arrived at the rooming house.[13]

There were some benefits to the job. After retiring in the early morning hours, DeVier slept usually until mid morning and had several hours to kill before reporting to work. He became friends with Duncan attorney Harold Garvin who allowed him to visit the courthouse and observe motion dockets and trials. It was important training for an aspiring lawyer.

The job as a roughneck could be dangerous. While pulling pipe from the hole, the little finger on DeVier's right hand was completely severed. He was taken to the infirmary in Duncan where DeVier insisted upon calling his father, who in turn, contacted Dr. Don O'Donaghue, a prominent orthopedic surgeon. Harold Garvin drove DeVier to Wesley Hospital in Oklahoma City at a high rate of speed. Dr. O'Donaghue reattached the severed finger. Decades later, it is still somewhat bent, but gives DeVier "a very fine interlocking grip" on the golf course.[14]

With the injury, DeVier decided he would have to find other ways to learn about oil and gas. He would leave oil field work to braver souls. He later found the law to be his contact with the oil and gas industry.

Back at OU, DeVier's decision to try for college academic success was paying off. At the end of his junior year, he had a 4.0 grade point average and was tied for top academic honors in his class with Hugh Roff, Jr., a Beta from Wewoka. Both were inducted into Phi Beta Kappa as juniors from the Class of 1953 and were joined by Willie Paul, Fred Harris, and David Hall from the Class of 1952. In addition to his membership in Phi Beta Kappa, DeVier was historian and rush chairman of his fraternity and a member of the League of Young Democrats.

OU buddies, left to right, Bill Bevers, Bill Robinson, and DeVier share iced teas at the Bachelor's Club dance at OU in 1953.

RIGHT: DeVier assists OU President Dr. George L. Cross in welcoming a new member of the Pe-et Society in 1953. *Courtesy University of Oklahoma.*

While at OU as an undergraduate student, DeVier was president of the Pe-et Society, Phi Beta Kappa, Honor Council representative, on the varsity debate team, a member of the League of Young Democrats, and held many offices in Phi Gamma Delta. *Courtesy University of Oklahoma.*

There were also some welcome tangible gifts. DeVier received the Robert Dean Bass Memorial Scholarship, given annually by a wealthy Dallas family in memory of their nephew, an OU student killed in World War II. It was a major award for DeVier, who said, "Being a Phi Beta Kappa was flattering, but the Bass award put money in the bank!" The $640 cash payment went a long way to finance his senior year.[15]

DeVier was chosen for membership in the Pe-et Society, the senior honor society for men, and was elected president of the group. Fittingly, his notice of membership came from his predecessor as president, Willie Paul. Being Pe-Et president was not overly time consuming. About the only tangible work he did, other than holding a flashlight for OU President

Dr. George L. Cross at the induction ceremony, was signing accomplishment certificates for more than 2,000 Oklahoma high school seniors. The ambitious undertaking took several weeks.[16]

To raise funds to finance his education, DeVier was creative. He noticed the OU student directory did not include home addresses and telephone numbers. Recognizing that students might want their friends' home information, particularly those of the opposite sex, he obtained such data from each fraternity and sorority house, published a Greek directory, sold advertising space in it, and sold the book for one dollar a copy. The official student directory did not like the competition and began including the same information. DeVier hiked his advertising rates and gave copies of the Greek directory to fraternities and sororities in bulk. By the time he completed school, he had raised nearly $7,000 from the publication, "an absolute fortune" which more than met his needs.[17]

DeVier had four years of Reserve Officers Training Command (ROTC) during his undergraduate years at OU. He was not enthusiastic at first, but clung to his ROTC assignment after the Korean War began and he was classified 1-A in the draft. The ROTC program had one major attraction—it provided an automatic deferment from the draft for four years.

Army ROTC and the Fighting Quartermasters were DeVier's choices. As a member of the Quartermaster Corps, he spent summer camp at Fort Lee, Virginia, close to both Richmond and Washington, D.C. At the time, he had never been east of the Mississippi River and had never flown on an airplane outside Oklahoma. During days off during the training, he and

DeVier reviewing the troops on the OU campus while he was ROTC cadet colonel. This photograph appeared in the 1953 *Sooner* yearbook. *Courtesy University of Oklahoma.*

several friends visited Washington, D.C., DeVier's first look at the nation's capital. He had no idea then that he would be a resident of Washington for most of his adult life.

The ROTC training broke DeVier's straight-A average when he received a B in Military Science. The instructor called him with news of the B and sounded apologetic. Frankly, DeVier was relieved—he feared the grade might be much worse.[18]

Even though he did not think of himself as much of a military man, DeVier was made a cadet colonel and commander of the ROTC brigade. He wondered if it was a practical joke, but did his best in the leadership role. On May 15, 1953, he received his certificate as second lieutenant in the United States Army.

DeVier received his diploma at OU's commencement on June 8, 1953. He marched across the stage with thousands of other students. He had been selected for *Who's Who in American Colleges* and was certifiable a "big man on campus." More important to him, he had made many friendships that would stay with him throughout life. It had been a wonderful four years.

CHAPTER SEVEN

YOU'RE IN THE ARMY NOW

*As a law student and old debater, I had a decent record
as a jailhouse lawyer during my time in Korea.*

—DeVier Pierson

As an undergraduate, DeVier had participated in a combined degree program that permitted him to take first year law school courses as his last year of undergraduate study. Even though he had received his Army commission, he was entitled to continue his deferment until the completion of law school. However, as he began his second year of legal studies, he felt "burned out"—he needed something new. He contacted the Department of the Army and requested that his name be placed in line for call to active duty as soon as possible. Law school could wait.

DeVier as a new second lieutenant in the United States Army when he reported for active duty at Fort Lee, Virginia, in February, 1954.

DeVier overestimated quick action by the Pentagon calling him for active duty. He waited for months. Finally, he was ordered to report to duty at Fort Lee, Virginia, on February 2, 1954. He loaded all his worldly belongings in his 1950 maroon and white hardtop Chevrolet and headed out on his first road trip east beyond the Mississippi River.[1]

Upon arriving at Fort Lee, named for Confederate General Robert E.

Lee, DeVier went directly to the Officer's Club. He sat down at the bar and was asked what he wished to order. Before DeVier could speak, a voice down the bar said, in a deep, Southern drawl, "That fine young man needs a martini and bring it straight up." The voice belonged to Burns Proctor of Birmingham, Alabama, who shortly would become one of DeVier's all-time good friends.

DeVier and Proctor lived together in bachelor's quarters on the post. Proctor's uncle was a lobbyist for the trucking industry in Richmond and was a "social lion" in Virginia's capital city. DeVier and Proctor became "extra men" at debutante balls and worked their way into the city's social structure. They also had memorable visits to the nation's capital just 100 miles away. After serving in the Army, Proctor returned to Birmingham and became a highly successful lawyer. He and DeVier were best men in each other's weddings and have remained close friends for life.[2]

DeVier completed a three month basic officer training course in which he learned to use an M-1 rifle, run obstacle courses, march long distances, and jump from a paratrooper tower. He remembered, "While they probably didn't think I would ever be much of a fighting man, they were determined to treat me like one."[3]

DeVier suffered only one significant setback during his year at Fort Lee. He was dating the daughter of the commanding general who invited him one Sunday morning to go skeet shooting. DeVier was apprehensive because he had never shot skeet. In fact, he had never fired a shotgun. DeVier also learned, to his dismay, that the general had been skeet shooting champion in the Army's European theater. In two rounds, the general shot 24 of 25 and 25 of 25. DeVier shot five and three, respectively, and was never invited back.

DeVier was able to make short visits to Oklahoma during the time he was stationed in Virginia. He became acquainted with General Oscar Senter, commander of Tinker Air Force Base in Midwest City, who was kind enough to offer DeVier transportation on military aircraft traveling from the east coast to Tinker. Several times DeVier was able to fly into Tinker on Friday evening, see his family and friends for the weekend, and catch a flight back to Fort Lee on Monday.[4]

Seemingly stuck at one Army base for two years, DeVier expressed that concern to a friend who worked at the Pentagon. The friend said, "I can fix that. Get released from your assignment and I will put you on the list for Europe." That sounded good to DeVier. The next day, DeVier met with his commander who appreciated the fact that DeVier wanted released so he could be closer to the action and sent the release to the Pentagon. Shortly thereafter, DeVier received orders to report to Korea—not exactly the European assignment he expected.[5]

In early December, 1954, DeVier's tour at Fort Lee ended. He drove to Oklahoma City in time for Christmas with family and friends. Before he was scheduled to report for duty in Korea, he was able to get orders cut to route him through San Francisco, California, and to Hawaii, where he would spend his accrued leave. It was a brave new world because he had never flown to California, never been to Hawaii, and certainly had not set foot in the Far East.

During the overnight stay in San Francisco, DeVier and

several other young officers arranged for a quick tour of the city's night life. At one bistro, the manager shined a spotlight on the young men, all in uniform, and announced them as heroes returning home after serving bravely in Korea. The manager also said drinks were on the house. Feeling there was little difference between "going to Korea" and "returning from Korea," the officers cheerfully accepted the hospitality.[6]

The following day, DeVier and other soldiers flew in a very noisy Lockheed Constellation to Honolulu and reported to Schofield Barracks in the nearby hills. The Army post, named for General John Schofield who recommended the establishment of a military base at Pearl Harbor, was famous as the setting for the epic novel and movie "From Here to Eternity."

Because DeVier was still on leave, he moved into Honolulu and rented a billet at Fort DeRussey, a famous military way station strategically located on Waikiki Beach. His bachelor officer's quarters (BOQ) was no more than 15 feet from sand. The Royal Hawaiian Hotel, with its renowned surfing area, was only a mile up the beach. DeVier leased a red MG convertible for the month and set out to see the sights.[7]

Oklahomans were everywhere in Honolulu. DeVier looked up Mo and Hank Simms and Pat and Jack Foster. All were OU graduates and DeVier had attended Classen High School with Mo. Jack was a very successful real estate developer on the island of Oahu. Hank was a Phi Gam and was famous as "Uncle Hank" on local radio and television. Among other duties, he managed a television talent show and asked DeVier to serve one memorable night as a judge.

Sherri Fain of Oklahoma City, who later would be DeVier's next door neighbor, arrived with her mother for a Hawaiian vacation. She and DeVier spent most of their waking daylight hours on the beach and hitting night spots in the evening, including seeing Nat King Cole perform at a local club. DeVier took Sherri surfing at what turned out to be a dangerous location. In a scary moment, Sherri was trapped by an undertow in the surf. DeVier's version was that he bravely rescued her, while Sherri contended that DeVier "left her in the lurch" and that she was saved by another man.

Sherri and DeVier chronicled their exploits in Honolulu in a long letter to Lavona Price in Oklahoma. Somehow, the letter was printed in *The Daily Oklahoman*. Sherri wrote, "All things must come to an end…This afternoon, the Oklahoman I am, bids aloha nui loi to Lt. Pierson who boards a plane for the Far East and the slightly cooler climate of Korea. We have tried to soothe the pain of his untimely departure."[8]

DeVier caught one more break before leaving paradise. The duty sergeant at Schofield Barracks asked him if he would like to take morning reveille for another week. It was an easy choice. Each morning, DeVier arose early, had the master sergeant assemble the troops in the courtyard made famous in the movies by Burt Lancaster, Montgomery Clift, and Frank Sinatra, called the troops to attention, dismissed them, and got back in his car to drive to Waikiki Beach.[9]

Finally, DeVier could no longer delay his departure. He boarded a military transport for Tokyo and promptly ran into Buck McPhail, a classmate and All American fullback at OU. After a brief tour of Tokyo, DeVier reported for duty at the Pusan Area Command (PAC) in Pusan, Korea.

Pusan, also known as Busan, was the second largest city in the Republic of Korea, or South Korea, and the largest port city in the country. The densely built up areas of the city were situated in a number of narrow valleys between the Nakdong and Suyeong rivers, with mountains separating some of the various districts. South Korea was struggling economically in the aftermath of three years of fighting between North and South Korean regimes. An armistice was signed on July 27, 1953, but tension continued along the 38th parallel, a tension that still requires the presence of American troops more than a half century later.[10]

BELOW: DeVier, as special services officer for the Pusan Area Command in Korea, dined with actress Debbie Reynolds in 1955. Reynolds was on a tour of American bases in Korea.

ABOVE: DeVier, right, and Dick "Bud" Zahm began a lifetime friendship while stationed in Pusan, Korea.

When DeVier arrived, the Panmunjong peace talks were underway. Pusan was a long way from any hostilities—DeVier was simply part of the army of occupation. The only time he was ever fired upon was when South Korean sentries mistook his group as intruders during inspection of a POL terminal.

The Pusan Area Command was a large military enclave of Quonset huts and other buildings erected and fenced off from a teeming Pusan suburb. DeVier's Phi Gam pledge brother, Lew Ground, already was stationed at PAC and welcomed DeVier. The entire complement of young officers, who looked like central casting for M.A.S.H., became friends. Among them was Bud Zahm, who became a lifetime friend, a lawyer for Mobil Oil Corporation, and one of DeVier's clients.

True to form, DeVier had another staff assignment of "questionable military value." He was appointed Public Information, Troop Information and Education, and Special Services Officer of the Pusan Area Command. Under his jurisdiction were the news operations, military education programs, the commissaries and PXs, movie theaters, and the officers' clubs. DeVier said, "It would have been wonderful training for a business executive, especially one interested in hotel or restaurant management, but it was of limited value to a future lawyer." [11]

One of the perks of his job was to screen arriving movies before they were shown to the troops. He also enjoyed supervising the continuing education programs which exposed the troops to cram courses in history, art, literature, and music. He was able to built Pusan's first tennis court, with the help of a general who was a frustrated tennis player. DeVier also edited the "A-Frame News," a bi-monthly publication for American troops in that part of Korea.

DeVier also became a *de facto* legal officer for the area command. Because he did not yet have a law degree, he was unable to try general courts martial. However, he kept busy defending soldiers on lesser offenses in which the penalty was only loss of rank or privileges or short periods of detention. The trials were conducted before a field grade officer with counsel appointed for both the Army and the defense. DeVier's record in defending the accused was fairly successful.[12]

An enjoyable duty for DeVier was facilitating visits of celebrities who came to Korea as part of the USO program to improve troop morale. He coordinated college choruses and individual entertainers passing through Pusan. His most notable assignment was accompanying actress Debbie Reynolds, fresh from a starring role in "Singing in the Rain," at several events in Pusan and other military posts in South Korea. *The Daily Oklahoman* published a photograph of DeVier and the actress having dinner at Pusan.

DeVier was proud of his Oklahoma roots and was always on the lookout for fellow Oklahomans, even though he was half way around the world. He lived in the same quonset hut with Lew Ground. On a visit to a Marine unit in the area, DeVier ran into Homer Paul, Bill Paul's younger brother and a fellow Phi Gam from Pauls Valley. At a press briefing, DeVier heard a familiar voice call his name. It was Harry Clarkson, a Phi Gam who was two years behind him at OU.[13]

When Ground was preparing to leave Korea, DeVier and

his friends threw him a farewell party and he presented a gift to a young Korean woman who was their favorite waitress at the officers' club. As the public information officer, DeVier had a "fetching" photograph taken of Ground and the waitress and sent it to his hometown newspaper in Midland, Texas, with a caption that Lieutenant Ground was presenting the annual award for outstanding food service provider. The photograph ran on the newspaper's front page, prompting inquiries to Ground's parents as to whether or not he was marrying a Korean girl. It was embarrassing for Ground because he was already engaged. "But," said DeVier, "good friendships weather these things." [14]

DeVier made several trips to Tokyo—some on official business and others for rest and relaxation. On one occasion, he was a military courier transporting confidential papers placed in a briefcase and locked to his arm. A jeep took him to the front steps of the Far East Headquarters which was at least a block from the entrance to the building. Military guards at ten-pace intervals lined the sidewalk. As DeVier walked toward the building, each of the guards suddenly snapped to attention and presented arms. DeVier thought it was an extraordinary display of respect for a young second lieutenant and returned the salutes as he sauntered toward the building. Still reveling in the respect, he glanced behind him to see four-star General Maxwell Taylor, commander of all Allied forces in the Far East, was walking behind him. Recognizing that the sentries were probably saluting the general, and not him, DeVier stepped out of the way and saluted as General Taylor passed. [15]

DeVier got closer to the action along the 38th parallel during his final months in Korea. He was temporarily assigned to the 21st Infantry Regiment of the 24th Army Division, a highly regarded regiment known as the Gimlets. The unit was stationed north of Seoul close to the truce line and was commanded by Colonel Glen Long, a graduate of Oklahoma A and M College, now Oklahoma State University. Long, a respected leader, had made bird colonel at age 36 and headed a superbly dedicated, trained, and boisterous group of men.[16]

DeVier shared an upscale tent with two very different young lieutenants. One was a West Point graduate whose father was a general in the Army. The other bunkmate was the son of a radio evangelist who, as a "real hellion," was rebelling against his upbringing. DeVier often accompanied the officers and enlisted troops while patrolling the truce line. Sometimes they passed North Korean and Chinese soldiers patrolling on the other side of the line.

There was one more off-beat assignment for DeVier. The biggest athletic event in the Far East each year was the annual football championship. Every division or equivalent unit stationed in Japan, Korea, Okinawa, and other places where American soldiers or sailors were serving in the Far East had a team that was often comprised of star collegiate players. In 1955, the finalists were the 7th Division and 24th Division, both stationed in Korea. It was the first time for an all-Korean championship. The game was scheduled to be played in the Bayonet Bowl, a stadium built to hold 25,000 troops north of Seoul.[17]

At the last minute, the Stars and Stripes Network that broadcast athletic events throughout the Far East tabbed

DeVier as the radio play-by-play announcer after a friend told network commanders that DeVier had "extensive broadcasting experience" at OU. After a brief studio interview in which DeVier was asked to make up details of a mythical football game, the officer in charge announced, "You're our man!" DeVier spent a week talking to the players and making arrangements to broadcast the game from a small booth built at the top of the Bayonet Bowl.

DeVier's maiden voyage as a play-by-play announcer went fairly well. He had a good offensive spotter and no problem following the ball on offense. On defense, it was more difficult and, when in doubt, he said, "another jarring tackle by Kowalksi," a hefty defensive tackle from Pittsburgh. After the game, DeVier went to the Gimlet Officers Club and listened to the replay of the game with his Army buddies until the wee hours of the morning. DeVier takes some satisfaction in the fact that Kowalski was selected the defensive player of the game.

The most violent episode witnessed by DeVier came in August, 1955, when 5,000 South Korean demonstrators launched a protest against Czech and Polish members of a neutral nations inspection team at Pusan. The South Koreans considered those two countries, as members of the Soviet Union-sponsored Warsaw Pact, to be enemies and objected to their presence in their homeland. American troops had to use fire hoses and tear gas to prevent the protesters from storming the military post. Hand to hand combat and rock throwing resulted in several injuries, although no one was killed. DeVier's commanders considered vacating the compound during the height of the attack, but final orders were given to defend it as United States property. After negotiations, tempers cooled and protesters went back to their homes. Years later, when DeVier was involved in the White House response to anti-war demonstrations in Washington, D.C., he remembered the anger and frustration he saw on the faces of the mostly young South Koreans at Pusan.[18]

In autumn, 1955, DeVier was promoted to first lieutenant and told he would be discharged in time to be home for Christmas, more than a month before his two-year active duty tour was scheduled to end. In November, he boarded a troop ship in Pusan harbor for a 17-day trip to Seattle, Washington. In preparation for resuming his life at the OU College of Law, his parents had shipped his law school notes and hornbooks so he could review them on the long trip home.[19]

In addition to refreshing his memory on the law, DeVier looked back on his two years in the military, counting his blessings that he was able to work and live, for the first time, with young men of many races and religions and with very different life experiences. He saw worlds that were totally foreign to his Oklahoma upbringing. He had to accept discipline and training and learned to lead and train others. Where he had been burned out on studying two years before, he now was "revved up" and ready to complete law school and become a lawyer. He had left OU as a "frat boy" and returned as a young man.

CHAPTER EIGHT

LIFE IN THE LAW BARN

The moot court national championship is as important
to OU as a national football championship.
—Bud Wilkinson

The OU College of Law admitted its first students
in 1909. OU Regents named Julien C. Monnet, a Harvard
University graduate, as dean; a position he held until 1941.
Monnet assembled an outstanding faculty, drawing from the
leading law schools in the nation. With an exceptional library,
the OU law school became a model for other state-supported
institutions. In the 1950s, most attorneys and judges in Oklahoma were graduates of the OU College of Law.[1]

The law school was located on OU's North Oval in Monnet Hall, affectionately known as the Law Barn. DeVier's
father had studied there as a member of the law school Class
of 1922. The Law Barn was strategically located adjacent to
the student union so that coffee breaks with fellow students
and faculty were only a few steps away.

When DeVier began his legal studies in 1952, it was the
Dean Earl Sneed era at the OU College of Law. Respected by
students, alumni, and the Oklahoma bar, Sneed presided over
a first-rate faculty. Dr. Maurice Merrill was one of the preeminent national authorities on constitutional law and oil and gas
law. Other outstanding faculty members included Elbridge
Phelps in contracts, Dale Vliet in evidence, George "Tiger"
Fraser in civil procedure, Eugene Kuntz in torts and oil and
gas, and "boy wonder" Frank Elkouri.[2]

Because some law students had come from undergraduate programs at other colleges and universities, and because he had taken two years away for his military service, DeVier had friends who graduated in five law school classes from 1953 to 1957. He started with the Class of 1955 that included friends from undergraduate days such as Bill Robinson, Tom Brett, Bill Bevers, Jerry Barton, Hugh Roff, Bill Rogers, Charles Johnson, and Paul Lindsey. He became great friends with Duke Logan from Vinita, Oklahoma. "Older" students at the school included John Mee, G.T. Blankenship, Randy Everest, Claude Mullendore, and Fred Harris. Although they were not in his class, DeVier spent a lot of time with his old mentor, Willie Paul, and others, including Lee West, later chairman of the Civil Aeronautics Board and a distinguished federal judge.[3]

Before DeVier had entered active military duty, he and Duke Logan had gone into business together to try to defray law school expenses. The venture was manufacturing seat cushions for use at OU football games. They noticed fans paying $1 to rent a bulky cushion that took up a lot of space. They reasoned that surely fans would buy an inflatable seat which could be used and then deflated and placed in a fan's pocket or purse. They found an industrial plant in Oklahoma City to produce the cushions for 50 cents each.

They pooled their money and ordered 2,000 cushions. Students were hired on a commission basis to sell the cushions at an OU-Notre Dame game for $2 each. The young entre-preneurs had it figured that if they grossed $4,000, they could split more than $2,000 in profit after the payment of manu-facturing and sales commissions. It seemed too good to be true—and it was.[4]

Without doing any market research on customer demand for inflatable seats, they began sales with high hopes. However, the salesmen sold only 17 of the 2,000 cushions. DeVier and Logan were stuck with both the cushions and the $1,000 manufacturing cost. They dissolved the business and used the remaining seat cushions as party favors and birthday gifts for several years.[5]

Duke Logan was involved in another business venture with DeVier. Because DeVier had dated Kelsey Browne, the daughter of Henry Browne, the Coca-Coca bottler in Oklahoma City, he had the inside track on an advertising idea. Fellow Phi Gam Dick Dial designed an OU cartoon with the football schedule printed on the back which could be affixed to an automobile windshield, prominently displaying the Coca-Cola logo. Logan and DeVier hired other students to put the sticker under windshield wipers of automobiles during football games. When the business grew profitable, they sold it to other enterprising OU students.[6]

After his two years on active duty in the Army, DeVier arrived back in Oklahoma in time to land a job as a Christmas season salesman at Joe Connolly's men's clothing store in downtown Oklahoma City. At that time, DeVier had only one good suit, a raw silk model he had custom made in Tokyo, which he noticed "seemed to glow in the dark" in his closet. When he wore the suit to work on his first day, the owner, a silver-haired fashion legend in Oklahoma City, quickly took DeVier upstairs and suggested that he use the 40 percent employee discount to purchase two new suits. So when DeVier returned to the OU College of Law in January, 1956, for the second semester of his junior year, he was 24 years old, dressed in his Connolly suits, and far more mature than he had been when he began taking law classes.

When DeVier returned to law school, most of the members of the Class of 1955 were long gone and he officially became a member of the Class of 1957. An exception was Tom Brett, DeVier's friend since high school, who had also taken time off between his undergraduate degree and law school for military service. DeVier made new friends. Arch Gilbert was a brilliant student from Eufaula and Pat Williams was DeVier's old campaign manager at Classen High School. Other new faces included Don Winn of Amarillo, Jerry Dickman of Tulsa, Jim Davis and Hardy Summers from Muskogee, his younger brothers in the Phi Gam house, and Jim George, who would become a good friend.[7]

To help with expenses, DeVier became the paid scholarship chairman of the Phi Gam house. The academic record of the fraternity had slipped in recent years, prompting a group of fraternity alumni in Oklahoma City to raise sufficient money to hire DeVier in the hope that he could help fraternity members raise their academic performances. With hard work, DeVier was able to raise the academic standing of Phi Gams significantly within the first year of the program.

The highlight of the spring of DeVier's junior year in law school was the annual moot court competition. Four junior law students were chosen to argue before the Oklahoma Supreme Court in observance of Law Day. Jerry Dickman, Pat Williams, Jim Davis, and DeVier were selected to prepare briefs and argue before the justices in a special session in the Law Barn.

DeVier, Jim Davis, Pat Williams, and Jerry Dickman, argued a case before the Oklahoma Supreme Court in the junior moot court competition.

At the Law Day ceremony, DeVier received the James F. Hawes Memorial Award as outstanding member of the second year class. It surprised DeVier because he had only been a member of the class for four months. His theory was that Arch Gilbert had received the award for highest grade point average and the faculty was simply "dividing the spoils."[8]

DeVier was known as a hard-working, hard-studying student. Future federal judge Lee West was a fellow law student. West said, "He was the hardest worker in the law school. With his many talents and abilities, I strongly suspected he could have achieved incredible academic success without working nearly so hard. I think it speaks well of him that he was never willing to take the chance."[9]

After the school year ended, DeVier returned to his job at Connolly's for the summer. Some of his law school classmates questioned why he did not take a job as a legal assistant or intern at a law firm. His response was that both the hours and money were better at Connolly's and "there would be plenty of time to be a young legal slave" after he graduated.[10]

But one more year of law school remained before he could be a lawyer. As a law school senior, DeVier concentrated on participating in the National Moot Court Competition. He believed it would be the most important thing he could do as a fledgling lawyer. It involved application of both writing and oral skills in competition with students from every other major law school in the nation. It was similar to debate because a legal position had to be organized by brief and then argued to an appellate court. It was what he hoped to do someday in the practice of law.[11]

The moot court topic that year was extremely interesting. The case involved the legal definition of insanity. The classic legal test for insanity was the McNaughton Rule, under which a defendant was found to be legally sane if he knew the difference between right and wrong when he committed the criminal act. A number of federal courts, including one court in the District of Columbia, had adopted the so-called "Durham Test," under which a criminal defendant might be found insane if his act was "the product of a diseased mind" or resulted from an "irresistible impulse." It was a timely legal issue because appeals courts around the country were in ferment as they struggled to find and apply the correct legal test. The result would be very important for the future administration of the criminal justice system.

After competition for the three slots on the moot court team, Jerry Dickman, Pat Williams, and DeVier were selected to compete for OU. Team members had to be prepared to argue both sides of the case—the side to be presented was determined by draw. Williams would argue the petitioner's side, Dickman would be prepared to argue the respondent's side, and DeVier was the swing man, arguing both sides of the case.

In the Southwest regional competition, DeVier and Dickman were successful in arguments against moot court teams from Louisiana State University in the quarter-finals and Tulane University in the semi-finals. They drew the petitioner's side for the finals against Southern Methodist University and stayed up most of the night to prepare for the shift of sides. The following day, DeVier and Williams won the regional final and qualified for the national competition.[12]

The national finals in New York City pitted 22 teams against one another. Wall Street law firms sent scouts to the competition to seek out talent for their firms. The judges were primarily from federal and state appellate courts of New York. As it turned out, the OU team drew the respondent's side for all arguments, so DeVier and Dickman argued each round.

The OU team survived the preliminary rounds as many teams from schools such as Harvard, Yale, and Stanford were eliminated. DeVier was pleased that many of the surviving teams were from state universities. OU defeated the University of Michigan, a very strong team, in the quarter-finals and the University of Colorado in the semi-finals to advance to the finals.

The final competition was like a football game—it was OU versus the University of Nebraska. The pressure-packed event was presided over by United States Supreme Court Justice Felix Frankfurter who interrupted the argument many times with questions. DeVier was certain Justice Frankfurter asked some of the questions just to throw the participants off stride. Many of the questions were lengthy and seemed to require a brief answer, the opposite of what he hoped to accomplish in the argument. After the argument closed, DeVier was uncertain how the OU team had performed.[13]

The court retired to deliberate while DeVier and his teammates "sweated it out." Justice Frankfurter returned with word that the 1956 national moot court champion was the University of Oklahoma. There was great relief and elation and the OU team went on the town in Lower Manhattan for a rowdy celebration of their new national championship.

The moot court team returned to Oklahoma on Christmas Eve as "conquering heroes." It was the first time OU had been the national moot court champion. A story in the *Oklahoma City Times* carried the headline, "Sooner Law Students Capture National Title." The three OU students posed for a photograph with Justice Frankfurter that appeared in several publications.[14]

The Oklahoma City alumni chapter of the Phi Alpha Delta legal fraternity held a dinner in honor of the moot court team. The affair was presided over by Alfred P. Murrah, Chief Judge of the United States Court of Appeals for the Tenth Circuit. Congratulatory letters came from near and far. Al Petite, a leading Wall Street lawyer wrote Oklahoma City attorney William J. Holloway, Jr., that "young Pierson has been making quite an impression." Holloway, who later became a judge of the Tenth Circuit Court of Appeals, passed the letter on to DeVier's parents.[15]

DeVier was a member of the 1956 national champion moot court team. Left to right, Jerry Dickman, Dean Earl Sneed, DeVier, and Pat Williams. The team was honored in a surprise tribute at the OU College of Law.

Lewis Ryan, a Syracuse, New York lawyer happened to be in New York City and saw DeVier's name. Having known DeVier's father, he attended the moot court finals and wrote W.D., "I shall never forget your son's performance and I would be amazed if he did not receive several offers from the large Wall Street firms before he was able to get out of the building." [16] DeVier also received laudatory letters from United States Senator Mike Monroney and Congressman John Jarman.

An interesting letter came from Dr. Caradine Hooton, general secretary of The Methodist Board of Temperance, a service agency of The Methodist Church. Dr. Hooton wrote:

While I am proud of the famous football teams for which we Oklahomans can everywhere root with solid satisfaction, I am especially pleased with your achievement, for it brings to the attention of the nation other excellencies of a great university and state all too generally known only for its prowess with the pigskin. [17]

Out of the blue came a letter from Judge Ben Cameron of the United States Fifth Circuit Court of Appeals. Judge Cameron, without ever having met DeVier, offered him a job as his clerk in the appeals court's office in Meridian, Mississippi, with a hefty salary of $4,525 annually.[18]

The OU College of Law hosted a surprise awards ceremony at Monnet Hall. Dean Sneed joined OU President Cross and other dignitaries to honor the moot court champions. The star guest was legendary OU football coach Bud Wilkinson who said, "with a straight face," that the moot court win was as important to OU as the national football championship his team had won. DeVier was proud of his victory, but said, "I personally felt that Bud lost a good deal of credibility with the audience at that moment." [19]

While Coach Wilkinson's characterization perhaps was exaggerated, there was no doubt the moot court team win was very good for the prestige of the law school. The team's success demonstrated that representatives of state colleges such as OU could successfully compete with premier Ivy League institutions. During his career, DeVier often told OU students that he may have been out-lawyered in a case, but he never believed he had been out-educated in contests with lawyers from the nation's best known law schools.

DeVier learned valuable lessons from his moot court championship. He applied his Boy Scout motto, "Be Prepared," and tried to go into any argument better prepared and better organized than the opposition. He believed in the old saying, "A victory is usually ten percent inspiration and 90 percent preparation." [20]

DeVier also learned that luck is a factor in any success. In the moot court competition, the OU team could have easily been defeated by fine teams from Southern Methodist University and the University of Michigan. He would not have been the least surprised if either of those teams had eliminated OU. Through the years, when a judge, jury, or regulator did not rule DeVier's way, he always tried to be philosophical and remember that he had won "some close ones" as well.[21]

A third lesson learned was that most of us in life are dependent from time to time on the kindness of strangers. After the OU win over Michigan in the quarter-finals, the premier member of the Michigan team came to wish the OU students luck and told DeVier that the judge in the semi-finals, the presiding judge of the New York Court of Appeals, had written an opinion in an unrelated case involving some of the legal standards of the moot court topic of legal insanity, and that the judge was "mighty proud of it." The Michigan student gave a copy of the case to DeVier.

During the semi-final argument, the New York judge, without identifying the opinion as his own, asked DeVier what he thought about the legal proposition he had articulated in the case. DeVier was able to respond that he had great respect for the court's opinion in that case, but that the OU position was distinguishable in specified ways. The judge beamed. That would never have happened without the kindness of the Michigan competitor at a time when he had to be disappointed in his own team's loss.[22]

As predicted by observers of the moot court team victory, DeVier received offers from several Wall Street firms during the spring of his senior year. The prevailing wage rate for new associates in New York City was about three times the prevailing rate in Oklahoma, so the offers were tempting in financial terms. But DeVier had never been interested in living in New York City and gave no serious consideration to the proposals. He believed his future was anchored in Oklahoma.

DeVier also spent time in his final year in law school as managing editor of the *Oklahoma Law Review*, a prestigious position. The board of editors wrote and edited legal articles and commentaries on a wide variety of subjects. Writing for the *Law Review* was a tremendous help in developing and honing the needed skills for organizing thoughts and putting them in writing.[23]

Harvey P. Everest, left, president of Liberty National Bank and Trust Company, presents DeVier and wife, Shirley, with a $500 check for the annual Liberty scholarship given to the outstanding student in the field of Estate Planning.

The success in the national moot court competition no doubt played a role in other high honors that came to DeVier. He became a member of Order of the Coif, received a $500 scholarship from Oklahoma City's Liberty National Bank and Trust Company, and received the S.T. Bledsoe Award as the outstanding law school senior. DeVier never fails to note that his friend, Arch Gilbert, was the class valedictorian by a substantial margin.

DeVier was proud of all his fellow students, but took particular joy in graduating from the OU College of Law in May, 1957, with John Green, the only African American in the class. Green served Oklahoma and the nation well for many years as a federal prosecutor in Oklahoma City. Their friendship has remained steady for the decades since receiving their diplomas in 1957.[24]

CHAPTER NINE

LOVE, MARRIAGE, AND A NEW LIFE

What I wanted to do more than anything else was to get into the courtroom without delay.

—DeVier Pierson

DeVier had occasionally seen Shirley Frost since she was a sophomore and he was a senior at Classen High School. When she came to OU, she was a regular at Phi Gam parties on the arm of others, but the age gap was still substantial. When DeVier was starting law school, Shirley began to "pop up" on his social radar screen more frequently. They dated before he left for active duty in the Army and while he was home before shipping out for Korea. They exchanged letters, although Shirley said his letters were not "very romantic" because they were "typewritten and chatty rather than soulful." There was no exclusivity of dating on either side of the relationship.[1]

Shirley Frost on a ski trip in Colorado. She had known DeVier since she was a 14-year-old sophomore at Classen High School, but they did not begin to date until much later.

85

When DeVier returned from Korea and prepared to enter his second year of law school, the chemistry between Shirley and him became more serious. They spent memorable evenings at the Beacon Club in Oklahoma City and danced to Frank Sinatra's "Tender Trap," frequently in the company of Fred and Nan Buxton. The only downside was that Shirley's father always seemed to be around when he took her home to obey the midnight curfew. Shirley's little brother, Paul, was famous for sneaking up behind DeVier's car and taking photographs of the young couple as DeVier was telling Shirley good night.[2]

DeVier may have been ready for a lasting relationship, but Shirley apparently was not. She and a college friend moved to Fort Lauderdale, Florida. Shirley and DeVier kept in touch, but Shirley was often reporting about her visits to nightclubs and a trip to Havana, Cuba, during the last throes of the Batista regime. Back in Norman, DeVier was "trying to fight fire with fire" on the social front.

Shirley's brother, Paul Frost, used stealth and his camera to record DeVier's good night kiss of Shirley in front of the Frost home.

Even in his busy schedule, DeVier greatly missed Shirley. He often visited Shirley's mother who gave photographs of Shirley to DeVier. To put pressure on Shirley, DeVier told her that if they were going to have a relationship, she needed to come home to Oklahoma. A few weeks later Shirley consented and DeVier picked her up at the airport. Shirley was very tan and seemed relaxed and happy. DeVier did not think that was a good sign. But, after constant companionship during the summer, DeVier "popped the martial question" in August.[3]

On September 1, DeVier and Shirley announced their engagement at a surprise party for friends at Shirley's home. In a responsible division of assignments, DeVier agreed to prepare for the moot court competition and stay afloat in law school and Shirley would plan their social life and prepare for a February wedding between law school semesters.

DeVier's parents were ambivalent about the wedding plans. They liked Shirley very much and were certain their son could do no better. But they were terrified that the weight of marriage might cause DeVier to pay less than adequate attention to his studies. Their wish was that the couple would wait until after DeVier graduated. DeVier's view was that being a young married man was bound to be more stable than spending one more semester as a bachelor on the OU campus.[4]

Reason prevailed. After several pre-wedding parties during the Christmas season, DeVier and Shirley were married on February 1, 1957, at Westminster Presbyterian Church in Oklahoma City. It was a beautiful white tie wedding with all the trimmings. DeVier's best man was Burns Proctor, his friend from the Army. His ushers included Phi Gam fraternity

DeVier and his beautiful bride, Shirley, at their wedding reception in Oklahoma City on February 1, 1957.

Shirley, center, with brother, Paul Frost, left, and sister, Marta Reynolds, on her wedding day.

brothers John Cox, Lew Ground, Earl Amundsen, Jim Berry, and Dick Van Cleef, and law school friends Bill Rogers and Duke Logan. Shirley's 12-year-old brother, Paul, was a junior usher.

The young couple spent their wedding night in the Pearl Mesta Suite of the Skirvin Hotel, a wedding gift of the owner. Shirley's father called early the next morning "to make certain his little girl was alright." DeVier and Shirley drove to Dallas for the next night and caught the new comedy duo of Dan Rowan and Dick Martin in the dinner club of the Adolphus Hotel. They spent the remainder of their honeymoon in New Orleans, where Oklahoman Virginia Eason Weinmann and her husband, Jack, "with typical thoughtfulness," threw a surprise dinner party for them, before DeVier returned to classes. They set up housekeeping in a rental home at 2757 Cambridge Court in Oklahoma City.[5]

DeVier had married into another pioneer Oklahoma family, but one with a very different heritage than his own.

DeVier and Shirley with their parents at the wedding reception. Left to right, Paul Frost, Alice Frost, Shirley, DeVier, Frances Pierson, and Welcome D. Pierson.

Shirley's paternal grandfather, Charles Frost, usually called Grosfader, was German and migrated to Oklahoma City at the beginning of the twentieth century when the community was a rough and tumble territorial town. He was a successful businessman who catered to every taste, owning a hotel, saloon, brewery, and even the water works. He was among the many immigrants who made the new state his home.

On a trip back to Germany, he fell in love with and married the 20-year-old daughter of his best friend and brought Clara to Oklahoma City. When she became pregnant, she refused to have her child in this dusty frontier land and insisted on returning alone by train and boat to her homeland to have the baby. Shirley's father, Paul Karl Frost, was born in Breslau, Germany, in 1905, but came to Oklahoma City when he was three months old.[6]

Charles and Clara lived in Oklahoma for the remainder of their lives. The family called Clara "Bim Bom," German for tick tock, because she swung a watch over the bed of her children and grandchildren chanting "Bim Bom." Clara once told DeVier that the first election she remembered was the 1912 presidential race between Theodore Roosevelt and Woodrow Wilson. The Frosts endured a good deal of prejudice toward Germans during World War I, but continued to live happily in Oklahoma City until Charles' death in 1935. Bim Bom, who became the faithful babysitter for Shirley and DeVier's children, lived to the ripe old age of 93.

Shirley's maternal grandfather, Charles Phelps, was another Oklahoma pioneer. He came from Canada shortly after the Oklahoma Land Run of 1889. He married Carrie Warren in 1902 and had seven children, including Shirley's mother, Carrie Alice. Phelps became a successful local real estate investor with one of his more striking parcels being the milk bottle triangle at Northwest 24th street and Classen Boulevard. Shirley's parents were married in 1933. Shirley was born on April 16, 1934 and was raised with siblings, Marta and Paul, on Northwest 21st Street.[7]

After their marriage, other than the proceeds from the Liberty National Bank scholarship, Shirley was the Piersons' sole means of support in the spring of 1957. She worked at the Cessna dealership at the old Tulakes Airport.

To keep the family going financially, Shirley worked at the Cessna airplane dealership in Oklahoma City. She took flying lessons while she was there.

DeVier began practicing law in Oklahoma City after his graduating from the OU College of Law in the Class of 1957.

Eager to begin private practice as a lawyer, DeVier caught a wonderful break at the beginning of his career. The Oklahoma legislature, "in their infinite wisdom," had passed a resolution allowing law students whose studies had been interrupted by serving in the military in Korea to be admitted to practice without studying for and passing the Oklahoma bar examination. So, while most of his classmates were burning the midnight oil studying bar review courses, DeVier showed up at the State Capitol and was immediately sworn in as a fully accredited lawyer by the Clerk of the Oklahoma Supreme Court.[8]

With the decision made to reject any offers from law firms in New York, DeVier looked for a job. He was tempted by an offer to be a clerk for Appeals Court Judge Alfred P. Murrah. Clerkships under Judge Murrah were coveted. However, even though the clerkship would have been a great professional experience and would look good on his resume, DeVier was anxious to begin practice. He declined Judge Murrah's offer, but the judge remained one of DeVier's heroes until his death.

Then, just the right opportunity came along. DeVier heard that Duke Duvall, a prominent Oklahoma City trial attorney, was forming a new partnership with Ben Head, a Phi Gam who had been an active alumnus when DeVier lived in the fraternity house. He went to the firm's new office, introduced himself, and announced that he wanted to be the firm's first associate. He told Duvall that they could pay him whatever they thought he was worth provided that he could try cases in the courtroom right away. Duval was amused, but honored both ends of the bargain. In June, 1957, DeVier began work for $300 per month. Two weeks after becoming a lawyer, he was impaneling a jury in a small case in district court.[9]

During the next two years, DeVier tried about 40 jury cases and assisted in many more in state and federal courts in Oklahoma City and throughout the state. He appeared before federal judges Fred Daugherty, Ross Rizley, and Stephen Chandler and made an argument before the Tenth Circuit Court of Appeals. He also was given the opportunity to make one of the infrequent oral arguments heard by the Oklahoma Supreme Court. Duke Duvall had given DeVier much more than a small salary; he had given him the chance of a lifetime to start his career in the courtroom.

In the heat of the litigation battle, DeVier learned the ropes of conducting proper discovery, taking depositions, and issuing interrogatories. Playing on his childhood practice of making scrapbooks of his Greek and Roman heroes, he pieced together all Oklahoma authority on evidence and compiled it in a three-ring binder he still has. He argued many motions in the days before copy machines when he actually took the volumes of reported cases with him to the courtroom and read from them as he referred to a particular case. He learned the trial lawyer technique of preparing a diagram of a jury during voir dire so he could memorize it and then put random questions to members of the jury and call them by name.[10]

DeVier thought he was at the legal pinnacle by having Duke Duvall as his mentor. While trying a case together in Seminole, they shared a room at a downtown hotel. At the end of the day, Duvall pulled out a flask of bourbon and poured both of them a shot. DeVier remembered, "As I sat there on the edge of my bed knocking one back with this accomplished lawyer, I thought I had now reached the legal big time!"[11]

Even as a brand-new lawyer, DeVier made good impressions upon other lawyers and judges at the courthouse. Marian Opala, now a justice of the Oklahoma Supreme Court, was a private practitioner who noticed DeVier. He said, "He stood out by both his dress and social manners. Impeccably dressed in the dark-suit attire of the day, he always wore a hat which was then fastly disappearing from the absolutely required accouterments of the male vogue." Opala continued, "DeVier's manner of speech was always formal, correct, and unaffected by the region's provincial dialect too often used by others. We became fast friends. A rare class act is the only fitting phrase to describe DeVier as a lawyer, a personal friend, and a human being."[12]

In courtroom work, DeVier especially enjoyed cross examining witnesses, particularly medical witnesses. He read several medical anatomy books to get some basic understanding of the human body and its parts. When he cross examined doctors who habitually testified for the plaintiffs, he allowed them to give a long explanation of why their patient's whiplash injury was so bad even though no diagnostic test showed anything wrong. After the doctor testified at length about his qualifications to give such an opinion, DeVier shot back, "Yes, I guess you are an expert on whiplash. In fact, isn't it true that you have testified for 14 plaintiffs in the past year and made a diagnosis of whiplash for each of them?" The jury often got the picture.[13]

DeVier's most unique case was in one of the few instances where the firm represented the plaintiff. The daughter of one of Duvall's good friends had been severely injured in an automobile accident. After the case was filed, DeVier discovered that the defendant's insurance company was represented by his father. At trial the judge determined in chambers that it was best that he refer to the lawyers not by name, but by "counsel." The jury apparently never knew that father and son were arguing for clients on opposite sides of the lawsuit.

Even though it was uncomfortable to be in combat with his father, it gave DeVier a wonderful opportunity to see his father in action at close hand. He came away with an increased admiration for his skill as a defense lawyer. DeVier won the case, but the judgment was far lower than he expected. His father's client probably would have considered it a victory.[14]

During a jury trial in Madill, Oklahoma, DeVier was concerned that he was away from home while Shirley was nine months pregnant and expecting their first child any day. After testimony and closing arguments in the trial on February 7,

1959, the jury was sent to deliberate. Moments after the jury left the courtroom the bailiff gave DeVier a note that Shirley had been taken to the hospital.

DeVier was determined not to miss the birth of his first child. He explained the situation to the judge who commissioned a member of the local bar who had been watching closing arguments to accept the verdict when it came in and told DeVier "to get the hell out of here." DeVier drove at a high rate of speed to Wesley Hospital where Jeffrey DeVier Pierson was born after he arrived. DeVier had mercifully decided not to saddle his son with the name, Welcome DeVier Pierson, III. DeVier believes Jeff was never sufficiently grateful for his restraint.[15]

In addition to trial work, DeVier prepared a few wills and worked on legal issues arising from the development of the new Quail Creek Addition to Oklahoma City. The firm represented Quail Creek Development Company and helped raise investment funds for the project. The units of participation were $50,000 each and were going fast. In his first entrepreneurial effort since the failed seat cushion business, DeVier took one of the Quail Creek units and sold it to ten of his friends at $5,000 each. In honor of his days at Camp Classen, he called it the "poor boys unit."

Shirley and DeVier settled down into the social life of Oklahoma City. They organized monthly get-togethers of the "Christmas Club" with Bill and Barbara Bevers, Jack and Joanie Catlett, Bill and Joy Rogers, Ed and Nancy deCordova, Barbara and Jack Coleman, and Randy and Faith Mary Everest. They had lots of low-budget dinners focused on bridge, burgers, Kentucky fried chicken, and movies.

With a growing family, the Piersons needed more room. They built a tract home at 2521 Kings Way in The Village, a north Oklahoma City suburb. The new area was a magnet for young couples of limited means. DeVier insisted on a wood burning fireplace in the living room, upping the cost of the house to $15,300. He financed the house with a borrowed $300 cash and a $15,000 FHA loan.[16]

Because of his involvement with the development of Quail Creek, DeVier was invited to be a charter member of the Quail Creek Golf and Country Club. Unfortunately, he did not have extra cash to pay the $500 initiation fee. He visited Penn Square Bank and borrowed $500 from the bank's young president, Bill "Beep" Jennings. The bank would later become famous when its collapse during a downturn in the oil and gas business reverberated through the nation's banking system.

In 1959, DeVier began working with Bill Whiteman, John Nichols, and other Oklahoma City businessmen who had formed a company to manage the assets of the infamous Selected Investments, a company that issued certificates of deposit with a guaranteed six percent return to thousands of Oklahoma investors. Selected Investments failed because its management was running a Ponzi scheme, able to meet obligations only from cash realized from new deposits. The collapse of Selected Investments was tied to their efforts to bribe members of the Oklahoma Supreme Court to get a favorable decision in a tax case. DeVier agreed to look at potential investments for the new Mid-America Corporation.[17]

In 1961, DeVier became heavily involved in plans by the same group to create a real estate investment trust, an investment vehicle that had favorable tax consequences for its owners and issued shares that could be publicly traded. DeVier took over the project and convinced his law school friend, Bill Bevers, to join him.

Deciding that Florida would be the best place to establish the trust, DeVier, Shirley, Jeff, and their newest addition, Elizabeth Frost Pierson, born on March 14, 1961, lived in Sarasota, Florida, for nine months. The trust, named Liberty Real Estate Trust, obtained an effective prospectus from the Securities and Exchange Commission. DeVier and Bevers, with the assistance of several real estate consultants, crisscrossed Florida looking for property owners who were willing to place their property in the trust in exchange for shares. In the end, they assembled properties with an equity value of approximately $10 million, a sum that seemed much larger then than it does now.[18]

After the trust closed, DeVier made a number of trips to New York City to find a public market for the shares. It was his first exposure to Wall Street and the investment banking community. Side trips to Broadway plays and helicopter rides from the top of the Pan Am Building in Manhattan to La-Guardia Airport were enjoyable first time experiences.

Other business opportunities came along because of the association with Whiteman and his group. DeVier and others backed a venture to computerize billing records of professionals using the main frame computers at banks. He also participated in the purchase of Cheatham Furniture Manufacturing

Company, a successful furniture manufacturer in Oklahoma City. The best part of that venture for DeVier was bringing in Dan Hogan as a partner to run the business. Not only did Hogan succeed in that and later ventures, he and his wife, Sarah, developed a lasting friendship with DeVier and Shirley.

Life was very good for the Piersons. The private practice of law and forays into the business world had been exciting. DeVier and Shirley had two beautiful children and a circle of close friends. He played golf at least once a week at Quail Creek. But, from time to time, he heard a small voice within asking, "Isn't there something more out there?" [19]

CHAPTER TEN

THE LURE OF POLITICS

*I am going to be a candidate for President of the
United States. Would you be willing to help me?*
—John F. Kennedy

DeVier's father was an Oklahoma "yellow dog Democrat," voting a straight party Democratic ticket "even if it was
headed by a yellow dog." W.D. Pierson's adult life experiences were shaped by the Great Depression, World War II,
and Democratic leaders Presidents Franklin D. Roosevelt and
Harry Truman. When DeVier was small, his father took him
to the Santa Fe Depot in Oklahoma City to catch a glimpse
of President Roosevelt waving from the back of a campaign
train.[1]

W.D. strayed from the party line only once in his life. He
had the great fortune of having Republican Ralph Thompson
and his wife, Barbara, as next-door neighbors. When Thompson was running for lieutenant governor of Oklahoma in
1970, W.D. called DeVier and announced, "after much soul
searching," he was voting for Thompson, the first and only
time in his life he cast a vote for a GOP candidate.

When DeVier was in high school and college he participated in campaigns on behalf of Congressman John Jarman
and United States Senator Mike Monroney. The campaigns
were "low tech." There was no television and candidates
campaigned in person at rallies and speaking events. The
candidates appeared at larger gatherings and surrogates made

their pitch to smaller groups. With his prowess at public speaking, DeVier was one such surrogate and spoke for his candidate at dozens of rallies in Oklahoma City and surrounding counties. Supporting a wide range of candidates from governor to county commissioner was, for DeVier, "an interesting and enjoyable field trip into Oklahoma politics."[2]

DeVier's first experience with machine politics and captive voters came in his freshman year at OU. Louie Trost, the Phi Gam president, ordered pledges to attend a meeting of the League of Young Democrats and were instructed to vote for a slate of officers that included David Busby as president and Fred Harris as secretary. Busby later became one of DeVier's closest friends in Washington, D.C., and Harris served Oklahoma as a legislator, United States Senator, and Democratic presidential candidate.

Other than traveling to Will Rogers Field to see Dwight Eisenhower at an airport rally in 1952, DeVier paid little attention to presidential politics for the remainder of the 1950s. He was preoccupied with law school and military duty and considered himself "a political agnostic" until the late 1950s.[3]

DeVier was lured into the political arena at the annual Jefferson-Jackson Day Dinner in Oklahoma City in 1958. The speaker was the young United States Senator from Massachusetts, John F. Kennedy. Kennedy had unsuccessfully pursued the vice presidential nomination in 1956 and his presidential ambitions were public knowledge. The Oklahoma visit was part of a two-year tour by Kennedy to expand his reputation and build a national organization to support a run for the presidency in 1960.

Two weeks before the dinner, DeVier received a call from Kennedy's Senate office inviting him to join the senator for lunch on the day of the dinner. The invitation was a surprise to DeVier. He was fresh out of law school and was not active in state party politics.

A dozen younger business and professional men joined Kennedy for the informal luncheon in a suite in the Skirvin Hotel. Kennedy made clear his political ambitions to DeVier and the other young men as they sat in shirt sleeves and ate club sandwiches. As DeVier left the suite, Kennedy took him by his arm and asked for a private conversation.

In the bedroom, Kennedy called DeVier by his first name and said, "I am going to be a candidate for President of the United States. Would you be willing to help me?" No doubt DeVier's name had been given to Kennedy by Ted Sorenson, who accompanied him on every trip. But, DeVier remembers, "It was still impressive."[4]

It was a "heady" moment for the 27-year-old DeVier, a scene that must have been repeated thousands of times as Kennedy garnered volunteers for his embryonic presidential campaign. DeVier quickly told Kennedy he would be honored to help. A few days later, DeVier received a letter from Kennedy and then a Christmas card from Kennedy and his wife, Jackie. The seduction was complete and DeVier was firmly entrenched as a member of the Kennedy team.[5]

At the 1960 Democratic National Convention in Los Angeles, California, DeVier joined Kennedy's campaign staff and was responsible for liaison to the Oklahoma delegation. Oklahoma Democrats overwhelmingly supported

Texas United States Senator and Majority Leader Lyndon B. Johnson. Oklahoma Senator Robert S. Kerr was very close to Johnson and led the Oklahoma delegation pledged to him. United States Senator Mike Monroney, and his closest aide, Tom Finney, supported the nomination for a third time of Adlai Stevenson. Finney, originally from Idabel, Oklahoma, would later develop a longtime friendship with DeVier in Washington, D.C.

The only prominent Oklahoma political leader supporting Kennedy was Governor J. Howard Edmondson who had lost control of the Oklahoma Democratic Party during his first two years as chief executive. Kennedy, a young, urban Catholic Democrat, was the last choice for the nomination among most Oklahoma Democrats.[6]

This became very clear at the convention. DeVier attended a 7:30 a.m. staff meeting each morning. Kennedy's brother, Robert F. "Bobby" Kennedy, presided over the meetings. One morning, the younger Kennedy sent DeVier on a mission to determine if there was any chance the Oklahoma delegation would support Kennedy if it became clear that Johnson could not get the nomination. When DeVier approached Senator Kerr, the elder statesman explained that the order of preference of Oklahoma Democrats was Johnson, Senator Stuart Symington, and Adlai Stevenson. Beyond them, Kerr said, "I don't know what the Oklahoma delegation would do." There was no mention of Kennedy, a fact not welcomed by Bobby Kennedy when DeVier made his report. DeVier was in the convention hall when Kennedy was chosen on the first ballot and when he selected Johnson as his running mate—a surprise choice with fateful implications.[7]

After the convention, DeVier was asked to serve as Oklahoma chairman for Citizens for Kennedy-Johnson, an "outside" group to provide a home for those voters not active in the state Democratic Party. Oklahoma was tough political territory for Kennedy's campaign. He was unlikely to do well among Republicans in Tulsa and northern Oklahoma. In Democratic Little Dixie, Catholicism was a big issue among rural Democrats. DeVier and his group opened a storefront campaign office on North Broadway Avenue in Oklahoma City and tried to build a Kennedy-Johnson following around the state. It was a standing joke that it was difficult to "get up a bridge game" of Kennedy supporters in most Oklahoma communities.[8]

Because the Democratic party machinery in Oklahoma was not overly fond of the ticket headed by Kennedy, DeVier and Shirley hosted Kennedy campaign staffers when they visited Oklahoma. Even though she was pregnant, Shirley was "a wonderful hostess" when Ted Sorenson, Ralph Dungan, Fred Vinson, and others came to Oklahoma City. One evening, she served them barbecued ribs with a very hot sauce, a shock to the culinary system of the young men raised on the East Coast. Vinson's father was the former Chief Justice of the United States. A decade later, young Vinson became DeVier's close friend and golfing companion in the nation's capital.

The Kennedy campaign never took life in Oklahoma. That is why DeVier was shocked when the Kennedy campaign headquarters called the week before the election in November, 1960, to announce an Oklahoma City appearance by the candidate. DeVier suggested that Kennedy was trailing badly in Oklahoma, but campaign officials said their internal polls showed the Democrat had a chance to carry the state if he made a personal appearance.[9]

Former Governor Raymond Gary was among the first politicians to show up at Will Rogers Field on the Thursday evening before the election to await Kennedy's cream-colored Convair, trimmed in orange and brown. By the time Kennedy arrived, DeVier was flanked by Democratic Party chairman Gene McGill, Governor Edmondson, House Speaker J.D.McCarty, and Senator Everett Collins.

Kennedy then went to the Municipal Auditorium for a high energy rally. Jim Young, a reporter for *The Daily Oklahoman*, wrote, "Kennedy, with a boyish grin on his face and confetti in his hair, stepped before a shouting, cheering audience…to try to pull Oklahoma back into the Democratic camp." The feeling that Kennedy was not an overwhelming favorite in Oklahoma was best said by a headline in *The Daily Oklahoman*, "City Crowd Cheers But Doesn't Swoon."[10] DeVier thought that most Oklahomans who intended to vote for Kennedy were probably in the audience that night.

DeVier and other Kennedy supporters did their best to create a spirit of enthusiasm. Spectators had a chance to see Kennedy along a motorcade route from the airport to the Municipal Auditorium. Bands played along the downtown route.

At the rally, Kennedy was belatedly endorsed by Senator Robert S. Kerr who was running for reelection. Polls showed Kerr would win with 80 percent of the vote. It was a safe bet for Kerr because the national election was close. DeVier sat next to Kennedy during the evening's program. After Kerr's endorsement, Kennedy took the senator by the arm and said, "Bob, you've just made me a hundred thousand votes." Kerr replied, "I hope so, Jack, I just lost a hundred thousand myself." [11]

Kerr's instincts were better than the internal polls of the Kennedy campaign. The following Tuesday, Kennedy was elected president by a razor-thin margin, but Richard Nixon swept Oklahoma with more than 60 percent of the popular vote. For years, Kennedy aide Sorenson, who hailed from Nebraska, and DeVier argued about which of the two states was the worst for Kennedy in the election. [12]

DeVier was asked if he wanted to join the Kennedy administration in Washington, but decided it was not the right time to leave Oklahoma City. He had little contact with President Kennedy and his staff except for occasional lunches at the White House mess with staff members he met in the campaign or in visits to the nation's capital.

There was a poignant coda. DeVier's next connection with Kennedy was on the fateful day of November 22, 1963. DeVier arrived at Love Field in Dallas about 1:00 p.m. for a downtown meeting. As his airplane landed, he noticed a Boeing 707 with "United States of America" painted on the side parked near the terminal and ringed with a military guard. He suddenly remembered that the morning newspaper had announced Kennedy would be in Dallas that day. [13]

DeVier was met at the airport by a friend who looked stricken and said, "President Kennedy has been shot and may be dead." Clusters of people huddled around transistor radios.

DeVier found a television in time to see newscaster Walter Cronkite say, "It's official, President Kennedy is dead."[14]

DeVier was numb, and just wanted to go home. However, when he approached the Braniff Airlines counter for a return trip to Oklahoma City, he was informed the airport was closed until further notice. He stood for the next two hours at a window and saw history unfold although he was too stunned to fully comprehend the historical events that unveiled before his eyes. A limousine drove up to *Air Force One* and a tense, grave Lyndon Johnson emerged and hurried to the plane. Then a hearse bearing the body of Kennedy pulled to the rear cargo door and, with the First Lady at its side, the casket was loaded onto the airplane.

A few minutes later, Sarah Hughes, a Dallas federal judge who was a friend of the Johnson family, arrived in a car and was escorted onboard to deliver the oath of office to the new President. Finally, *Air Force One* began to move, turned on to the main runway, and soared into the Texas sky with two presidents on board, one dead and one facing a sad journey back to Washington, D.C. As he returned to Oklahoma City, DeVier had no idea of the important role that the new President would play in his life a few years later.[15]

In 1964, DeVier learned a valuable lesson in practical politics when he agreed to co-chair the Democratic Council for an Effective Legislature (DCEL) with prominent Capitol Hill businessman Jim Lookabaugh. The group was formed after the United States Supreme Court ruled in a "one man-one vote" decision that the state legislature had to be reapportioned to reflect population. The effect was to create a large number of new State Senate and House of Representatives seats in urban areas of Oklahoma City and Tulsa. Oklahoma County would elect eight senators and 19 House members by countywide election.[16]

Initially, DCEL had wide support. District chairmen included attorney James R. West, medical clinic administrator Dwight Mitchell, attorney C.H. Spearman, Jr., Dr. Allan Stanley, businessman Fred Schilling, banker Robert Empie, and Dr. W.H. Porter.[17]

DeVier and many other leaders were concerned that all 27 seats being elected at large by all county voters might leave large pockets of the electorate unrepresented. There was also the concern that with potentially more than 100 candidates filing for the 27 positions, voters would have little chance to look at their qualifications. DCEL proposed that nominating committees be created for each of the eight senatorial districts to recommend one senatorial and two House candidates for each district with the approval of the entire DCEL council.

It was a sensible approach, but it did make kingmakers out of the DCEL. DeVier, Lookabaugh, and other leaders of the effort encountered a firestorm of opposition from incumbents and others who believed that the DCEL picking candidates amounted to elitism. Such criticism caused the proposal to fail, although DCEL did come forward with a slate of candidates in some districts.[18]

Having now dabbled in the elections of state legislators and one President of the United States, DeVier returned to professional life in Oklahoma City. That was about to change.

CHAPTER ELEVEN

OFF TO WASHINGTON

I knew I wanted to be closer to the historic events unfolding in Washington, D.C., but I was baffled as to how do to so.

— DeVier Pierson

DeVier's long friendship with Oklahoma United States Senator Mike Monroney changed his career path in 1965. For years, DeVier had enormous admiration and affection for Monroney who he saw as "an unusual kind of political figure," with a journalist's background and a warm and humble personality. Monroney was sometimes disorganized, not flamboyant, and labored for a long time in the large shadow of Senator Kerr.[1]

The Piersons had family ties with the Monroneys. Shirley's mother was first cousin to Monroney's wife, Mary Ellen Monroney. They grew up like sisters and traveled together when they were teenagers. Mary Ellen often invited Shirley and DeVier to visit them in Washington.

DeVier had been impressed with one of Monroney's legislative achievements while Monroney was still in the United States House of Representatives. He and Senator Robert LaFollette co-authored the LaFollette-Monroney Legislative Reorganization Act of 1946, the first time in the twentieth century that Congress had made fundamental changes to its organizational structure. For his efforts, Monroney received the Collier Award as the outstanding member of Congress. It gave rise to DeVier's feelings that Monroney was sometimes more appreciated in the nation's capital than he was in Oklahoma.[2]

Shortly after the 1964 election in which President Johnson was elected to a full term and Oklahoma Democrat Fred Harris rode Johnson's coattails to defeat Republican Bud Wilkinson for the United States Senate seat, Monroney invited DeVier to lunch in Oklahoma City. The senator said he wanted to revisit the area of congressional reorganization because he believed a number of additional reforms were needed. He said such reform could not be accomplished through the work of standing committees in the Congress. Monroney wanted to seek authorization for the creation of a Joint Committee on the Organization of Congress. He thought the Joint Committee's work might take one or two years.

DeVier liked the idea, but was shocked when Monroney said, "If I can get the Joint Committee authorized, would you come to Washington as chief counsel to head up the staff and let us work together on this project?"[3]

It was a perfect offer at a perfect time. It would give DeVier a unique opportunity to be in Washington and to look at all aspects of Congress, to get what amounted to a doctorate in political science, without having to make a permanent commitment to leave Oklahoma. After talking to Shirley about the possibility, DeVier called Monroney the following day to accept.

Shirley was very supportive. She knew DeVier was "fidgety" and wanted to be involved in national issues. Although she loved her Oklahoma family and friends, she "was willing to take the plunge." In fact, DeVier learned that Shirley had been talking with Mary Ellen Monroney about how wonderful it would be for them to spend more time in Washington. For years, when asked how the appointment came about, DeVier responded, "It combined all the best attributes of patronage and nepotism."[4]

Shirley knew that if DeVier was not stimulated or intellectually challenged, he would not be happy. She saw him as "restless" in his law practice and business endeavors in Oklahoma City and recognized that the intrigue of the nation's capital would be exciting for him.[5]

Even though DeVier was a student of American history, he knew little about the operation or organization of Congress. As Committee counsel he would be dealing with some of the most powerful members of the Senate and House without being well qualified to do so. While Monroney was seeking legislative approval for the Joint Committee, DeVier began a cram course on Congress. He reviewed the LaFol-

United States Senator Mike Monroney, left, welcomes DeVier to Washington, D.C. Monroney was DeVier's mentor in his work as Chief Counsel of the Joint Committee on the Organization of Congress.

lette-Monroney Act, reports of the committee's hearings, and scholarly articles written by political scientists on the state of Congress. He also immersed himself in books on the history of the Congress.

Allan Cromley wrote in the Oklahoma City Times*: Pierson was given a stack of books and reference material and told to become an overnight expert. Since last November, Pierson has been burning midnight oil to catch up with Capitol Hill veterans, who for 20 and 30 years have been soaking up knowledge that Pierson is acquiring almost overnight...If he performs spectacularly in the committee job, he'll be wooed by government agencies as well as private law firms.*[6]

Monroney was successful in obtaining authority and a budget for the new Joint Committee on the Organization of Congress (Joint Committee) on March 11, 1965. It was to be a bi-partisan, bicameral committee of 12 members—six from the Senate and six from the House—half Democrat and half Republican. A strong committee was appointed and DeVier was named chief counsel. Senate members of the Joint Committee were Monroney, John Sparkman of Alabama, Lee Metcalf of Montana, Karl Mundt of South Dakota, Clifford Case of New Jersey, and J. Caleb Boggs of Delaware. House members were Ray Madden of Indiana, Jack Brooks of Texas, Ken Hechler of West Virginia, Thomas Curtis of Missouri, Durward Hall of Missouri, and James Cleveland of New Hampshire, who resigned during the process to be appointed to the United States Senate.[7]

Immediately after the legislation establishing the Joint

Committee was approved, DeVier left for Washington. Jeff
and Libby were in school in Oklahoma City, so DeVier was
a bachelor for a few weeks. He stayed with the Monroneys
and commuted to the Capitol each day with the senator. They
often had breakfast and lunch together and discussed organization of the Joint Committee, pending legislation, and the
world in general. DeVier could not have asked for a better
mentor.[8]

While staying in the Monroney home, DeVier became
the extra man at a series of dinner parties. Mary Ellen was
legendary as a hostess and many Washington "movers and
shakers" dined with the Monroneys. DeVier was in awe of
the dinner guests. One evening he found himself having dinner with United States Supreme Court Justice Potter Stewart, Chairman of the Joint Chiefs of Staff General Maxwell
Taylor, and prominent journalist William S. White and their
wives. DeVier mustered the courage to tell General Taylor
about his brief encounter with him in Tokyo ten years before
in the "saluting" incident. The general was mildly amused.
For someone who had barely seen the major tourist sights of
the nation's capital, the dinner parties provided DeVier an
incredible introduction to life in Washington.

Because both houses of Congress wanted the Joint Committee to be on neutral ground, DeVier's office was located in
the exact center of the United States Capitol. The view from
behind his desk was from the north front of the Capitol to the
Mall, past the Smithsonian buildings, and on to the Washington Monument and the Lincoln Memorial. It was the best
office view in Washington. DeVier said his office views went

steadily downhill in the more than 40 years since.[9]

DeVier's role as chief counsel was somewhat murky in the beginning. He had three other professionals on the staff, and each of them had far more government experience. One staff member was a former Michigan congressman who planned to run again to win back his seat. Another was a longtime aide to Senator Karl Mundt, the ranking Senate Republican. The final staff member was a political scientist who had spent many years working with various congressional committees on legislative matters.

DeVier's first challenge was to develop a division of responsibility among staff members, although one staffer arrived for work at 10:00 a.m., left for an extended and "highly liquid" lunch, and left the office for the day at 4:00 p.m. "They at least tolerated me as their nominal boss," DeVier remembered, "and eventually began to follow my lead."[10]

DeVier set out to meet the congressional leaders whose good will would be critical to the Joint Committee's success. He recognized that he needed to assure chairmen and staff directors of each congressional committee that it was not the Joint Committee's purpose to relieve them of their power—the idea was to make their jobs easier and more efficient. The meetings with committee chairmen tended to be brief and courteous. However, DeVier began establishing ongoing relationships with staff directors, the daily drivers of their committee's agenda. DeVier asked for their concerns and priorities. He hoped they would become his tutors in learning about Congress. He wanted their opinions as to whether any proposal was sensible or unrealistic.[11]

The Joint Committee began hearings on May 10, 1965, in the old Supreme Court chamber, one of the most historic rooms in the Capitol. The room had been used by the Senate in the early years of the republic and then became the chamber for the Supreme Court. As DeVier looked around the room, he could almost hear the voices of early Senate giants at the beginning of the nineteenth century. He could also imagine the Supreme Court sitting in the chamber to decide historic cases such as Dred Scott prior to the outbreak of the Civil War.

After Senator Monroney gaveled the hearings into session, and other committee members made opening statements, senators and congressmen begin giving testimony. The first Senate witness was Senator Joseph Clark of Pennsylvania, "a congressional reform gladfly" with a host of unrealistic proposals. Clark was a thorn in the Joint Committee's side for the entire process and was miffed that he had not been asked to serve on the committee. The first House witness was Oklahoma Congressman Ed Edmondson.[12]

It had been 20 years since senators and congressmen had the opportunity to express their views on the structure and functions of Congress, so there was a good deal of interest in the hearings. One of DeVier's responsibilities was to talk to witnesses in advance of their testimony, understand their views, and prepare possible questions for Senator Monroney and other committee members. In some cases, these meetings led to friendships that have continued over the years.

One such witness was Senator Thomas Kuchel of California, the assistant Republican leader in the Senate, who later asked DeVier to join him in his Washington law practice. Other witnesses included Representative Bob Ellsworth of Kansas, who DeVier subsequently met with when Ellsworth was a member of Nixon's White House staff; Representative Melvin Laird of Wisconsin, later Nixon's Secretary of Defense; Representative Bob Michel, later House Republican leader, and Representative George Mahon, the powerful chairman of the House Appropriations Committee. DeVier later had a number of dealings with Chairman Mahon while he was in the Johnson White House. Laird, Michel, and Mahon were also sometime golf companions.

There was some comic relief. Representative Robert Dole of Kansas, later Senate Republican leader and the GOP presidential nominee in 1996, had a wicked sense of humor. DeVier listened to Dole closely when he espoused serious proposals for the reorganization of Congress, but was at first "taken aback" by Dole's tongue-in-cheek suggestions that the Joint Committee oppose free haircuts for members of Congress and prohibit senators from announcing federal grants until members of the House had made them public.[13]

Another early witness was Senator James Pearson of Kansas. The same last name, although with a different spelling, created a standing joke between DeVier and the senator. One day when DeVier was going to a meeting in the Senate Office Building, the young elevator operator said, "Good afternoon, Mr. Pierson." DeVier asked the young man how he knew his name. It turned out that the operator had previously heard someone in the elevator call DeVier by name and the operator mistook him for Senator Pearson. The next time he took someone up to Pearson's floor he asked, "Is Senator Pearson that young nice-looking fellow? The passenger said, "No, I'm Senator Pearson." After that, DeVier and Senator Pearson kidded each other as to which of them was actually the "young, nice-looking fellow."[14]

The Joint Committee was interested in strengthening congressional participation in the budget process and invited Charles Schultz, director of the Bureau of the Budget, to testify. DeVier and Schultz became friends. Schultz invited DeVier to moonlight as a member of the task force on the organization of the new Department of Transportation, an interesting interlude that led to a lifelong friendship with Alan Boyd, the first Secretary of Transportation.

From a historical perspective, perhaps the most interesting witness was a young congressman from Illinois, Donald Rumsfeld, who was concerned with the allocation of power between the President and Congress in foreign policy and war-making authority. Rumsfeld later left Congress to serve as White House Chief of Staff and Secretary of Defense in the Gerald Ford administration and Secretary of Defense in the administration of President George W. Bush.[15]

Rumsfeld's spoken views as a young congressmen were very different from his views in the Bush administration. Among Rumsfeld's proposals were broadening the congressional treaty power, creating a permanent joint committee for national security to oversee executive branch actions, and revisiting the practice of a President pursuing military actions without a formal congressional declaration of war. He also raised the issue of whether there were adequate congressional checks on executive actions in the areas of intelligence, counterinsurgency, and covert military actions. Rumsfeld said:

> *With the improbability of wars on the scale of the 19th and early 20th century conflicts and the increased likelihood of so-called cold wars, and the resulting use of programs of counterinsurgency, do we need to define the various war situations that we are likely to face and evaluate the desirable congressional role—which might vary considerably in each?* [16]

Rumsfeld was ahead of his time on the debate concerning the role of Congress and the President in making war. There was a constitutional ambiguity with Congress having the power to declare war under Article I and the President being given power as commander in chief in Article II. Later, in 1973, Congress passed the War Powers Act as a result of the open-ended commitment in Vietnam. Because the act puts a time limit on commitment of troops without congressional authorization, most scholars believe it to be of dubious constitutionality. No President has since acknowledged the Act's efficacy. In 2009, a special commission headed by former Secretaries of State James Baker and Warren Christopher recommended a new War Powers Consultation Act to require consultation with Congress before a President takes military action of any duration. [17]

Late in the hearings, there was considerable testimony and materials put in the record with regard to limits on the doctrine of executive privilege as a bar to presidential advisors testifying before Congress. While DeVier paid very little attention to it at the time, these statements would come back to haunt him three years later.

Twenty-one senators and 85 congressmen, about one-fifth of each body, testified in person or gave written statements to the Joint Committee. There were proposals dealing with every aspect of the legislative branch of the federal government—relations with the executive branch, terms of office, committee functions, mechanisms to deal with the annual budget, enhanced sources of information for members, regulation of lobbyists, housekeeping functions such as supervision of the Capitol police and other congressional employees, appointment of postmasters, and many others. Sorting out these proposals would be a massive undertaking.

CHAPTER TWELVE

THE SENATE ACTS

*Everyone was for congressional reform in the abstract,
but the devil was in the details.*

—DeVier Pierson

After the hearings were completed, DeVier's assignment was to reduce months of testimony from members of Congress into a cogent, comprehensive report. Although there appeared to be much interest in congressional reform, DeVier recognized that intense opposition would arise from specific proposals of the Joint Committee. Some of the opposition would come from powerful committee chairmen who would perceive correctly that some reforms might lessen their power. Any changing of committee responsibilities meant there was jurisdictional turf to be gained and lost.

After formal testimony was concluded, DeVier and the other staff members interviewed more than 100 members of Congress and their surrogates to obtain additional ideas and sound them out on specific proposals. Senator Monroney and DeVier began preparation of a structure for the Joint Committee's final recommendations. While DeVier worked on the report, Monroney began lobbying his colleagues. They had a series of sessions to review tentative proposals and attempt to resolve the conflicts, especially those between the Senate and the House. An interim report was prepared for members of the Joint Committee.[1]

By early 1966, the Joint Committee had agreed in principle on its recommendations. DeVier's biggest job was to prepare the final report that would be the basis for legislative language in an omnibus reorganization bill. Committee members began pushing their positions on pet issues and sending their staffers to make sure their viewpoints were heard. To get any work done, DeVier closeted himself in one of the small rooms called "hideaways" on the Senate side of the Capitol where senators could have private meetings. Monroney's hideaway was down an obscure hallway close to the middle of the Capitol. It was a perfect place for DeVier to dictate the final report.

There was one memorable event during this time. One day, as DeVier hurried from the suite of hideaways with a bundle of papers, the door suddenly opened and he ran, literally, into Richard Nixon. Nixon was visiting Senate Republican leader Everett Dirksen to discuss the 1966 congressional elections, an important part of Nixon's return to political prominence. Both DeVier and Nixon were knocked backward and DeVier's papers flew in all directions.

DeVier apologized profusely while picking up the papers. Then DeVier noticed something strange. Nixon had trouble making eye contact and muttered something about it not being a problem. DeVier observed that Nixon, one of the most prominent figures in the nation as former senator, vice president, and presidential nominee seemed to be more ill at ease than he was. DeVier never forgot the brief encounter and always thought the moment spoke volumes about Nixon's personal insecurity.[2]

Senator Monroney reviewed each proposal in the final report which the Joint Committee approved and issued on July 28, 1966. It was a tribute to Monroney's leadership skills that this bi-partisan Joint Committee of Republicans and Democrats, senators and congressmen, could come together in a unanimous report.

The Joint Committee made important recommendations for the improvement of the organization of the Congress. They included strengthening committee procedures to give a majority of the committee, rather than the chairman, the right to move legislation through the committee and to the floor; the realignment of some committee jurisdictions; augmentation of personal and committee staff resources; strengthening fiscal controls by reorganization of the General Accounting Office (GAO), the office that advises Congress on financial matters; strengthening the operation of the Legislative Research Service; broadening the lobby registration requirements; and significantly strengthening the congressional review of the annual budget submitted by the President.[3]

With the report now public, the task turned to selling the proposals to the Senate and House. Monroney had hoped that the bill could be taken to the floor before the end of the session. However, many members of Congress wanted to get home early for congressional elections and the leadership cut short the list of items to be considered before the recess. DeVier used the time to put the Joint Committee's final report into legislative language with a promise from the Senate leadership that the matter would be taken up when Congress reconvened in January.

Floor consideration of the measure began in January, 1967, and "was a three-ring circus." DeVier sat on the Senate floor with Monroney for seven weeks while the bill was being debated. More than 100 amendments were offered. The bill was under attack from a collection of "old bulls" who did not want any change and from reformers who did not believe the Joint Committee had done enough. The issue was in doubt for several weeks.

Monroney patiently dealt with every amendment, accepting a few and rejecting others. Senator Joseph Clark was a "constant thorn in our side" with a plethora of amendments that had no chance of passing, but could have derailed the bill. DeVier remembered, "I often wondered if we were going to die by a thousand cuts."[4]

Monroney argued strongly against efforts to knock lobbying restrictions from the bill. With uncharacteristic heat, Monroney told fellow senators, "Adopt this amendment and you will have the same old club...making sure that the public interest is not going to prevail."

The turning point came when Senator Dirksen and Senator Russell Long, a colorful senator from Louisiana and chairman of the Senate Finance Committee, joined in a motion to return the bill to committee to consider the floor amendments that had been offered. It was a transparent disguise to kill the bill. Surprisingly, the motion was defeated by a lopsided 70-18 vote. It was an icebreaker because the vote signaled that Monroney had the votes for congressional reform.

The bill passed on March 7, 1967, by a 75-9 vote, after an eloquent plea by Monroney:

The road to congressional reorganization is never a short or smooth one...I can say without qualification that no bill with which I have been associated has received such painstaking and length consideration on the floor of the Senate...

I hope, and I believe, that the members of this body will seize this opportunity to say with a loud clear voice that it is unafraid of change and prepared to enact those measures which will make our Congress a more efficient, thoughtful, and well-informed decision-making body.[6]

The actual margin of passage was 91-9 because all those not present had publicly announced they would vote aye if they were present. It was an overwhelming victory. Even Senator Clark voted for the bill with the caustic comment that the committee had "labored and brought forth a mouse, but a pretty healthy mouse." The final Senate approval of the bill was a reflection of Monroney's standing and popularity. Few members of the Senate could have achieved this result.[7]

Following passage, Monroney received a torrent of well-deserved praise from members of the Senate led by Democratic leader Mike Mansfield. Senator Caleb Boggs of Delaware, a member of the Joint Committee who had been especially committed to the effort, took the unusual step of recognizing DeVier's work as chief counsel. Boggs said, "He has been a source of great strength throughout the long consideration which this legislation has received."[8]

The battle then moved to the House of Representatives. Monroney turned the process over to Representative Ray Madden, the House co-chairman of the Joint Committee.

DeVier was in a holding pattern, ready to help the effort when it reached the House floor, but the schedule was indefinite.

Before the end of the Joint Committee assignment, DeVier and Shirley had assumed that their time in the nation's capital would be short and decided to put Jeff and Libby back in school in Oklahoma City. For nine months, DeVier was a commuter, hopping back and forth on weekends between Washington and Oklahoma City. It was tough on the family, but convenient from a work standpoint. He lived during the week at the old Capitol Hill Hotel about two blocks from his Capitol office. It was a handy location because of the long and erratic hours, especially during the preparation of the final report. At that time, there were very few security restrictions in effect at the Capitol and DeVier could move freely between his hotel and office.

When it appeared in 1966 that the Joint Committee's work would be extended, DeVier and Shirley leased their Oklahoma City home and rented a house in the Maryland suburbs. They would have never predicted it at the time, but the move was far more than temporary. They have lived in the Washington, D.C. area ever since.[9]

DeVier and Shirley enjoyed an active social life in Washington because of their ties to the Monroneys. Mary Ellen Monroney was a grande dame of Washington who had known every president since Franklin Roosevelt. There was still an air of social grace and less partisanship, a far cry from the Washington of a few decades later. Mrs. Monroney's idea of a nice dinner party was to have a Supreme Court justice, one or two Cabinet officers, senators and congressmen from both parties, and at least one journalist. Shirley said, "If you were at a Monroney dinner, you were automatically surrounded by big names." [10] DeVier asked Mary Ellen once if she considered having all Democrats to a dinner, to which she replied, "How boring!" [11]

The Piersons were especially close to other Oklahomans in the area. Monroney had brought several of them to work at the Capitol. Tom Finney of Idabel came in 1955 to work for Monroney on natural gas deregulation, became his adminis-

When DeVier arrived in Washington, D.C., one of his best friends was David Busby. Busby had left Oklahoma for the nation's capital a few years before. DeVier and Busby were members of the "Oklahoma Mafia" in Washington.

trative assistant, and then joined the law firm of Clark Clifford in 1963. David Busby came to Washington to work on automobile legislation and stayed to become a highly successful trade lawyer. John Burns of Pauls Valley left Monroney's staff to be a career diplomat in the State Department. John Burzio of Blackwell became counsel to the Senate Post Office Committee, chaired by Monroney, and eventually became one of DeVier's law partners. In addition to the former staff members, Mike Monroney, Jr., the senator's son, had lived in Washington for many years, but "was a devout Oklahoman." DeVier called the Oklahoma group the Monroney School of Public Administration, but others referred to the men as the "Oklahoma mafia." [12]

Tom and Sally Finney, David and Mary Beth Busby, and Mike Monroney, Jr., and his wife, Jocelyn, were the Piersons' constant social companions. Finney was DeVier's close friend and adviser until his tragic death in 1978. The Busbys and Mike, Jr., have remained good friends for decades.

With the congressional reorganization work in abeyance, DeVier and Shirley prepared to return to Oklahoma. But Tom Finney urged DeVier to consider staying in Washington to look at a possible position in the Johnson administration. DeVier had moonlighted as a member on the task force on the organization of the federal Department of Transportation and had been become well acquainted with Alan Boyd, President Johnson's selection as the first Secretary of Transportation.

Boyd asked DeVier to be his chief of staff, but still the Piersons thought they would return home to Oklahoma.

Then a call came from the White House and the Piersons' lives and DeVier's career changed forever. [13]

CHAPTER THIRTEEN

WHITE HOUSE COUNSEL

*I hired him as my lawyer in the White House because
Mike Monroney said he was the best damn young lawyer
in Washington, D.C.*

—Lyndon B. Johnson

In early 1967, DeVier received a telephone call from
Harry McPherson, President Johnson's Special Counsel and
longtime adviser, inviting DeVier to a White House meeting with him and Joseph Califano, Johnson's chief domestic
policy adviser. At the meeting, DeVier thought he might be
under consideration for a staff position, but he had no idea
what to expect and, while flattered, still planned to resume his
law practice in Oklahoma City.

A week later, a secretary at the White House called with
a specific time for a meeting on a Saturday afternoon. When
DeVier arrived at the White House gate and showed his identification, the guard looked at the visitor list and said, "Oh
yes, you are meeting with the President." That was big news
to DeVier who had assumed he was meeting with McPherson
and Califano.[1]

He was ushered into the Roosevelt Room across from the
Oval Office. Marvin Watson, the President's appointments
secretary, said President Johnson had an emergency meeting and would be delayed. The delay turned out to be several
hours so DeVier read a handy copy of William S. White's bi-

ography of Johnson. Having never met the President, DeVier thought it would be a good idea to know more about him.

At about 7:00 p.m., DeVier was taken into the Oval Office and met alone with the President. His first impression was that Johnson was "a big man, a formidable presence." For almost an hour, Johnson talked about politics, the nation, and his affection for Senators Kerr and Monroney. Then abruptly, Johnson said, "I need your help. Here's what I want you to do," and took it as a given that DeVier was joining his White House staff. DeVier was shocked. The case was closed. The Piersons were staying in Washington.[2]

Although it was an exciting prospect, DeVier had apprehensions as well. Johnson was a giant in the capital but was known as a demanding boss who was tough on his subordinates. He had been a masterful Senate Majority Leader during the Eisenhower years, had loyally served as vice president, and took over leadership of the country with great strength when President Kennedy was assassinated. After Johnson defeated Goldwater in 1964, he rammed through Congress the most sweeping collection of social programs—civil rights, Medicare, aid to education, and much more—since President Franklin D. Roosevelt's New Deal during the Great Depression.

DeVier also understood that Johnson's most glowing moments might be behind him. Republicans had made major gains in Congress in 1966 and were far less amenable to the President's dictates. The conflict in Vietnam was becoming increasingly unpopular. President Johnson was more beleaguered. DeVier did not know what to expect.[3]

DeVier talked about the White House opportunity with

Senator Monroney. There was no immediate need for DeVier to continue his work on the reorganization of Congress. Monroney told DeVier he simply could not turn down the opportunity to work in the White House. Later Monroney told DeVier that he had discussed DeVier's qualifications with the President and was assured that if the reorganization bill came up again in Congress, he would be allowed to assist Monroney.

DeVier accepted the rare opportunity to serve the President when he was appointed Associate Special Counsel to the President in March, 1967. To this day, it is still a mystery to him as to how he got the job. He assumed that Harry McPherson and Joe Califano had made a favorable recommendation. He knew President Johnson talked to Senator Monroney about him, but he never learned who his other sponsors may have been. DeVier had no prior ties to Johnson, had never been active in any of his campaigns, and had indeed never been face-to-face with the President until the day he was hired.[4]

A senior staff position was open because incumbent special counsel, Harry McPherson, was "stretched beyond his available time" to perform the needed legal work for the President. After Bill Moyers had left the Johnson White House and McPherson became the chief speech writer, in addition to his other duties, he often asked the President for help.[5]

There was one other Oklahoman on the President's staff when DeVier arrived. James Jones of Muskogee had worked on Johnson's 1964 campaign as an advance man and came to the White House as a personal aide. In 1968 he became Appointments Secretary and was a powerful member of Johnson's senior staff. He later served as congressman from

Oklahoma's First Congressional District and United States
Ambassador to Mexico in the administration of President Bill
Clinton.[6]

The White House Counsel's Office was "a lawyer's
dream come true." Unlike subsequent administrations in
which the Counsel's Office became a large institution, there
were only three lawyers in the office in the Johnson White
House. McPherson was special counsel and became DeVier's
great friend and mentor. In addition to DeVier, the third
lawyer was Cliff Alexander, who later became Secretary of
the Army and was the highest ranking African American on
Johnson's staff.

McPherson was impressed with DeVier's organizational
abilities. He said, "He was not only a great lawyer, he had an
outstanding business and organization sense. He was careful
and precise. We made a good team because I moved into ad-
vising the President on major policy issues and DeVier took
care of the business side of the White House."[7]

The White House Counsel's Office had a huge responsibility. It gave legal clearance on every governmental act
requiring presidential action, including review and approval
of legislation, signing or veto statements, presidential proclamations, and executive orders. The counsel also provided legal
and policy advice on other issues that bubbled up through the
cabinet bureaucracy and were eventually resolved by the President. DeVier assumed responsibility for liaison with the protective agencies serving the President and White House—the
Secret Service, FBI, National Park Service, and security forces
of the military and the District of Columbia government.

In 1968, Johnson appointed DeVier Special Counsel to
the President, the most senior legal position on his staff. He
also was designated as Counselor of the White House Office
and became responsible for the implementation of standards
of conduct for all persons in the Executive Office of the
President. DeVier was in regular personal contact with the
President during his final year in office.[8]

DeVier and President Lyndon Johnson look over the proclamation appointing DeVier as Special Counsel in the
Oval Office in the White House.

President Johnson had a unique work schedule. He awoke before dawn and often worked in his bedroom for an hour or two become coming to the Oval Office for appointments with staff, other members of the administration, and visitors. After a late lunch, he undressed and took a full-fledged nap for one to two hours. He began another workday around 4:00 p.m. and attended to his duties into the evening. He then left for a late dinner in the living quarters and reviewed his "night reading," memoranda from staff and government officials. In the wee hours of the morning, he went to bed for a few hours' sleep before repeating the process. Because of the irregular schedule, staff members had to adapt, except for the afternoon nap.[9]

There often was a temptation to forget that White House staff power is derivative only. DeVier and all staff members were sometimes guilty of telling a Cabinet official, "The President wants" or "The President has decided" a certain matter when a final decision of the President himself was at least debatable.

Direct access to the President was extremely important. But DeVier believed that the most important component of staff power in many presidential decisions was "the power of the final memorandum." During his two years as Counsel, DeVier prepared more than 100 memoranda summarizing agency views with a recommendation of the decision the President should make. The final memorandum was placed on the top of other documents submitted by the Cabinet departments. Often, the President read only the summary memorandum in his "night reading" before making a critical decision.[10]

An example is a December 1, 1967, memorandum about the President's strategy for grains reserve legislation. DeVier pointed out four ways to boost grain prices, cited support from major farm organizations, but warned that Senators George McGovern and Eugene McCarthy were "getting attention" with their own bill. DeVier's recommendation was that the "right" sponsor be found for Johnson's own bill. DeVier wrote, "This strategy protects our political flank and leaves your options open. I recommend that we ask Monroney to introduce the bill and permit Agriculture to testify in favor of it if hearings are held." The President apparently agreed with DeVier's assessment of the situation and wrote on the bottom of the memo, "Get Russell and a good House member to go along."[11]

On another occasion, DeVier began a memorandum with the brief statement, "The oil import program is a mess." DeVier told the President that Senator William Proxmire was making speeches regularly on the Senate floor and that Congressman Ed Edmondson was holding hearings in the House Interior Committee. When DeVier recommending the naming of a study group to look into the problem, President Johnson wrote, "Call me."[12]

Often, DeVier's memoranda to the President involved unusual situations. Johnson was left $1,000 by the last will of a Chicago man who was a great admirer of the President. DeVier, as White House counsel, said the President's policy of not accepting cash gifts did not apply. DeVier wrote, "A testamentary bequest presents a somewhat different situation since the donor is deceased and obviously could not be seeking favor by making the gift." DeVier found several instances of previous presidents facing a similar situation. President Theodore Roosevelt was bequeathed cash and two white angora cats in the will of a lady who committed suicide. Roosevelt turned down the cash but accepted the cats on behalf of the White House. President Johnson chose to follow DeVier's recommendation that the $1,000 from the Chicago man's estate be donated to the LBJ Library.[13]

President Lyndon Johnson in his rocking chair discussing the day's events with aides, left to right, Harry McPherson, Doug Carter, and DeVier.

DeVier saw firsthand how correct President Truman was when he said, "The buck stops here!" The most difficult federal government decisions are "bucked to the President." One of the most challenging and sensitive roles of White House staff was to umpire cabinet-level disputes on issues that had be resolved by the President. As others on the senior staff, DeVier often presided over meetings with representatives of agencies, sometimes including cabinet secretaries, to hear pros and cons and make a final recommendation to the President.

In one bizarre case in 1968, DeVier met with the Attorney General, the deputy secretaries of State and Defense, the director of the Bureau of the Budget, and the director of the

It was not unusual for President Johnson's grandchildren to frequent the White House. Luci's son, Lynn Nugent, sits with DeVier, right, while Secretary of Commerce and American Airlines founder, C.R. Smith, briefs the President.

Office of Emergency Planning to review the adequacy of government contingency plans for the continuity of government in the event of nuclear attack on Washington. After receiving several differing views, DeVier had to make the final recommendations to the President. DeVier believed that making decisions on that subject was "somewhat above my pay grade."[14]

President Johnson also assigned members of his staff to act as liaison with cabinet officers and their immediate subordinates who looked for presidential attention to one or more of their perceived problems. At various times, DeVier was assigned as liaison to the Departments of Agriculture, Commerce, Transportation, and Interior, and the Office of the United States Trade Representative. He worked with a premier group of cabinet secretaries—Agriculture Secretary Orville Freeman, former governor of Minnesota; Commerce Secretary C.R. Smith, the founder of American Airlines; Transportation Secretary Alan Boyd,, former chairman of the Civil Aeronautics Board; and Interior Secretary Stewart Udall, former congressman from Arizona and an early environmentalist. While DeVier sometimes had stormy sessions with the cabinet secretaries on particular issues, all became good friends and colleagues.[15]

There was irony in his assignment to look after the matters at the Department of Agriculture for the President. DeVier grew up as a city boy and had spent very little time on a farm. Law school classmate Duke Logan always said that DeVier's view of the outdoors was simply a long tunnel between two buildings. President Johnson apparently assumed a Pawhuska boy should be well-suited for dealing with agricultural issues. Soon, DeVier was thrust into a world of support prices, quotas, allotments, set-asides, and other agricultural programs.[16]

In Washington, one of the devices used to study problems that involved more than one federal agency was to create an inter-agency task force. Johnson was not overly impressed with task forces and insisted that each involve a member of his senior staff to keep in close touch with task force committee chairmen and leading members.

DeVier was the principal author of a presidential message on communications policy, including the establishment of a task force. He occasionally met with officials of the communications industry who were concerned that the federal government might delve into its business. In the end, the President declined to issue the task force's recommendations in late 1968 because he did not want to bind his successor.

Johnson used his staff to achieve a variety of ends, and he was not above deception. During the fight over the 1968 tax bill, Johnson asked DeVier to join him at a meeting with Congressman Wilbur Mills of Arkansas and a group of rice state congressmen. The President said, "When you are asked for your view, report favorably on plans at the Department of Agriculture to reduce rice allotments." Johnson knew that such news would cause an adverse reaction from representatives of rice-growing states because such a reduction would lower domestic support prices.

When DeVier delivered an extensive report on why the lower rice allotment was necessary, he received cold stares and heard muttering from the congressmen as he left the

During a cabinet meeting, President Johnson signs a position statement prepared by DeVier.

room. DeVier knew that the President had no intention of lowering the allotment, but surely told the congressmen, "You see the problem I have at Agriculture on rice, but I'll get it fixed if you can give me some help on my tax bill." [17]

DeVier did not consider himself a very eloquent presidential speech writer. Harry McPherson wrote most of the President's major speeches. When DeVier was asked to prepare a speech on farm policy, he was apprehensive, but did his best. His worst fears were realized when President Johnson critiqued his effort by saying it read like a "[expletive deleted] legal memorandum." Johnson never asked him to write a major public speech again. [18]

DeVier worked with another Oklahoman, Jake Simmons of Muskogee, in policy related to the fortunes of the oil and gas industry. Because President Johnson had close ties in Texas with the oil industry, he recused himself from any decision-making on oil issues and delegated responsibility for such actions to Interior Secretary Udall. Even so, Johnson took a private, but lively, interest in what was happening to oilmen, especially independent producers, and asked DeVier to make certain that no federal action be taken that would unduly expand oil imports. Each morning, DeVier received a call from Simmons at Interior to confirm that there was no unanticipated increase in the imports of foreign oil. Compared with the complicated energy policy of recent years, the Johnson fear was simply that any substantial increase in foreign imports would do harm to domestic producers.[19]

DeVier also spent a lot of time resolving disputes in the foreign trade area. Since the founding of the nation, trade matters have been highly political. Senators and congressmen are protective of industries or economic interests in their states or districts. On the other hand, presidents, after they are elected, take a more national view and usually promote "free trade." Consequently, when issues arise, they often pit the President against the Congress. In addition, there are conflicts among the cabinet secretaries who are sensitive to the wishes of their constituencies. It is the President who is called upon to make the final decision on trade agreements, quotas, import tariffs, and other trade penalties.[20]

It seemed that every week a new trade dispute arose. There were existing import quota programs in place for steel, textiles, shoes, sugar, and dairy products. Someone always wanted to expand, reduce, terminate, or initiate one or more of the programs. DeVier sat in meetings where cabinet representatives sometimes shouted at each other. To resolve the issues, DeVier had many captains of industry, representatives of organized labor, agricultural interests, and internationalists, such as David Rockefeller, visit his office, arguing for presidential action one way or another.

Sometimes, the President met with cabinet secretaries on

major quota and other trade issues. But usually the final decision came after staff meetings and "the last memorandum" that appeared in Johnson's night reading with a final recommendation. DeVier wrote many such memoranda on trade issues during his tenure at the White House.[21]

The President of the United States has sweeping powers of executive clemency under the constitution through pardons and commutations of sentences. Johnson saw the exercise of this power as necessary, but politically explosive.

During the Johnson administration, a strict process was followed to make certain there was no abuse of the pardon power. The Pardon Attorney, a career civil servant at the Department of Justice, made the initial review of pardon requests, obtaining recommendations from the prosecutor, sentencing judge, and the Bureau of Prisons. Then, the Attorney General's office reviewed pardon recommendations before sending them on to the White House. With the applications already intensely screened, the clemency requests came to the White House Counsel's office for a final recommendation to the President.

President Johnson wanted to exercise his pardon authority in deserving cases, but was always concerned about political appearances. A significant number of the requests that came to DeVier for final clearance were on behalf of young, often first-time offenders who had been convicted of drug violations. Some were in federal penitentiaries solely as a result of possession of marijuana. DeVier recommended favorable consideration of many of these applications. During the time that he had major responsibility for the administration of the clemency process, President Johnson granted many pardons and commutations of sentences, but stopped doing so in late 1968. No clemency application ever began in the White House. All were processed initially by the Justice Department.[22]

DeVier believed strongly that the use of safeguards was important to protect the integrity of the presidential pardon authority and to avoid any politicization of the process. For this reason, while he admires President Bill Clinton in many ways, he was highly critical of the eleventh-hour pardons granted by Clinton in the last days of his presidency to fugitive Mark Rich and others. That heated topic was the subject of several speeches by DeVier, including a 2001 address to the American Inns of Court in Tulsa.[23]

CHAPTER FOURTEEN

THE AGONY OF VIETNAM

I was deeply disturbed that we were virtually at war with
our own people, as well as the North Vietnamese.

—DeVier Pierson

During DeVier's years in the White House, the ongoing struggle in Vietnam cast a pall over the Johnson administration and America itself. There was never a day that work at the White House was not interrupted, and sometime influenced, by some development in that tiny country halfway around the globe.[1]

American involvement in Vietnam began in the 1950s when President Eisenhower authorized military advisors to enter the country after the French left following their defeat at Dien Bien Phu. President Kennedy increased the American presence with more advisors. There is a historical debate whether or not Kennedy would have continued the American commitment in Vietnam had he lived. In any event, President Johnson ordered a sharp escalation in 1965, including massive bombings known as "Rolling Thunder." A large number of combat forces were committed. By the time DeVier arrived at the White House in 1967, the United States had deployed nearly 500,000 combat forces in Vietnam.[2]

The Vietnam War was a proxy fight in the Cold War and a significant link in the American policy of containing communism. Many foreign policy experts both in and outside the federal government subscribed to the "Domino Theory," that theorized that any failure to contain communist influence in Vietnam would lead to similar communist takeovers throughout Southeast Asia, the Indian subcontinent, and beyond. Some believed Vietnam was the logical extension of the containment of North Korean communism in the Korean Conflict.[3]

At the time DeVier joined the White House staff in March, 1967, the subject of Vietnam preoccupied the Johnson administration. The President held weekly luncheon meetings with Secretary of State Dean Rusk, Secretary of Defense Robert McNamara, Chairman of the Joint Chiefs of Staff General Maxwell Taylor, and his National Security Advisor, Walt Rostow. The coordination of Vietnam policy in the White House was the responsibility of the National Security Council and its staff. DeVier played no role in developing White House policy on Vietnam—a fact he relished both at the time and in the decades since.[4]

The Pierson family visit Oklahoma City while DeVier is giving a speech during his tenure in the White House. Left to right, Shirley, Libby, Jeff, and DeVier.

DeVier, like most Americans, initially "bought into" the Domino Theory. He made a number of speeches in 1967 in support of Johnson's Vietnam policy. At a speech to a YMCA group in Oklahoma, he made the point that it was easier to fight communists on the other side of the world "than closer to home." He received skeptical looks from the younger people in the audience.

By the middle of 1967, the Vietnam War was tearing the United States apart. The draft was in full force and young people faced the prospect of involuntary service in a war they hated. Demonstrations erupted on college campuses, large and small, religious and secular. At the White House there were daily demonstrations. Sometimes the crowds mushroomed to thousands of people making peaceful and not so peaceful protests. On days when the crowd was rowdier than usual, DeVier, in his West Wing office, could hear shouts of, "Hey, hey LBJ, how many kids have you killed today?"[5]

In his role as liaison to the Secret Service and protective services, DeVier was in the middle of the response to the protests. After one large demonstration, the head of the Secret Service detail was so concerned that the fence around the White House might be breached, he suggested electrifying the fence along Pennsylvania Avenue. DeVier asked, "What if someone tried to climb the fence? Would he be electrocuted?" When the Secret Service chief was ambiguous in his response, DeVier declared, "We will have to find a better way of protecting the White House than electrocuting demonstrators."[6]

DeVier helped law enforcement authorities "keep a cool head" during the protests. One afternoon, several thousand protesters led by a group called the Women's Strike for Peace converged around the White House fences. DeVier was stationed behind a large tree on the White House lawn with a walkie talkie communicating with the Secret Service, District of Columbia police, and federal troops stationed down Pennsylvania Avenue.

As the crowd grew, someone suggested using fire hoses or tear gas to disperse the protesters. "Wonderful!" DeVier thought, "We'll just use the same tactics employed in Birmingham against the civil rights demonstrators." Fortunately, less distasteful options were chosen. A handful of token arrests were made and the remaining demonstrators concluded they had made their point and left.[7]

President Johnson was at war with himself over implementing the draft to fill slots in the American military and granting deferments to college students. On one hand, he believed that all young men of the same age should bear the same burden to fight for their country. But he also realized that drafting the educated pool of young Americans would cause even more protest and opposition to the war. He became so concerned about the matter that he decided to set up a Saturday afternoon debate in the Oval Office.[8]

DeVier was asked to present one side of the debate and another staff member would take the other view. When DeVier arrived, he found that the President had brought in two of his friends to judge or comment upon the debate—Clark Clifford, the prestigious Washington lawyer who later would be named Secretary of Defense, and Homer Thornberry, a judge on the United States Court of Appeals for the Fifth Circuit, who

Johnson would later unsuccessfully nominate for an open position on the United States Supreme Court. While it was an interesting afternoon of discourse, it did little to satisfy the President's quandary and most student deferments continued.

In late 1967, White House dynamics on Vietnam began to change. Defense Secretary McNamara, a leading proponent of the 1965 escalation, became increasingly troubled over the bloody consequences of the decision and seemed to be visibly disturbed at meetings of the cabinet and National Security Council. The President was concerned that McNamara might have a mental breakdown; he accepted his resignation and appointed him to head the World Bank. Johnson then appointed Clark Clifford as Secretary of Defense.[9]

The Clifford appointment received mixed reviews. He had been a strong supporter of Johnson and was a member of the "kitchen cabinet" who met frequently and informally with the President to discuss Vietnam and other issues. Senator Edward Kennedy commented, "Why didn't he just appoint Atilla the Hun?" assuming that Clifford would be a hardliner in every way. Surprising to many, Clifford was far more sophisticated and would prove to be a surprise in his handling of the war.

The seminal event on Vietnam policy was the Tet Offensive on New Year's Day, 1968. Viet Cong soldiers staged military attacks throughout South Vietnam, making it to the front lawn of the American Embassy in Saigon before being turned back. Although North Vietnam did not gain any permanent military advantage from the attacks, the psychological effect was profound. Decision makers and in and out of the government began questioning whether the United States could ever have any success in Vietnam. DeVier could see the questions on the faces of cabinet members when they met with the President.[10]

The nation's news media began questioning the prudence of the President's Vietnam policy. An essay in *Time* Magazine said, "Attitudes at home set more stringent limits as a rising number of Americans demand to know why they must commit their strength on distant frontiers." [11]

Secretary Clifford was asked to make a fact-finding trip to Vietnam and report back to the President. On the ground in Vietnam, Clifford talked to senior American and South Vietnamese military and political leaders. When he returned, he was asked to brief the cabinet and presented the President three options:

(1) Sharply increase the troop strength to as many as one million fighting men;

(2) Concentrate American forces in a few areas that could be effectively defended; or

(3) Begin planning for withdrawal of troops from Vietnam.[12]

DeVier was seated directly behind Secretary of State Dean Rusk at the meeting. When Clifford mentioned the word, "withdrawal," Rusk's neck turned "beet red." Clifford was using a lawyer's device to say that in effect that withdrawal was the only viable option and that a profound shift in American policy was necessary. At that moment, DeVier remembered, "The battle for the heart and mind of Lyndon Johnson began." [13]

It was a three-month battle in the White House and during meetings of the cabinet and National Security Council. Opposition to Johnson's Vietnam policy began to dominate the political scene. Senator Eugene McCarthy was the peace candidate and many anti-war protesters flocked to his campaign. Some in the White House suspected Senator Robert Kennedy would run against Johnson in the 1968 primaries. Those closest to Johnson knew nothing would be worse for the President than losing to Kennedy who had been his bitter rival since the 1960 election.[14]

DeVier became involved in a series of events that could have had a dramatic effect on Vietnam policy. One of Kennedy's advisors was Ted Sorenson, DeVier's longtime friend from the 1960 campaign. At a February, 1968 luncheon in the White House Mess, Sorenson revealed to DeVier that he was urging Kennedy not to run for president and volunteered to help Johnson keep it that way. DeVier was uncertain about Sorenson's sincerity, but they agreed to stay in touch.[15]

In a few days, Sorenson called DeVier to arrange an appointment with the President. Johnson agreed to meet Sorenson on March 11. DeVier sent Johnson an extensive memorandum suggesting that Sorenson had political ambitions of his own, wanted good relations with the White House, and might be helpful in keeping Kennedy out of the race. In any event, DeVier wrote, "You can be certain that Ted will report your conversation to Bobby very quickly."[16]

After the meeting with Sorenson, the President told DeVier that Sorenson's real purpose was to float a proposal for the creation of a high level commission to review Vietnam policy and make public recommendations for changes.

Johnson was willing to expand his group of Vietnam advisors. However, he was understandably not willing to give up the presidential authority of making a final decision. The President was also concerned about the political implications of a commission filled with public figures, including Kennedy and other potential presidential candidates.

On the evening of March 13, DeVier again talked with Sorenson who believed the idea of a high level Vietnam study commission would be appealing to Kennedy. Sorenson agreed that the commission should not include political figures, should function independently, and make a public report. He said he would call the following day with a list of possible commission members. Johnson remained very skeptical, but directed DeVier to pursue it and to memorialize the contents of his meetings and telephone calls with Sorenson.[17]

The following day, March 14, was memorable. Rather than getting back with DeVier, Sorenson and Senator Ted Kennedy went to Defense Secretary Clifford's office at the Pentagon and made the same proposal to him. Clifford immediately contacted the President. Johnson told Clifford that any commission that was given independent powers and the right to make a public report would not be approved by him. The President was not willing to "pay a bribe" to keep Kennedy out of the presidential race. Johnson's feelings about the issue were communicated to the Kennedy emissaries by Clifford in a short telephone call. History records the fact that Johnson and Robert Kennedy were both secretly listening to the call, an example of how much they distrusted each other.[18]

DeVier was directed by the President to contact Sorenson and deliver the same message. Johnson would not play politics with Vietnam, even if it meant Kennedy entering the fight for the Democratic nomination. Sorenson said he hoped a Vietnam commission would be helpful in keeping Kennedy out of the race. He said he was concerned that such a candidacy would divide the party. When DeVier told Sorenson the President's decision was final, Sorenson responded, "I guess Bob will run now." As always, they agreed to stay in touch.[19]

In the meantime, administration policy on Vietnam was under intense review. President Johnson had scheduled a speech on Vietnam for March 31. The speech became a vehicle for arguments between those who wanted to continue existing policy and those seeking change. Clifford and Harry McPherson, who was writing the speech, wanted to see change, and they prevailed when the President signed off on their final draft.[20]

DeVier and other senior staff members assumed the President would run for reelection. Even though Vietnam was weighing heavily upon Johnson, and First Lady Lady Bird Johnson was worried about her husband's health and life expectancy, a campaign team was assembled by the Democratic National Committee and DeVier and others began discussing likely campaign issues. DeVier believed that Johnson would never willingly give up power that he had worked his entire life to attain.

Wanting to take his family on vacation, DeVier asked the President for time off in late March. Johnson said, "That's fine, it's a good time for you to be away." The Piersons took advantage of a White House perk and flew to the Virgin Islands to stay in the Government House at St. Croix for a week of beautiful weather, golf, swimming, boating, and fishing.[21]

DeVier watched the March 31 presidential speech while still in the Virgin Islands. President Johnson announced a temporary bombing halt, the desire to commence peace negotiations with North Vietnam, and no increase in troop levels. In the final paragraph of the speech, added in Johnson's own hand, the President stunned the country by announcing that he would not be a candidate for reelection because he did not want political considerations to interfere with the effort to seek peace in Vietnam.[22]

Robert Kennedy sought an immediate meeting with the President. Johnson asked DeVier to attend, but he could not get back from the Virgin Islands in time. He missed the historic meeting which turned out to be the last time the two Democratic leaders would talk in person.[23]

The Vietnam War raged on throughout the remaining months of the Johnson presidency. DeVier visited the President about six months after he left office as he was writing his memoirs. Johnson shared minutes of the National Security Council in 1965 when escalation of the war was discussed. For the first time, DeVier discovered that Johnson rejected the McNamara proposal for escalation three times before finally adopting it and making the war his own. There was no doubt Johnson received conflicting advice. Johnson's old Senate friend, Richard Russell, urged him not to commit substantial ground forces in Vietnam. DeVier said, "The sad fact is that the President was not sufficiently secure with respect to his own national security instincts to override the advice he was receiving in 1965 from his military and civilian advisors."[24]

In the more than 40 years since the first three months of 1968, DeVier often has looked back to "what might have been." He wonders if the Vietnam commission might have made a difference if Johnson had been willing and able to negotiate the terms of such a study group in an acceptable way. If he had such a group, it might have been a tool for more consensus between Johnson and Robert Kennedy—and even a different result in the 1968 presidential election.[25]

It took seven more bloody years—through the Nixon administration and after President Gerald Ford took office—to finally end the Vietnam conflict. The end was anything but the way Johnson would have wanted, with the final remnants of American forces being helicoptered out of the American Embassy in Saigon as Viet Cong and North Vietnamese forces were entering the city. The agony of Vietnam had not only bitterly divided the country, it had brought down the Johnson presidency.[26]

When Johnson's memoirs were published, the President wrote on the title page of DeVier's copy, "To DeVier Pierson, a devoted friend and counselor who made my responsibilities bearable. Lyndon Johnson."

CHAPTER FIFTEEN

UNSETTLED TIMES

Daddy, Senator Kennedy has been shot.
— Jeff Pierson

As if the heaviness of the war in Vietnam was not enough to strangle the country, the level of domestic violence in America in 1967 and 1968 rose to record and deplorable levels. As peaceful demonstrations organized by Dr. Martin Luther King, Jr., gave way to more militant Black Power rallies, riots struck major cities such as Detroit. A command post was established in the White House to monitor the riots and determine if federal military forces should augment local law enforcement.

President Johnson did not believe he should send federal troops into a state unless requested by the governor. As nightly news reports showed increasing violence in Detroit, the President considering breaking his policy because Michigan Governor George Romney was reluctant to request federal troops. Romney was planning to run for the Republican presidential nomination and did not want to appear to be a weak governor who needed federal military assistance to handle internal problems.[1]

To buttress his case for not sending federal troops to Detroit without a request from the governor, the President asked DeVier to find precedent. DeVier found, with the help of attorneys at the Justice Department, an instance in 1794 when

President George Washington waited on a request from the governor of Pennsylvania before sending troops to put down the Whiskey Rebellion. DeVier passed the information to the President who had private meetings with prominent Washington journalists to explain the historical perspective for his position, embellishing the Whiskey Rebellion precedent at one point to "The Great Debate of 1794." Ultimately, Governor Romney requested federal help and they were promptly sent. Johnson felt vindicated.[2]

On April 4, while still in the Virgin Islands on vacation, DeVier and Jeff were returning from fishing when they saw the American flag being lowered to half staff over Government House. DeVier asked the guard, "What's this?" The guard replied that Dr. Martin Luther King, Jr. had been assassinated in Memphis, Tennessee. When the Piersons returned to the nation's capital that night, they could see portions of the downtown area in flames. The killing of Dr. King had sparked violent protests in Washington and across the country. The country would remain in turmoil the remainder of the year.[3]

The political world was also in limbo. Senator Eugene McCarthy and Robert Kennedy were already in the race and Vice President Hubert Humphrey was certain to throw his hat into the battle for the nomination after the President made his announcement that he would not run. McCarthy had a host of young volunteers, many of whom shaved their beards and trimmed their hair to be "clean for Gene" as they blanketed the primary states. Kennedy was considered to be a strong candidate as the heir to his brother's unfinished Camelot. Ironically, Humphrey, the former youthful firebrand reformer, was now the candidate of the old guard of the Democratic Party. Johnson was officially neutral and had separate briefing sessions with each of the three candidates. Inside the White House, everyone assumed that the President was a Humphrey supporter.

As the campaign heated up, Johnson believed that the time had come to provide Secret Service protection for presidential candidates, a practice that had not yet been implemented so that candidates were dependent on private bodyguards. At the President's direction, DeVier prepared a proposed bill that provided for certification of a person as a bonafide candidate by a committee headed by the Secretary of the Treasury. A roadblock was opposition from Senator James Eastland, chairman of the Senate Judiciary Committee, who thought the bill was an unnecessary expenditure of taxpayer money. The bill was bottled up in Eastland's committee.[4]

At 7:05 a.m. on June 5, 1968, while still at home, DeVier received a call from the President. Johnson said, "Where's that bill for Secret Service protection?" DeVier replied, "It's in my office." The President said, "Get your ass down here and bring it to the bedroom!" It was a puzzling request that was made clear when Jeff yelled at his father when he was leaving the house, "Daddy, Senator Kennedy has been shot."[5]

The official White House log, a historical preservation of each moment's activity of the President, confirms the call to DeVier. The log shows presidential calls to Senator Edward Kennedy at 6:45 a.m., breakfast at 7:00 a.m., and the call to DeVier at 7:05 a.m. The log indicates DeVier arrived at the presidential bedroom at 8:00 a.m. and stayed until 8:50 a.m.[6]

When DeVier arrived at Johnson's bedroom, the President was on the telephone with Senate Majority Leader Mike Mansfield and Republican Leader Dirksen to arrange for immediate Senate consideration of the bill. Johnson directed the assignment of Secret Service agents for each candidate in the interim, although there was no presidential authority to do so. The President then called two Oklahomans, Mike Monroney and Tom Steed, who, respectively, chaired the Senate and House appropriations subcommittees with jurisdiction over the Secret Service.[7]

Deputy Treasury Secretary Joe Barr took the bill to Capitol Hill to secure immediate committee and floor action. DeVier talked to Senator Monroney several times during the day to follow the progress of the bill that passed both houses of Congress the following day unanimously.

The remainder of that day was a grisly death watch. Secret Service agents on the scene reported to the President that Kennedy was for all purposes dead, but the Kennedy family did not make a formal announcement until later that evening. There was no love lost between Johnson and Kennedy, but the President was very shaken by the acts of violence directed at the Kennedy family. The day ended with DeVier having a late evening drink in the small study off the Oval Office with the President, Harry McPherson, and Joe Califano. The White House log showed DeVier arrived at the Oval Office at 10:54 p.m. The next activity for the President was with "Mrs. Johnson" at 11:40 p.m. The President did not have a lot of time for his wife. The log shows Senator Roman Hruska of Nebraska returned Johnson's call one minute later.[8]

During tough times such as this, DeVier noted the "soothing influence" upon the President by his wife, Lady Bird Johnson. In a subsequent interview for the oral history collection at the LBJ Library, DeVier said, "She was present in these times of great stress…whether they were saying anything to each other, she was always a present influence… she was a constant counselor and had great impact upon her husband."[9]

The violence continued through the summer and fall. The Democratic National Convention in Chicago was chaotic and ugly. The President, an unpopular figure because of the burden of Vietnam, did not attend. The symbol of the convention was the beating of young anti-war demonstrators by Chicago police. Robert Kennedy's delegates were divided between Humphrey and Senator George McGovern. Finally, the vice president, who had not entered any primary, emerged as the nominee of a divided and beleaguered Democratic Party.

DeVier and other White House staff members had no role in the Humphrey campaign. However, DeVier played a significant role in presidential action on the 1968 Farm Bill. Both houses of Congress passed the bill and it lay on the President's desk. Humphrey fervently appealed for its signing, feeling its veto would hurt his efforts against Republican nominee Richard Nixon in farm states. Johnson did not like the bill because it did not provide multi-year authority for basic commodity programs.[10]

The President asked DeVier to prepare both a "signing statement" and a "veto statement." Johnson had not signed the bill on the last day he could officially act upon it. He called DeVier from Air Force One on his way to see former President Harry Truman in Independence, Missouri. Johnson said, "I like the veto statement better than the signing statement." DeVier suggested that the President sign the bill and use the language of the veto statement to express his reservations. Remarkably, that is what Johnson did. DeVier said, "He signed the bill with the most tepid presidential signing statement in modern American history."[11]

DeVier became embroiled in Johnson's controversial nomination of Abe Fortas to be Chief Justice of the United States. The President was already a lame duck and there was talk that the Senate would delay consideration of Fortas to give the new president the opportunity to make his own selection. Fortas was already a member of the high court as an associate justice and had a distinguished legal career before his appointment. A problem was that many senators knew he and Johnson were close and that Fortas was a frequent visitor to the White House.

Fuel was added to the fire when Senator Gordon Allott told the Judiciary Committee during the Fortas confirmation hearing that Treasury Undersecretary Barr, who had taken the Secret Service protection bill to Capitol Hill following the Robert Kennedy assassination, had said, "The bill has been approved by DeVier Pierson and Abe Fortas and is what the White House wants." If the statement was true, it raised serious separation of powers issues because a sitting Supreme Court justice should not be participating in executive and legislative decisions. The Senate Judiciary Committee immediately requested that DeVier and Secretary Barr appear as witnesses at the confirmation hearing.[12]

DeVier was very willing to testify. He knew he had written the bill and had never talked about it with Justice Fortas. DeVier had discussed the bill with the President but there had been no significant change in the language. The notion that Fortas was in the loop did not ring true with DeVier.

However, Attorney General Ramsey Clark believed strongly that no White House aide should testify concerning conversations with the president under the doctrine of Executive Privilege. Johnson agreed, so Secretary Barr and DeVier sent letters to the Justice Department declining to testify on grounds that their testimony would involve matters relating to their official duties on behalf of the President and confidential communications with him.[13]

The refusal to testify set off a firestorm. The Judiciary Committee considered issuing subpoenas and contempt citations if DeVier and Barr refused to appear. DeVier made headlines in both major newspapers in Oklahoma. He liked the headline in *The Daily Oklahoman*, "Sooner has Role in Constitutional Drama." But he was not crazy about a headline in the *Tulsa Tribune*, "LBJ's lawyer slams the door on Congress." The Tulsa newspaper article was especially embarrassing because it correctly noted that DeVier had been chief counsel for the Joint Committee on the Organization of Congress and had argued that Congress be given full information to facilitate sound decision making. DeVier was concerned that his brief period of public service might end on a very sour note.[14]

The entire controversy "died with a whimper rather than

with a bang." It became clear that the Senate would not act on the Fortas nomination. Fortas eventually asked that his name be withdrawn for other reasons.

DeVier had other interesting assignments in 1968. President Johnson had appointed Clark Clifford to replace Robert McNamara as Secretary of Defense. Clifford was the quintessential Washington insider, having been counsel to President Truman and founding a very successful Washington law firm. He had a melodious voice and his verbal judgments on a matter sounded like the ultimate wisdom "from an oracle on high."

DeVier, as White House ethics officer, was charged with "vetting" Clifford, to make certain there were no financial or other problems that might prove embarrassing to the administration. At the time, DeVier had no personal relationship with Clifford, and, at their first meeting, asked the new appointee to provide financial statements, tax returns, and other documents related to his business affairs.[15]

Clifford was "aghast at the notion" that young DeVier would have access to his private financial matters. Instead, he proposed that he simply go to Capitol hill and discuss his finances with important members of the Senate, all of whom he knew very well, and report back to DeVier if they perceived any problem. Understandably, DeVier did not believe that was a practical approach.

When DeVier told Clifford it was absolutely essential for him to turn over his financial records "to protect the President" in making this key cabinet appointment, Clifford grudgingly complied. DeVier found some defense stocks in

Clifford's portfolio which the nominee cheerfully divested. Later, Clifford and DeVier would become good friends.

On a personal note, DeVier asked for time off in the final days of the 1968 general election to be with his mentor, Senator Mike Monroney, who was involved in an uphill battle for reelection with former Oklahoma Republican Governor Henry Bellmon. GOP presidential nominee Nixon was running strong in Oklahoma, making it difficult for Monroney to carry the state. DeVier felt he should be with his old friend on election night.

When Monroney lost, DeVier was by his side when the senator received a call from President Johnson. In a memorandum thanking the President for the call, DeVier correctly predicted Oklahoma's political future. He wrote, "Sad to say, Oklahoma is well on its way to becoming a solid Republican state. Oklahoma and Tulsa counties gave Nixon more than a 70,000-vote edge in the presidential race."[16]

CHAPTER SIXTEEN

WHITE HOUSE PERKS

*Lyndon Johnson was a tough boss who could, and would,
verbally skin your hide when he was unhappy with
your work, but he was also very loyal to his staff.*

— DeVier Pierson

One day in 1968 DeVier received a telephone call from his longtime friend and fraternity brother, Lee Allan Smith, who was working on the Stars and Stripes show, a July 4th celebration in Oklahoma City. Smith wondered if the President could record a message of congratulations and best wishes to Oklahoma and the nation. DeVier was pessimistic because the President received hundreds of such requests each year. However, he told Smith he would try.[1]

DeVier put a note in the President's night reading saying that the request came from a very good friend with a good event for a good home state. DeVier finished the note with, "I hope you will give this consideration." To his happy surprise, DeVier read Johnson's response the following morning, "I'll do it! Set it up!" DeVier arranged for a taping in the White House recording studio. Johnson showed up on time and delivered the prepared message. DeVier was happy for this particular White House perk because he knew Smith had devoted his entire adult life doing great things for Oklahoma.[2]

DeVier was able to use his position of influence to help his native Oklahoma City when it was involved in sensitive negotiations with the federal Department of Housing and Urban Development (HUD) for loans and grants for urban renewal. When the Oklahoma City Urban Renewal Authority received approval of major requests for funding, its executive director, James B. White, wrote DeVier, "No one knows better than yourself that this downtown renewal project is a vital step in the economic and cultural revitalization of our community…we are deeply aware of the importance of your support in this matter."[3]

DeVier occasionally helped old friends navigate problems that may or may not have needed White House assistance. Duke Logan wanted to visit the World's Fair in Montreal and could not find a hotel room anywhere. He called DeVier, who responded, "You think I'm up here to pimp hotels internationally?" After recalling old times, DeVier used his influence and found Logan a hotel room in Montreal.[4]

When Marian Opala needed tickets for a White House tour for his son and him, DeVier not only made special tickets available, but spent nearly an hour on the telephone talking about mutual friends in Oklahoma City.[5]

Larry Nichols, son of Oklahoma City oilman John Nichols, a longtime friend who DeVier admired greatly, was completing a clerkship with United States Supreme Court Chief Justice Earl Warren when he sought DeVier's recommendation to be a special assistant to the Attorney General of the United States. DeVier was glad to assist his fellow Oklahoman who greatly appreciated "DeVier's help in identifying and securing that position."[6] Later, Nichols left the law and co-founded Devon Energy Corporation, Oklahoma's largest public company. DeVier had urged Nichols to consider staying in Washington and joining his law firm, but said with a smile that he thought Larry had probably made the right decision.

In 1968, DeVier was involved in a bizarre incident involving reclusive billionaire Howard Hughes. At the time, Hughes was living in a hermetically sealed penthouse in Las Vegas, Nevada, and was paranoid about contact with any source of germs, including human beings. From his own sealed world, Hughes was upset about government nuclear tests at the White Sands test range near Las Vegas and was trying everything in his power to prevent them.

Hughes' lawyer for many years was Clark Clifford. But with Clifford as Secretary of Defense, Tom Finney, DeVier's longtime Oklahoma friend, became legal spokesman for Hughes. Finney called DeVier and said Hughes wanted to talk with the President to relay his opposition to the nuclear tests. DeVier said it was unlikely that Johnson would discuss such a sensitive national security issue with a private citizen. Instead, DeVier suggested that Hughes write Johnson a personal letter with his views.[7]

A few days later, Finney appeared at the White House with a sealed envelope, a letter from Hughes who had requested that no one read the letter but Johnson himself. DeVier agreed and sent the unopened letter to the President. The nuclear test went forward as scheduled and without incident. A few days later, DeVier asked the President if Hughes' letter had been interesting. Johnson just smiled. DeVier asked if he had talked with Hughes on the telephone after receiving the letter. Again, Johnson just smiled.[8]

DeVier shouldered the major responsibility in 1968 to review and recommend presidential action in the largest international air route case since World War II. Senior aides Califano and McPherson were looking to the future, and talking with Washington law firms with airline clients, so they could not participate. DeVier had decided he would not discuss future employment with any law firm that has business with the administration until he left the White House.

In the days before deregulation of the airlines, the Civil Aeronautics Board (CAB) made recommendations for international routes, but the President made the final decision. Billions of dollars of anticipated revenue were at stake on the carrier selections in the Trans-Pacific route case because of the need for carriers to fly to rapidly growing Asian markets. Every major carrier wanted one or more of the routes—it was inevitable that some would happy and some would be very disappointed.[9]

The Trans-Pacific case was a "political hot potato" because President Johnson had many friends either in the airline industry or as lawyers representing airline clients. Worst of all, Johnson's close friend and Secretary of Commerce C.R. Smith had founded American Airlines and was anxious for American to have a new route to Japan. The CAB had approved such a route. Johnson and DeVier discussed the problem and the President opted to not discuss the route decisions with anyone—American Airlines, other airlines, and their lawyers would have to talk to DeVier.

DeVier reviewed the matter with CAB Chairman John

Crocker and met with officials of the relevant cabinet departments, especially Transportation Secretary Alan Boyd.

DeVier finally recommended that the President approve all proposed new routes to Asia except for American's much-desired route to Tokyo. The Japanese government had strongly objected to the establishment of a new route for American. Because of the Japanese opposition and other policy considerations, the Department of State and the Department of Transportation also supported the denial of the route for American. DeVier believed the denial of the route was the right result

DeVier, Shirley, Jeff, and Libby at the White House Christmas Party in 1968.

and also would insulate the President from any accusation of making a political decision. The President agreed and approved DeVier's recommendations.[10]

Even before Nixon was elected president in November, 1968, the White House was in a transition mode. Cabinet heads had been directed to refrain from last minute decisions that would bind their successors. After the election, DeVier and other senior staff prepared status reports on pending matters that could be shared with incoming counterparts in the Nixon White House.

In December, DeVier and other Johnson aides met with new Nixon staff members to talk about their roles. After a stiff beginning, the ice was broken by a warm statement from Bryce Harlow, a distinguished Oklahoma City native who had gone to Washington and served as President Eisenhower's speech writer and who was Nixon's first staff appointment. Harlow stressed how much Nixon's people wanted to collaborate with the Johnson White House in a good transition of power.[11] It was a harmonious transition, although DeVier reflected that it is always easier to graciously assume power than to cheerfully give it up.

President Johnson was a tough boss who expected perfection. But he was loyal and interested in the futures of his staff members who would be leaving the White House with him. In the last month of the administration, a large California law firm wanted to talk to DeVier about opening an office in Washington. DeVier sought and received Johnson's permission to take two days off and fly to Los Angeles to meet the principals of the firm.

DeVier was meeting with the firm's executive commit-
tee in a large, luxuriously-paneled conference room when a
very flustered secretary rushed into the room and said, "Mr.
Pierson, the President is on the phone and says he needs to
talk with you right away." The lawyers cleared the room for
DeVier who thought the President assumed he was in his
office down the hall from the Oval Office. DeVier said, "Mr.
President, I am not in Washington, I am in Los Angeles."
Johnson replied, "I know, I didn't have anything to talk about.
I just thought the call might help."[12]

Although DeVier decided not to join forces with the California firm, an urgent call from the President of the United
States was probably a useful recommendation.

DeVier and Shirley had developed a warm relationship with the Johnson family. Shortly after DeVier became a
member of the President's staff, they were invited at the last
minute to a reception in the White House. Shirley had been
at a local nursery buying shrubs and a tree. With only an
hour's notice, she arrived at the White House in their station
wagon with the tree and shrubs sticking out the back. Despite
the unique arrival, she was thrilled to be at the White House
as a guest rather than a tourist and went from room to room
soaking in the beautiful furniture, furnishings, paintings, and
photographs.

At the reception, DeVier introduced Shirley to Mrs.
Johnson for the first time. She greeted Shirley warmly, saying
that she hoped she was having a good time, and then added,
"And I know you are making our other guests feel right at
home in the White House." It was a not-so-subtle reminder to

Shirley that she had some staff duties as well. Shirley quickly turned around and began shaking hands with each person she saw.[13]

DeVier and Shirley maintained their Oklahoma ties while he served in the White House. They made several trips to Oklahoma City to visit family and friends. He spoke to the Oklahoma City Chamber of Commerce, the YMCA, and the annual banquet of the Phi Beta Kappa alumni association. In Washington, he hosted a number of Oklahomans at the White House for lunch, including Harvey Everest and Earl Sneed. The Piersons attended summer cruises on the Potomac River sponsored by the Oklahoma State Society and their guests. On one such cruise was a young state representative from Oklahoma, David L. Boren.[14]

Shirley had a huge job at their home, spending much of her time raising the children. DeVier often did not arrive home until after the children were in bed. She took the children to baseball games, piano practice, and other family activities. Frankly, living in Washington, D.C., was a big adjustment. DeVier tried to spend as much time with the family as possible on weekends. Because they assumed they would be in Washinton for only a short time, DeVier and Shirley planned active weekends to see all the historic sites in the area.

Having daily access to the President of the United States, the most powerful man on earth, was only one of many perks of working at the White House. DeVier officed in the West Wing, a short walk to and from the Oval Office. He had a private telephone line, called the POTUS line, which rang in one uninterrupted ring in the office or at home until the phone was picked up. He often met privately with the President, rode in White House limousines, flew on Air Force One and the Presidential helicopter, visited the LBJ Ranch and Camp David, attended cabinet meetings, and flourished in a social scene that only a White House staff position could embellish. Shirley's favorite moment may have been during entertainment following a White House state dinner when Robert Goulet knelt in front of her and sang "If Ever You Should Leave Me."[15]

President Johnson greets DeVier and Shirley at a state dinner in the White House in 1967.

At the final cabinet meeting in January, 1969, Johnson looked at DeVier and referred to him, as he often did the previous year, as "the best lawyer in the White House." Wanting the meeting to end on a light note, Johnson looked at his cabinet and said with a smile, "I commend him to any of you who may be investigated in the next few months."[17]

DeVier had one last matter to complete. In the final months of the Johnson administration, Interior Secretary

Udall proposed that the President exercise his authority under the Antiquities Act to add more than seven million acres to the national park system. Johnson was skeptical about taking such action without congressional approval. The President also suspected that Walter Hickel, governor of Alaska and Nixon's choice as Secretary of the Interior, might oppose the move because the largest tracts of new park land were in Alaska. It became a major and highly contentious issue.[18]

Finding strong opposition in the Congress, DeVier believed it would be a mistake for Johnson to add the full amount of this land to the national park system in such a manner. The President asked DeVier to prepare proclamations for each parcel of land while he continued to reflect on the matter. Udall was unhappy with the President's inaction and demanded to see him at the White House the Saturday before Nixon was inaugurated. When Johnson would not see Udall

The Pierson family came to the Oval Office to say goodbye to President Johnson during his last Saturday in the White House.

immediately, he left the White House "in a huff."

A few minutes later, President Johnson called DeVier to have him look at the wire service ticker for a story that quoted Udall as saying the land addition was "a done deal." Johnson was outraged and ordered DeVier to call Udall and have him retract the story. Udall said he would, but he was resigning at that moment as Secretary of the Interior. DeVier told Udall that would be a miserable way for him to end his distinguished career as a public servant. Udall grudgingly relented.[19]

On the same Saturday afternoon before he left office, President Johnson had DeVier, Shirley, Jeff, and Libby into the Oval Office for family photographs. On the evening of January 19, the President and First Lady hosted a dinner for senior staff in the living quarters of the White House. The dinner lasted past midnight with Johnson making his final remarks before leaving office the next day.

On his last morning as President, Johnson asked DeVier to bring the national park documents to his bedroom for final decisions in his final hours as chief executive. There were eight parcels of land proposed as additions to the national park system and DeVier delivered a draft presidential proclamation for each. Together they spread them out on the bed and "cherry-picked" four of them totaling 300,000 acres which established one new national monument, Marble Canyon in Arizona, and enlarged three others. Johnson signed the four proclamations and asked DeVier to bring back the executed copies with a signing statement.[20]

When DeVier returned, Johnson had dressed for the inaugural and was visiting with the First Lady and their daughters,

Luci and Lynda. DeVier rode the elevator with them downstairs. The President wrote in his memoirs, *The Vantage Point*, that he signed the proclamations prepared by DeVier in the elevator as they descended to the ground floor of the Executive Mansion. Johnson noted that he was proud of the fact that he had added four million acres to the national park system during his time in office.[21]

As the elevator doors opened, President-Elect Nixon and his family were arriving through the front door. DeVier turned, shook hands with President Johnson for the last time as president, and said good-bye.[22]

DeVier returned to his office and packed away his remaining files. On the desk was a nice farewell letter from the President. There was also a more mundane bill from the White House mess for his outstanding balance.

DeVier's office had been assigned to Daniel Patrick Moynihan, born in Tulsa, who had been appointed President Nixon's Special Assistant for Urban Affairs and who later would serve as Ambassador to the United Nations and United States Senator from New York. DeVier put a note on his desk wishing Moynihan luck, turned in his White House pass, and left the building.

That afternoon, DeVier and several Johnson friends and officials of the administration went to Andrews Air Force Base to see the Johnsons off for their return to Texas. Even with a huge Republican celebration going on in downtown Washington, a Republican congressman, George H.W. Bush, was there to pay respects to his fellow Texan.

Air Force One took off, headed west for Texas, and DeVier was a full-fledged private citizen.

CHAPTER SEVENTEEN

BECOMING A WASHINGTON LAWYER

*Washington, D.C., is truly the intersection of law
and public policy.*

— DeVier Pierson

It was again decision time for the Pierson family. A few friends in Oklahoma suggested he return to his native state and run for public office. Although he respected public service and admired those who had endured the rigors of public life, DeVier believed his calling was the practice of law. While he had many friends in private practice in Oklahoma, the broader and more interesting practice seemed to be in the nation's capital.[1]

He knew he did not want to be a lobbyist. He had lunch at the Capitol with Tommy Boggs, the scion of a prominent Louisiana political family, who was establishing a lobbying firm. When Boggs told DeVier that he assumed he would be seeing him every night at some political fundraiser, DeVier told Boggs that was not how he wanted to spend his life. Boggs told DeVier that the only way he could be a successful Washington lobbyist was to commit to nighttime events by the hundreds each year, often more than one a night. Boggs knew what he was talking about; he has been one of the premier lawyer/lobbyists in Washington for 40 years.[2]

DeVier did not want his law practice based upon who he knew rather than what he knew. In a town that had more than its share of "rainmakers" and "fixers," he wanted to move in a different direction.

During the past four years, he had been counsel to two very important clients—the Congress and the President of the United States. He had been exposed to a wide variety of legal and policy issues. Now he wanted to counsel those who had matters before the government and those whose interests or businesses were affected by government actions. He hoped for an opportunity for broad advocacy—to present matters on behalf of clients to trial and appellate courts, administrative bodies, and executive branch officials. He wanted to deal with matters of substantial importance.[3]

Because he had chosen not to have serious discussions with law firms until his White House tour of duty was completed, DeVier's future was an open issue on January 20, 1969, when he became a private citizen. He had overtures from a number of large Washington firms, but was concerned they were too large and bureaucratic. Clark Clifford was returning to his law firm and talked to DeVier, but nothing came of that. His good friend, David Busby, offered him a partnership in his firm, an attractive possibility. Harry McPherson's new firm also made him an offer.

DeVier's job search was interrupted by a sudden, short, and unpleasant firestorm. The Trans-Pacific route case was reopened amidst charges of political impropriety. Ever since

President Johnson made his decision on new Asia airline routes in December, 1968, a number of airlines had lobbied the incoming Nixon administration for reconsideration. They made the argument that the airlines that were awarded the routes had political ties to Johnson. On January 21, one of President Nixon's first acts was to reopen the case.[4]

DeVier knew Johnson was getting "a bum rap." The President had denied the coveted Tokyo route to American Airlines, founded by one of his closest friends. In other awards, Johnson followed CAB recommendations to the letter. DeVier knew more about the subject than anyone at the White House because the President had deflected all conversations about the case to him.

Robert Novak, co-author of the daily Evans and Novak column in the Washington Post, called DeVier and said he understood that DeVier was going to join a law firm representing Trans World Airlines (TWA). DeVier told Novak that was not true and that he had not discussed affiliating with any firm while still in the White House. Novak asked DeVier to pledge to never represent an airline as a lawyer. When DeVier said that pledge was ludicrous because he hoped to practice law in Washington for a long time, the columnist said, "Then I am going with the story."[5]

The result was a syndicated column published in many of the nation's leading newspapers identifying DeVier as a "rainmaker" whose handling of the Pacific route cases was under "clouds of suspicion" if he became an attorney for one of the airlines involved. Rainmaker was the term often used to describe lawyers who use their high government contacts to bring about magical solutions for their clients.

The column was all conjecture. It never accused DeVier of any wrongdoing but danced around the issue. Novak and Evans wrote, "Here, then, is a delicate conflict-of-interest question. If Pierson does not represent TWA, his work in the White House on the Transpacific case will be considered suspect, unfairly."[6]

DeVier was offended by the article, told Novak so, and noted in his response that he still had not decided which law firm he would join. He succinctly pointed out why the allegations of politics in President Johnson's decision had no merit. In a story about the controversy in Newsweek Magazine, DeVier said the rumors of political giveaway were "phony baloney…poisonous stuff" circulated by "a rather fascinating coalition of the disappointed."[7] Still, DeVier was "clearly stung."[8]

The controversy had a typical Washington ending. After the initial political posturing, the Nixon White House was unable to find any basis for radical change to Johnson's decision. DeVier, at their request, met with Bob Ellsworth and Peter Flanagan, the Nixon White House aides with responsibility in that area, to confirm that it was a tempest in a teapot. Months later, Novak ran a very small retraction at the end of a column conceding that DeVier did not join a law firm that had TWA or any other airline as a client. As his career unfolded over the next 40 years, DeVier never represented an airline.[9]

DeVier continued to consider his future. He had been admitted to practice before the United States Supreme Court in 1966 when he was counsel for the Joint Committee. At the end of 1968, he was admitted to practice before all courts in the District of Columbia after submitting an application with requisite letters of recommendation, including a very nice letter from President Johnson. Best of all, he was admitted to the D.C. Bar without having to take a bar examination. They accepted the results of his 1957 admission to practice in Oklahoma.[10]

After weighing the options, DeVier made a career decision he has never regretted—he decided to start his own law firm. While he had attractive offers from existing Washington firms, he wanted to run his own show. It was a high-risk decision because most new firms established in Washington did not succeed—their problem was the lack of clients who wanted to move from older firms.

The firm of Sharon Pierson and Semmes opened for business on April 1, 1969. DeVier's fellow risk-takers were John Sharon, who had left Clark Clifford's firm; David Semmes, a former CIA agent who had an intellectual property law practice; Theodore "Ted" Crolius, a former legislative assistant to Senator Jacob Javits of New York, and William T. "Tom" Finley, Jr., a former associate deputy attorney general at the Department of Justice. Soon, Knox Bemis, a trial attorney in the Justice Department's tax division, joined the firm.[11]

David Semmes was pleased to team with DeVier and
Sharon in the new firm. Semmes said, "We were launching
out in a new effort at a time when many law firms were clam-
oring for available clients. But our hard work and reasonable
results brought clients our way." [12]

From his first week as a lawyer in the firm, Bemis knew
DeVier demanded a high standard of both legal analysis and
legal writing. He said, "It was an incredible learning experience because DeVier demanded the same near-perfection
from us that he expected from himself. In working for a client, only the best was good enough." [13]

The group of lawyers that launched out on their own in
1969 practiced law together for the next 30 years. Six years
after its formation, the firm name was changed to Pierson
Semmes Crolius and Finley, as the result of Sharon's retirement and untimely death. Following the retirement of Crolius
and the tragic death of Finley, the firm was reconstituted as
Pierson Semmes and Bemis. Many of the young lawyers who
came to the firm as associates in the 1970s and 1980s remained with the firm for its entire existence.

After a short stay in downtown Washington, the firm's
office was moved to the Canal Square Building in the Georgetown section of the District of Columbia. It was a lovely Civil
War era building, originally a warehouse, abutting the historic
C&O Canal that was built after the Revolutionary War as the
young nation's first public works project. The core building
was brick with exposed beams. DeVier's office was in the old

After his years in the White House, DeVier began the private practice of law in Washington, D.C. His firm flourished from the beginning.

DeVier, right, and his law partner, John Sharon, left, meet with the President of Mauritius during a 1971 trip to discuss world sugar policy.

section looking down the canal toward the Potomac River and the Washington Mall. The view was exceeded only by his first Washington office in the Capitol.[14]

With beautiful offices and fine lawyers, all that was needed was clients. Fortunately, they came quickly. DeVier's first client was an Oklahoma company, Lee Way Motor Freight, which he represented on a matter before the Interstate Commerce Commission. Lee Way's general counsel, Sidney Upsher, was a Phi Gam and entertained DeVier with stories of meetings with Jimmy Hoffa on Teamster issues. It was not a

big case, but DeVier was pleased to start his law practice with
a client from home.

In his first year of practice, DeVier began the representation of a group of petrochemical companies led by Union
Carbide, Dow, and Monsanto in their dealings with the government to obtain access to crude oil under the strictures of
the Mandatory Oil Import Program (MOIP), a program that
had become familiar territory during his time at the White
House. The work for Union Carbide led to a broader relationship in which DeVier's firm advised the company on many
issues. Other partners in the firm were working on matters for
the Penn Central Railroad, the mutual fund industry, the title
insurance industry, and General Electric Company. The firm
was off to a good start.[15]

One of DeVier's most interesting early clients was located on the tiny island of Mauritius in the Indian Ocean. In
the first week that the law firm was open, DeVier was asked
by a prominent sugar broker to handle an emergency matter
for the sugar industry of a Central American country. The
country's right to import sugar into the United States was
lapsing unless an emergency petition was filed the next day
with the Economic Division of the National Security Council.
DeVier worked all night with a team of economists to prepare
the petition and supporting economic tables. The following
day, DeVier presented the petition to the National Security
Council official in charge of the program and it was granted.
There was a buzz in international sugar circles that DeVier

and his firm were miracle workers.[16]

This early success led to the firm being retained by the Mauritius Sugar Syndicate, the organization of sugar producers in this island nation. Despite its tiny size, Mauritius was one of the ten largest sugar producing countries in the world. DeVier spent a great deal of time with representatives of the Syndicate in London and Washington and presented the Mauritius interests at both the State Department and by testimony before the Senate Finance Committee. DeVier was successful in obtaining a large country quota for Mauritius each year until the country quotas were abandoned in favor of global arrangements.[17]

In 1971, the Pierson family grew with the birth of Steve. Shirley gets his attention while Libby, Jeff, and DeVier watch.

The Mauritius representation enabled travel to exotic places. In 1972, the Pierson and Sharon families spent several days in London, followed by a week on camera safari in Uganda, Kenya, and Tanzania, and ending with a flight from Nairobi across the Indian Ocean to Mauritius.

The week in Mauritius was very interesting. The country had been a French colony for generations and most of the sugar planters on the island were of French descent. Even the newspaper accounts of the Pierson and Sharon visit was in French. DeVier and Sharon met with the president of the country, exchanged customary gifts, and toured the sugar plantations. DeVier appeared on Mauritius TV to explain the importance of the United States sugar program. The hospitality of the sugar producers was abundant.[18]

Although generally unenthusiastic about a lobbying practice, DeVier's firm undertook one legislative assignment for the El Paso Natural Gas Company. El Paso had merged with Northwest Pipeline Company, another interstate pipeline. The merger was embroiled in litigation for a decade, having gone to the United States Supreme Court three times. El Paso's position was upheld each time by the high court until the last appeal by a consumer activist in California. In a decision written by Justice William O. Douglas, generally viewed as an aberration of antitrust law, the merger was overturned.

El Paso retained the firm to determine if there was a legislative solution to the problem. For example, was it possible for Congress to pass legislation to overturn the Supreme

Court decision and allow the merger? Most natural gas producers and consumer groups supported the merger and there
was considerable political sentiment for such legislation.

DeVier discussed the matter at length with the chairman
of the Senate Commerce Committee and determined there
was substantial support for the bill in the Senate. However,
the House leadership was not enthusiastic, and the effort
eventually was abandoned. DeVier's only enduring recollection of the matter was convincing El Paso's chairman that
they should not visit members of Congress on Capitol Hill in
his long black company limousine. DeVier thought that image
to be "at war with the representation of consumer interests." [19]

Surprisingly, one of the new firm's best sources of business was other law firms. At the time, very few large firms in
other cities had Washington offices. DeVier traveled to the
headquarters of a number of major firms to discuss Washington aspects of their practice and to establish correspondent relationships. In the early 1970s, the firm became the Washington correspondent for the Ely Bartlett firm in Boston; Baker
& Botts, Houston's largest law firm; and Gibson Dunn &
Crutcher, located in Los Angeles and the largest firm in California. Until larger firms began establishing branch offices in
D.C., it was a lucrative relationship for DeVier's firm. [20]

DeVier kept his ties with Oklahoma. The firm was
retained by Oklahoma Natural Gas Company (ONG) to
advise them on Washington issues. DeVier enjoyed his trips
to Tulsa to talk to company management. He developed a

close personal relationship with ONG CEO Charles Ingram and worked with him on a wide array of natural gas issues when Ingram was chairman of the American Gas Association. Ingram was an avid golfer and he and DeVier often slipped away for quick rounds at Burning Tree on his Washington visits.[21]

DeVier also handled several matters for Mobil Corporation. He had met Mobil's general counsel on an Aspen Institute executive retreat. After the firm had been retained, DeVier's principal contact in the company was his friend from Korea, Dick Zahm, Mobil's in-house point man on a number of federal issues. The representation included dealing with the State Department on issues of international law arising from a Mobil concession in Egypt, a South American trade dispute, and one of the early controversies with the federal government over federal oil and gas leases off the California coast. Other lawyers in the firm represented Mobil in arbitration matters before the United States-Iranian Claims Tribunal.

Another Oklahoma client provided some comic relief. One day DeVier received a telephone call from Pody Poe, his debate partner at Classen High School. Poe, who had been in trouble with the law on several occasions, wanted legal advice on legislation that might have an adverse affect upon his bookmaking business. When asked what specific legislation, Poe replied, "The Omnibus Crime Control Act of 1968."[22]

Poe startled the law firm's receptionist when he appeared

in a lavender jumpsuit. DeVier introduced Poe to Tom Finley who had participated in the drafting of the crime control legislation when he was with the Justice Department. When Poe came back to DeVier's office to say goodbye, he said he was happy with the legal advice, thanked DeVier, dropped an envelope on the desk, and rushed out. When DeVier opened it, he found $10,000 in crisp $100 bills.

DeVier had no idea where the money came from, but knew the firm was not going to touch it. He re-sealed the envelope, enclosed it in a package with a letter stating the firm only accepted fees by check or wire transfer, and sent it to Poe. DeVier never heard back from Poe. DeVier said, "Discretion being the better part of valor, we never sent him a bill." [23]

CHAPTER EIGHTEEN

FINISHING CONGRESSIONAL REORGANIZATION

*It was gratifying to return to the work which had
brought me to Washington in the first place.*

— DeVier Pierson

DeVier had not forgotten about the assignment that had
brought him to the nation's capital—the efforts of the Joint
Committee on the Organization of the Congress. There had
been a disappointing series of developments after the passage
of the Legislative Reorganization Act in the Senate in March,
1967, under Senator Mike Monroney's leadership;. The bill
had been defeated in the House of Representatives because
of the opposition of a number of House committee chairmen.
The Joint Committee itself had gone out of existence at the
end of 1968. Monroney had been defeated in his re-elec-
tion bid in 1968 by Henry Bellmon and was no longer in the
Senate. DeVier was very anxious to see the congressional
reorganization effort completed successfully as a tribute to
Monroney.[1]

In 1970, DeVier received a telephone call from Senator
Lee Metcalf of Montana who had served on the Joint Committee. He was hopeful that he could resurrect the congressional reorganization bill and pass it in both houses of Congress.
Metcalf asked for DeVier's help, which he gladly offered
without compensation.[2]

DeVier had a series of meetings with Senator Metcalf and other members of the Senate who had continued their interest in congressional reorganization. He also met with House members leading the reorganization effort in that body. Unlike the situation in 1967, a significant number of "Young Turks" in the House were now actively campaigning for congressional reform. Prospects for the Legislation Reorganization Act now appeared promising in both the Senate and House.

Sure enough, the House came through, passing the bill 326-19 on September 19, 1970, under the sponsorship of the Young Turk reformers. The margin was deceptive. There was still substantial opposition by most committee chairmen and the bill was approved after the longest debate on any single legislative measure in the House within the three previous decades.

The bill moved to the Senate. With the help of Majority Leader Mansfield, Senator Metcalf was appointed floor leader after the legislation won approval of the Senate Government Operations Committee. During debate on October 5, Senator Metcalf paid tribute to Senator Monroney as the greatest champion of congressional reform in the twentieth century. As Monroney had done in 1967, Metcalf beat down a number of crippling amendments. On the following day, the Legislative Reorganization Act of 1970 was passed by an overwhelming margin. Following passage, Metcalf praised DeVier's work without pay on the project, perhaps viewed as contrary to the norms of a Washington lawyer.[3]

The bill was signed into law by President Nixon on November 13, 1970. Bryce Harlow sent DeVier one of the pens used by the President in the signing ceremony. DeVier was extremely happy that Monroney's hard work had been vindicated and his enormous contribution to the quality of Congress had been achieved. On a personal basis, DeVier thought it nice to successfully ring down the curtain on the matter which had enabled him to come to Washington in the first place.[4]

DeVier completed the congressional reorganization work with much admiration for most members of Congress. He believed that, with a few exceptions, the senators and congressmen with whom he worked were persons of intelligence, integrity, and dedication to their work. He noted that throughout the nation's history, Congress had been the branch of government most accountable to the people and that it was not surprising that members were "political" in the sense that they were highly conscious of their constituents' views. He believed that many members of Congress had made substantial financial sacrifices to serve the American people and that they deserved more credit for that sacrifice. He was grateful for the years he had spent on Capitol Hill.

CHAPTER NINETEEN

REPRESENTING BIG BUSINESS

We met with Attorney General John Mitchell in his
football-field-sized office at the Justice Department.

— DeVier Pierson

During the 1970s, DeVier's law firm was very active
on antitrust matters on behalf of America's steel industry.
The firm was retained by National Steel Corporation, the
fourth largest United States producer, to advise its leadership
concerning a prospective merger with a smaller company.
Although DeVier's first thought was that the combined market share of National Steel and the smaller company should
not raise any anti-trust concerns, the Antitrust Division of the
Department of Justice under President Nixon had been surprisingly hostile to mergers in the steel industry. Indeed, the
Assistant Attorney General for the Antitrust Division advised
DeVier at their initial meeting that Justice would oppose the
merger. [1]

DeVier met with National Steel CEO George Stinson and
his senior staff to plot a strategy. DeVier suggested a four-part
plan—prepare an exhaustive trial brief, with supporting economic studies, to show the Antitrust Division that National
Steel was serious about the merger; talk to a White House
staff member who could discuss the merger behind the scenes
with Antitrust Division lawyers; obtain a letter to President
Nixon from I.W. Abel, president of the Steelworkers Union,

supporting the merger; and meet with Attorney General John Mitchell to ask reconsideration of the Justice position. National Steel agreed to DeVier's plan of action.

With a trial brief filed with the Antitrust Division and a letter in hand from Abel, DeVier arranged for Stinson to meet Nixon economic aide Peter Flanagan. DeVier sent Stinson to the White House alone—he thought Flanagan would be more at ease talking about the situation with Stinson if the steel company's lawyer was not present. The meeting was productive. After a debriefing over lunch, Stinson said, "In all my years dealing with Washington lawyers, this is the first time one ever suggested that he not attend a meeting at the White House." DeVier took that as a compliment.[2]

The next stop was Attorney General Mitchell's large office at Department of Justice headquarters. Mitchell sat at the end of a conference table puffing on his pipe. Justice Department lawyers were on one side and Stinson, a consulting economist, and DeVier were on the other. When DeVier said that the merger was pro-competitive and that he believed the steelworkers would benefit from it, Mitchell gave him a smile, reached into his pocket, and waved a copy of the letter from Steelworkers Union President Abel to President Nixon.

The meeting produced an unqualified victory. Based upon the Attorney General's final decision, the Justice Department concluded it would not oppose the merger. The two companies consummated the deal shortly thereafter. National Steel remained one of DeVier's clients for a decade.[3]

In 1981, National Steel's Stinson asked DeVier to come to Pittsburgh to discuss a far bolder proposal. U.S. Steel, the largest American steel producer, had proposed a merger with National. In previous years, a merger between the number one and number four producers would have been unthinkable on antitrust grounds. But the administration of President Ronald Reagan had a more open view toward business mergers. DeVier began orchestrating a series of meetings in Pittsburgh and Washington to discuss the possibility of merging U.S. Steel with National Steel.

At that time, trust-busters used the so-called Herfindahl Index to determine permissible and impermissible combined market shares on a product-by-product basis. Looking at just the steel market in the United States, the Herfindahl Index exposed percentages that would kill any U.S. Steel-National Steel merger. Many of U.S. Steel's principal competitors were in Europe and Japan. DeVier suggested the merger be presented based upon world market shares because major steel producers now competed freely on a global basis. U.S. Steel's general counsel agreed the merger should be tested on the world market basis.[4]

It was the early days of wide computer use, but a young associate in DeVier's office had mastered the new technology on an Apple computer to piece together a series of tables of market share using published data for total worldwide production, National's market share, and estimates of U.S. Steel's share. While there may have been some Herfindahl Index violations, any negative test of the merger looking at world market figures was slight.[5]

When DeVier showed the information to U.S. Steel, its general counsel said DeVier's "sophisticated program" clearly was superior to information developed thus far by U.S. Steel. DeVier said, "The sophisticated program consisted of one associate producing a string of tables on his Apple in his tiny office." U.S. Steel proposed that DeVier and his firm act as the buffer for market share data for both companies in talks with the Justice Department. In effect, DeVier's firm would be in the enviable position of representing both companies.

The plan moved forward. However, the size of the two companies and the novelty of the global market analysis were simply too much for the Antitrust Division. When its lawyers announced the Justice Department would vigorously oppose the merger, it was abandoned. DeVier's only consolation was that the concept of a global steel market proved to be accurate and American producers, including U.S. Steel and National Steel, consistently lost market share to foreign steel producers in future years.[6]

DeVier was happy with his firm's success in representing a broad spectrum of clients in many different industries. But energy problems, particularly those of the natural gas industry, began to dwarf other areas due to a special client relationship.

In the early 1970s, the firm handled several matters for Pennzoil Corporation, a Houston-based company controlled by Hugh and Bill Liedtke who had grown up in Tulsa, Oklahoma. DeVier and other lawyers in his firm handled a trade matter for Pennzoil's sulfur subsidiary involving the Anti-Dumping Act and Interstate Commerce Commission issues for the company's oil pipeline subsidiary. DeVier personally represented a senior Pennzoil executive in a criminal antitrust investigation.[7]

When President Nixon initiated the ill-fated wage and price control program in 1971, the firm made Knox Bemis the guru of price control issues. The firm represented Pennzoil on all matters arising under the Economic Stabilization Act.

In late 1971, DeVier received an envelope from Pennzoil General Counsel Baine Kerr containing a copy of a lawsuit filed in federal court by Texas Gulf Sulfur Company (Texas Gulf) against United Gas Pipe Line Company (United), a Pennzoil subsidiary. Pennzoil had acquired United in the late 1960s after the company had built one of the largest pipeline systems in the country and served much of the natural gas market in the South, especially along the Gulf Coast.

There was no letter attached to the copy of the complaint, so DeVier called Kerr. The Pennzoil lawyer said, "This is some kind of strange little case that won't amount to much, but I would appreciate it if you would handle it." [8] The "strange little case" turned out to be the opening bell of the largest economic dispute in the history of the natural gas pipeline industry, a dispute that raged for the next 15 years.

In late 1973, DeVier conferred in Houston with Pennzoil executives who had decided to spin off United into a separate public company. Because there might be conflicts between the two companies, Pennzoil proposed that the Houston law firm of Baker & Botts represent Pennzoil and that DeVier's firm represent United from that time forward. In terms of development of legal business, it was "the deal of the century." [9]

To DeVier's amazement, the new CEO of United was his longtime OU classmate in undergraduate and law school studies, Hugh Roff. Roff, who DeVier considered one of the smartest persons he had ever known, had opted for the business world rather than private practice after law school. He became one of DeVier's most important clients and a very close friend.

The first order of business was to get the necessary regulatory approvals for the spinoff and the creation of United as a separate public company. Since United was classified as a natural gas company within the meaning of the Natural Gas Act, the Federal Power Commission (FPC), later the Federal Energy Regulatory Commission (FERC), had jurisdiction to determine if the spinoff would have any adverse affect upon consumers.

In evidentiary proceedings before the FERC, DeVier represented United and Baker & Botts was counsel to Pennzoil. The spinoff was approved. United became an independent company, but with many problems.[10]

United's most pressing problem was the lack of gas. At the time, interstate gas transmission companies such as United were "merchant pipelines," buying gas from producers in the field for transmission through its pipelines for sale to customers. As a result of market conditions and Federal Power Commission control of wellhead prices, natural gas production had declined, resulting in a nationwide gas shortage.[11]

United found itself in a very unpleasant situation of having less gas under contract from producers than it was obligated to deliver to its customers. The dilemma was complicated further because many of United's customers were electric utilities that used natural gas to generate electricity to residential and commercial customers. It was a recipe for disaster.

The first issue was how United would allocate its scarce gas supplies among its various customers. In regulatory terms, it was known as "curtailment," an issue over which the FPC had asserted jurisdiction. At the first meeting with United's general counsel to discuss the curtailment issue, DeVier "talked a good game," but clearly did not fully understand the curtailment situation. After the meeting, he told associate and longtime partner, Peter Levin, "Find out what a curtailment is and how we deal with it." [12]

Levin began to delve into the complicated world of gas supply and pipeline transportation. Over the next few years in the litigation involving United, Levin worked under DeVier's scrutiny. He said," If my work passed his very exacting standards, then I had a good, solid argument. He was much tougher than our adversaries in picking out weaknesses in our position. If a young lawyer missed something, DeVier cut to the chase and corrected it quickly." [13]

The FPC ordered a plan to spread the scarce gas supply among United's customers. The power plant companies objected to the FPC's action and took the legal fight over the federal agency's authority to the Fifth Circuit Court of Appeals and ultimately to the United States Supreme Court. DeVier helped prepare the briefs for the litigation. Fortunately, the high court upheld the FPC's jurisdiction under the Natural Gas Act, establishing the authority for allocating United's limited gas supplies in a sensible way. [14]

After the FPC jurisdiction was established, United initiated the first contested curtailment proceeding of any interstate pipeline. DeVier's firm represented United in the matter.

In addition to United, other pipelines, gas producers, electric utilities, municipal distributors, and several public interest groups entered the fray, described by DeVier as "a three-ring circus with a cast of thousands that would take almost four years to resolve." [15]

DeVier and his partners were forced to add a number of lawyers to the firm to staff the gigantic administrative action. DeVier recruited a brilliant young lawyer, Ross Hamachek, who had been engaged in weapons system analysis for the Department of Defense and the Senate Armed Services Committee. Hamachek headed the firm's curtailment team and fashioned a system for obtaining end-use data from United's thousands of direct and indirect customers. After protracted hearings and the filing of "enough briefs and economic studies to destroy several forests," a curtailment tariff was approved by the FERC to provide an order of priority for United's service to its customers and a roadmap as to how United would implement the plan. The method became the model for the entire pipeline industry. [16]

Several appeals from these FERC orders were hotly-contested matters. DeVier argued three of the appeals before the Fifth Circuit Court of Appeals and Levin argued another. Finally, United's curtailment program became final, giving some certainty to its future deliveries.

But there was a lurking problem of gigantic proportions. What was United's liability for the shortfall between the amount of gas promised under contract and the volume actually delivered under the curtailment program? Was United liable for the difference between its contract price and the amount paid by customers for alternative fuels? If the answer was yes, the liability for United would run into the billions. One estimate placed potential liability at $6 billion. It was obvious that United could not survive damages of that magnitude.[17]

The lawsuits began. The first one was the small lawsuit that Baine Kerr had handed to DeVier as "the strange little case" filed by Texas Gulf Sulfur. Major suits were filed in 1974 by electric utilities in Texas, Louisiana, and Mississippi. DeVier and his team of lawyers faced enormous discovery obligations and eventual trials. The life of United Gas Pipe Line Company was at stake.[18]

CHAPTER TWENTY

DAMAGE CONTROL

*It was a delight to see DeVier take apart the most complex
legal situation and put it into business terms which
our non-lawyers were able to grasp.*

— Hugh Roff

For several years, the United Gas Pipe Line curtailment
cases were the biggest items on DeVier's legal agenda. The
cases were unique because there were so many parties and the
stakes were so high. Pierson Semmes assembled a defense
team headed by its partners and associates and working with
other lawyers in Texas, Louisiana, and Mississippi. A central
databank for discovery purposes was established and research
teams were organized to analyze each of the relevant legal
issues.

Peter Levin, who considers DeVier his mentor, applauded DeVier's leadership of the defense team. He said, "He is
one of the best oral advocates I have ever seen, one of the
quickest studies. I was rarely at a meeting with him where he
was not the dominant person. He could command the room
and everyone would look up to him."[1]

United's principal defense was that allocating scarce gas
supplies under a FERC-approved tariff was an absolute defense to damage liability. But this result was far from certain.
DeVier and Hugh Roff also initiated discussions with the
major electric utility plaintiffs at both the management and

legal level about the possibility of settling the dispute without litigation. DeVier argued that the plaintiffs would never be able to collect the amount of claimed damages and that the destruction of their gas supplier would not be in their long term best interest.[2]

Most of the curtailment damage suits had been filed in various state courts and asserted claims under state law. DeVier's legal team removed the cases to federal court, but then had to prove that a significant federal question was present. They argued that curtailing gas supplies pursuant to FERC-ordered tariffs made the dispute a federal issue, controlled by federal standards for contract damage liability. But the damage suit petitions were simply for breach of contract under state law and said nothing about federal authority.

After the cases were in federal court, a petition to consolidate them was filed with the Judicial Panel on Multidistrict Litigation. To DeVier's delight, the panel was chaired by retired Tenth Circuit Court of Appeals Chief Judge Alfred P. Murrah, DeVier's longtime friend and mentor.

However, Judge Murrah was skeptical of DeVier's position. After asking DeVier a series of probing questions as to how he could square removal with prior federal question authority, Judge Murrah denied the request to consolidate the cases and sent them back to state court. DeVier was later told that Judge Murrah said, "DeVier is a very good lawyer, but he sure didn't have much of a case." After the hearing, United's general counsel left DeVier's office and returned with a gift. He had gone to a sporting goods store and bought DeVier a protective cup.[3]

Left to right, Doyle Cotton, Hugh Roff, Bill Cassin, and DeVier celebrate their 50th birthdays on a business trip to Italy in 1981. Roff was DeVier's OU classmate and chairman of the board and CEO of United Energy Resources, Inc.

After years of discovery and pre-trial jockeying, the lawsuits brought by the three largest power plants, New Orleans Public Service, Inc., Gulf States Utilities, and Louisiana Power & Light Company, went to trial in 1982 in a consolidated proceeding in state district court in New Orleans.

Any Louisiana trial is unique because Louisiana is the only state in the United States that operates under the French civil law rather than the English common law. In addition, this case was especially unusual because there were so many parties and the stakes were so nigh. The three plaintiffs claimed damages of approximately $1.5 billion, plus interest. The case would be tried to a judge, without a jury.[4]

DeVier and 16 other lawyers, drawn from his firm and other firms in Louisiana and Mississippi, descended on New Orleans for the trial. A full-fledged litigation center was housed in an office building in downtown New Orleans near the courthouse. The trial lasted two years, "in fits and starts, with long breaks in between," while all parties put on a long list of fact and expert witnesses on liability and damage issues.

"Even in high tension moments, DeVier was calm," said United CEO Hugh Roff. "I think the stress was actually a challenge for him. The more complex the litigation was, the more in control he seemed to be."[5]

United's most memorable witness was Edwin Edwards, the former governor of Louisiana who was preparing to run again. He was asked to testify as to the pervasive nature of the natural gas shortage in the state throughout the 1970s in order to establish that United's shortfall was part of an existing industry problem rather than the fault of the company or its management. DeVier met with Edwards several times to prepare him for trial. They reviewed the documents during his time as governor that acknowledged the dimensions of the gas shortage.

"Governor Edwards was a very smooth and articulate man," DeVier remembered. "He had a photographic memory, but he was a rascal." DeVier was satisfied with his testimony at trial, then held his breath, wondering if something bad might happen in cross-examination. Edwards was subsequently re-elected Louisiana governor and then was caught up in questionable activity and was ultimately indicted, convicted, and sentenced to a term in federal prison.[6]

During the lengthy trial, some things began to fall United's way. During a recess, Hugh Roff and DeVier negotiated a settlement with Gulf States Utilities, the largest claimant among the three plaintiffs, for just over $100 million, less than ten percent of its claim. There was great psychological value in settling the largest claim for "a dime on the dollar" and set the stage for a subsequent settlement with New Orleans Public Service, Inc., for $75 million. That was a lot of money, but United could survive the payments.

In August, 1984, judgment was entered for the final plaintiff, Louisiana Power & Light Company for $40 million, far below its claim of $700 million. United was happy with the result, although the Louisiana Court of Appeals increased the award to $90 million and the Louisiana Supreme Court refused to review the case. DeVier thought the Court of Appeals raising the award by $50 million was "a very hometown decision for a local company."[7]

When the United States Supreme Court declined to intervene in the case, United ended the 17-year curtailment damage saga by paying Louisiana Power & Light approximately $200 million for its judgment and accrued interest. The litigation had, literally, been a matter of damage control. The remaining cases in Mississippi were either settled or dropped. The totally payments by United to customer plaintiffs were approximately $400 million, only a fraction of the bankrupting claims of several billion dollars. Hugh Roff said, "The final disposition was a victory. We were able to stay in business. DeVier held the wolves at bay for long enough for us to do what was best for the shareholders."[8]

By the time the United litigation ended, DeVier's firm in Washington, D.C., was well regarded. The curtailment proceedings and related damage litigation had received a good deal of attention in the Washington energy bar. Year after year, DeVier's firm was listed as number one in the nation's capital in legal fees from pipeline companies. DeVier was interviewed several times by reporters and tried to explain the groundbreaking nature of the United curtailment litigation. Skeptical reporters just looked at the large legal fees and wrote that the fees had "built a lot of second homes on the Eastern Shore and put a lot of kids through college."[9] When DeVier was asked to comment, he simply denied that he had a second home on the Eastern Shore. Years later he and Shirley did add a second home to their residential holdings—and it was on the Eastern Shore of Maryland.

The shortage of gas in the 1970s had another perverse result. United and other pipelines began to offer higher prices to producers for gas and agreed to contract provisions that required the pipeline to take minimum quantities of gas or to make advance payments, a "take or pay" contract. When customers' demand for gas fell in the early 1980s so that pipelines could not buy all the gas, producers began to sue pipelines to enforce the contracts.

Hugh Roff had a whimsical response to United's dilemma. He said, "Now I understand the purpose of a natural gas pipeline. If it has too little gas, it is sued by customers. If it has too much gas, it is sued by its producers. The purpose of a gas pipeline seems to be to act as an agent for the service of process."[10] Humor aside, the change in gas demand had resulted in a new threat to the ongoing financial viability of pipelines.

Other changes affected United. The company entered into talks with MidCon, a larger gas pipeline company head-quartered in Chicago, Illinois, and serving Midwest markets. Initial negotiations centered around a "merger of equals," but soon it was clear that MidCon intended to acquire United. DeVier represented United and Roff, individually, in weeks of day-long talks and all-night drafting sessions in New York City.

In August, 1984, MidCon and United merged, with Mid-Con as the surviving company. Roff was to retire and MidCon to take over management of United. As Roff and DeVier were driving to the airport to fly back to Washington, D.C, after the merger agreement was signed, Roff said, "Well, DeVier, this is the end of an era for me." DeVier thought his days of repre-senting the old United were also over. The negotiations with MidCon had been highly adversarial and he did not expect them to be a client.[11]

A few months later, DeVier received a telephone call from MidCon general counsel Joe Wells asking for a meeting in Chicago for an undisclosed purpose. When DeVier arrived, he was shown a lawsuit filed against Natural Gas Pipeline of America, a MidCon subsidiary, and two other smaller pipe-lines. It was one of 30 "take or pay" lawsuits filed against MidCon, United, and its subsidiaries in the past 90 days. Wells told DeVier, "No one understands these suits or what we should be doing about them."[12]

To DeVier's great surprise, Wells asked him to take over

the lawsuits and to handle all of MidCon's take or pay problems. It was a mammoth task because litigation was pending in ten states with billions of dollars in claims. DeVier said he would accept the job if his firm would have total control, that all local counsel would report directly to him, and that Wells would write a letter to the local counsel confirming the agreement. Wells agreed, the letters were sent that day, and DeVier returned to Washington with a very big new client.

DeVier began to use his superb talents in organization to develop a strategy. He visited local counsel in the various states to assure them that this would be a collaborative venture. He wanted their cooperation and good will. Back in his own law firm, DeVier added lawyers and directed Rich Yarmey to create a central computerized document bank. DeVier's lawyers became frequent flyers to Chicago, Albuquerque, Salt Lake City, Dallas, Kansas City, Houston, New Orleans, Atlanta, Tulsa, and Oklahoma City.

There was also a regulatory component to the take or pay issue. Because of the enormity of the claims by producers, the viability of the entire pipeline industry was at risk. The FERC was concerned that the industry would be permanently disrupted by pipeline companies enduring the "rough justice" of individual lawsuits. FERC initiated Order 500, a proceeding to get comments on how the agency could exercise its jurisdiction under the Natural Gas Act to reach a fair resolution of the problem. DeVier spent a lot of time with MidCon executives, the Interstate Gas Association of America, and the America Gas Association to fashion industry positions on the matter.

Meanwhile, the take or pay litigation was moving from the discovery and pre-trial motion stages to the setting of trial dates in some jurisdictions. DeVier convinced Joe Wells and other MidCon executives that the first priority should be to keep any case from going to trial while the FERC was looking for a way to intervene. DeVier reasoned that if one jury rendered a huge verdict against MidCon, it would have a ripple effect on the rest of the litigation. Every legal move was made to delay a trial.

While in the delay mode, DeVier asked for authority to try to settle some of the larger claims. He was given $200 million settlement authority and began talking with plaintiffs. He was able to settle some of the most troublesome cases for $75 million, a small percentage of the actual claims. The settlements brought a buzz in industry circles and established a precedent for low dollar settlements.[13]

FERC finally came through with an order which was a creative way to spread the risk of excess gas costs to all segments of the industry. DeVier said, "It was a brilliant way to answer a problem that could have ruined the gas pipeline industry that was involved in a $12 billion transfer of gas each year." With the regulatory assistance, most of the other take or pay plaintiffs fell into line and accepted low dollar settlements. Although the last case was not dismissed until 1995, the serious take or pay litigation was over and MidCon survived as a viable company.[14]

The resolution of the take or pay issue brought cosmic changes to the gas pipeline industry. The traditional pipeline function of acting as merchants who bought and sold gas was changed. Producers were permitted to make direct sales to large customers and pipelines served primarily as transporters. In a less regulated environment, pipelines began to experiment with new profit centers based upon trading rather than pipeline transportation. Two such pipelines merged a few years later and created a company named Enron.

Looking back on the issues that had been handled by DeVier's law firm since its founding in 1969, he was pleased at their breadth and scope. He had been given the opportunity to work on a wide variety of substantial legal problems, including trade matters, antitrust issues, foreign arbitrations, oil industry problems, and major litigation and regulatory issues confronting the natural gas pipeline industry. He had taken matters to the United States Supreme Court, argued before a number of federal and state appellate courts, and had taken the lead in several major trials. With these high-stakes cases involving major economic issues, the time had passed quickly.[15]

CHAPTER TWENTY-ONE

UNPOPULAR CAUSES

If the practice of law is to be a profession rather than a trade,
we lawyers have a professional obligation to
take on the representation of unpopular clients and
causes we would not join.

— DeVier Pierson

DeVier's belief that a lawyer should be willing to represent an unpopular client or legal cause, sometimes without compensation, manifested itself in the one notable foreign policy failure in the administration of President Ronald Reagan.

One of the last proxy battles in the Cold War was America's support for the Contras, a resistance movement against the Marxist Sandinista government in Nicaragua. Congress was skeptical about aid to the Contras and passed a series of measures which either limited or prohibited federal government funding of the Contras through appropriated funds.

The Reagan administration believed in the Contras' fight and looked for ways to get money to the resistance other than by means of congressionally- appropriated funds. Lieutenant Colonel Oliver North, a second-level staff member at the National Security Council, headed the administration's covert effort to raise private funds from individuals, organizations, and other nations. The Central American policy was coordinated by a Restricted Inter-Agency Group (RIG), comprised of North, Central Intelligence Agency (CIA) officer Alan

Fiers, and Assistant Secretary of State Elliott Abrams. There were frequent rumors that the American government was helping fund a secret war in Nicaragua, but Reagan officials always denied it.

In November, 1986, a series of events, including the downing of an aircraft delivering supplies to the Contras, resulted in public disclosure of the remarkable event that United States arms had been sold secretly to Iran and that proceeds of the sale had been diverted to the Contras. President Reagan ultimately appeared on television and apologized to the nation.

A firestorm consumed Washington, D.C. Both houses of Congress began formal investigations of the scandal that became known as Iran-Contra. The Justice Department appointed former federal judge and American Bar Association president Lawrence Walsh as Independent Counsel to investigate any criminal activity. Walsh had recently moved to Oklahoma City.

Every official in the Reagan administration who had responsibilities in the area—including the Vice President, the Secretary of State, the Secretary of Defense, and the National Security Advisor—were at legal risk.

DeVier's first contact with the scandal came when several members of the Senate Select Committee asked him to consider serving as chief counsel for the investigation. DeVier met twice with senators but decided that, even if asked, he could not afford the extreme disruption that such an assignment would have on his law firm and pending litigation. The Committee chose Arthur Liman, a distinguished New York attorney, for the job.

Then, DeVier became involved in Iran-Contra in a totally different way. He received a call from Harry McPherson, his friend from LBJ White House days, asking if he would be willing to meet with Assistant Secretary of State Elliott Abrams who was looking for legal representation. Abrams had worked briefly at McPherson's firm and was close enough to McPherson to share his difficulties and his need for counsel. McPherson was already representing others who might become involved in the scandal, and recommended DeVier to Abrams.[1]

At a breakfast meeting with Abrams, DeVier agreed to represent him. DeVier found Abrams to be a brilliant young man. He was the youngest Assistant Secretary of State in American history. In his job as Assistant Secretary for Inter-American Affairs and member of the RIG, he was certain to be a prime target of Walsh's investigation. In addition, Abrams was a brash and outspoken proponent of Reagan administration policy and had made many enemies on Capitol Hill and elsewhere.

DeVier had several reasons for agreeing to represent Abrams. He clearly needed legal help. Second, DeVier was instinctively opposed to the criminalization of policy disputes and believed that any lack of candor with Congress should be dealt with on a political basis, not in a criminal proceeding. In addition, the chance to work with congressional committees and the Independent Counsel would be a change of pace from his other legal assignments and the subject matter was a fascinating public policy debate. It was too good to pass up.[2]

From first blush, Abrams was comfortable with DeVier

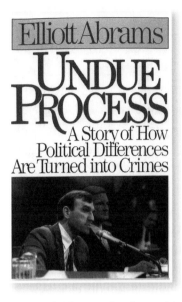

Elliott Abrams
UNDUE PROCESS
A Story of How Political Differences Are Turned into Crimes

The photograph of DeVier sitting beside Elliott Abrams while testifying to a congressional Iran-Contra investigating committee appeared on the front of Abrams' 1992 book, *Undue Process*.

as his lawyer. He said, "Here was somebody who was straight as an arrow, highly intelligent, and who was extremely knowledgeable. None of this was foreign to him, and so it was love at first sight for me. He became not just a lawyer in the narrow sense of the term, but in a broader sense, a true counselor. My future depended upon his skills."[3]

In his memoirs of the event, the 1992 book, *Undue Process, A Story of How Political Differences are Turned Into Crimes*, Abrams said of the first meeting at the Four Seasons Hotel, "My immediate first thought…was that he was a ringer for Jimmy Stewart, and as I came to know him better that impression only deepened. Tall, silver-haired, with the polite and old-fashioned manners and speech of a well-bred Oklahoman, he is the central casting Western lawyer who talks slowly and quietly, then exits the room leaving everyone feeling satisfied and friendly, and wondering how it is they have all just agreed to give it up and see things his way."[4]

Abrams had spent most of his adult life as a public servant and had no financial means to pay a huge legal bill. DeVier was uncomfortable with "running a legal meter" on this young man who was trying to support his wife and two children on a government salary. DeVier agreed to represent Abrams in the initial investigation without charge. If the representation became a protracted matter, the issue of fees could be revisited.[5]

DeVier asked Abrams to prepare a detailed chronology of his actions that might in any way bear on aid to the Contras. Abrams was directed to obtain a copy of all relevant files from the State Department and his prior testimony before congressional committees.

DeVier reapplied for the government security clearance he had enjoyed at the White House. Armed with the new clearance, he asked for access to the Senate Intelligence Committee document room and all State Department or other government files related to the matter. He spent several days poring over hundreds of significant Top Secret and even more sensitive Code Word documents. The issue was to what extent Abrams was involved and if he had testified truthfully to Congress.

As anticipated, Abrams was called to testify before a joint hearing of the Senate and House Iran Contra committees. DeVier advised Abrams that if his principal concern was avoiding criminal liability, he should take the Fifth Amendment because his congressional testimony would be used in subsequent grand jury appearances or matters before the Independent Counsel. On the other hand, if Abrams' first priority was to keep his job at the State Department and preserve his career, he should testify. Abrams chose the latter, and heavy preparation began.[6]

Abrams was the first Reagan official to testify at the Iran-

Contra hearings. One newspaper called his testimony "defiant and elusive."[7] Senator Howell Heflin told Abrams, "You are well-schooled in word-dancing. Is that something they teach you at the State Department?"[8]

"Elliott certainly stood his ground," DeVier remembered. In the all-day, televised hearing, Abrams was on the receiving end of tough questions about his knowledge of the Contra resupply effort and the accuracy of his previous testimony to Congress. DeVier told Abrams in advance that he did not plan to object to any questions unless absolutely necessary. DeVier did not want it to appear that Abrams was being "propped up by counsel." DeVier never said a word.[9]

DeVier's greatest disappointment during the hearing was Oklahoma Senator David Boren's scalding attack on Abrams which ended with Boren's question as to whether or not Abrams should continue his job at the State Department.[10] When DeVier returned to his office, he had a telephone call from Boren who said, "I know you think I was tough on him. I wanted you to know I am not trying to get him fired." Pierson ruefully told his longtime friend, Boren, "Well, you disguised that sentiment very well."[11]

Abrams was subpoenaed to appear before a federal grand jury twice in 1987. As in all grand jury proceedings, counsel cannot be present, so Abrams was alone when he was asked about his knowledge of the aid to the Contras scheme.

The Independent Counsel turned his attention to Colonel North and National Security Advisor John Poindexter. Both were indicted and convicted of several felony counts of perjury but the convictions were subsequently overturned because the Iran-Contra Committee had granted limited use immunity to both of them and it was difficult to segregate their congressional testimony from the evidence used at trial.[12]

After meetings with Judge Walsh, DeVier was notified in early 1988 that the Independent Counsel did not intend to take any action against Abrams. Although he had been roughed up in congressional hearings and before grand juries, Abrams had weathered the storm and continued as Assistant Secretary of State until the end of the Reagan administration.

Three years later, in the summer of 1991, DeVier began hearing rumors that Abrams had again become a criminal target of the Independent Counsel. CIA officer Fiers, another member of the RIG, plea bargained and entered a guilty plea to misdemeanor counts of withholding information from Congress. DeVier believed that move was an ominous sign for his client, Abrams.

On September 6, 1991, DeVier sent a letter to Judge Walsh reminding the Independent Counsel that a previous agreement with the office entitled Abrams to advance notice if there was a change in his status. DeVier wrote:

Since a number of recent news stories have mentioned Mr. Abrams in connection with your ongoing investigation, I felt it was appropriate to bring to your attention the understanding I have with your office. I assume that this understanding remains in effect so that I would be advised—and given the opportunity to meet with you—if there were to be any change in Mr. Abrams' status.[13]

Four days later, Walsh's new chief assistant, Craig Gillen, called DeVier and said, "There is movement." A very concentrated negotiation with the Independent Counsel's office took place during the next month. DeVier met with Gillen who said he was convinced that Abrams knew that secret aid was being provided to the Contras and had testified falsely to congressional committees in 1985 and 1986.

It was DeVier's assessment that Abrams was in serious legal jeopardy. He had to appear again before the grand jury. On September 26, 1991, DeVier met with Judge Walsh to present Abrams' case. For two hours he summarized the evidence supporting his position that Abrams had not been aware of North's illegal activities and had not intended to mislead Congress. DeVier urged that the matter be resolved on a noncriminal basis.[14]

While DeVier thought from time to time that he was making progress with Judge Walsh, Walsh and Gillen eventually took the position that Abrams must either agree to a misdemeanor plea bargain or they would file felony charges. Judge Walsh said a misdemeanor plea would "hardly make a ripple" in the press. DeVier replied that "the papers will find room for it" and told them he would discuss it with his client, not making any promises.[15]

Abrams was in personal torment. He later wrote, "I sensed the trouble I was in here. Walsh was a zealot, I thought, a legal Calvinist, and this was not politics to him. If I had made a mistake...I had to be punished."[16]

DeVier presented the options to Abrams and his wife, Rachel, telling them that punishment would be very light under a misdemeanor plea bargain, but that a felony conviction would mean mandatory prison time of several years under the sentencing guidelines. After a private husband-wife talk, "with plenty of anger and tears," they agreed to the plea

Elliott Abrams Admits His Guilt To 2 Counts in Contra Cover-Up

Elliott Abrams leaving court in Washington yesterday after his guilty plea. With him were his wife, Rachel, and lawyer, W. DeVier Pierson.

Paul Hosefros/The New York Times

Plea Accord May Open New Avenues in Inquiry

DeVier's photograph was on page one of the *New York Times* as he left the federal courthouse after Abrams pleaded guilty to a misdemeanor for his part in the Iran-Contra affair. Shown with Abrams and DeVier is Abrams' wife, Rachel.

bargain. At the October 7, 1991 court appearance to enter the plea, contrary to Judge Walsh's prediction, a photograph of Abrams and DeVier leaving the proceeding appeared on the front page of the *New York Times*.[17]

A probation officer and the Independent Counsel's office recommended leniency, as promised. At the sentencing hearing, DeVier quoted the probation officer's report to Judge Aubrey Robinson, "Mr. Abrams has paid a tremendous price, both personally and professionally; and it is unfortunate that his distinguished career in public service has been blemished by what appears to be a momentary lapse in judgment."[18] Judge Robinson was clearly sympathetic. He gave Abrams a suspended sentence, a $100 fine, and ordered him to spend 100 hours of community service. There was joy and relief in the Abrams family.[19]

The day after the sentencing, Shirley and DeVier were invited to a celebratory dinner hosted by Abrams' close friend, Irving Kristol, a powerful intellectual force in the conservative movement, and his wife. The guests included leading conservatives such as then Secretary of Defense and later Vice President Dick Cheney, former congressman and presidential candidate Jack Kemp, Judge Robert Bork, Gary Bauer, Bill Kristol, former Nixon aide Leonard Garment, longtime Republican congressman Henry Hyde, and others. DeVier was certainly the dinner curiosity as the Democratic lawyer who had steered Abrams through the ordeal. DeVier said to Shirley on the way to the dinner, "Be sure to talk to everyone because it's very unlikely that we will ever be asked to have dinner with this group again!"[20]

Reflecting many years later, DeVier said it was "very wise" for Abrams to accept the plea bargain and avoid a felony trial. Abrams was able to survive as a public servant and an active participant in international affairs. Just before he left the presidency, George H.W. Bush granted Abrams a full pardon. He was an active intellectual voice on the conservative side during the President Bill Clinton years. When George W. Bush was elected President, he chose Abrams as Deputy National Security Advisor with responsibility for policy on Israel and its neighbors in the Middle East.[21]

DeVier and Abrams do not agree on many policy issues. However, DeVier has never regretted his representation. DeVier said, "I still feel it was wrong to criminalize his actions and that being persona non grata to some people of importance, especially on Capitol Hill, would have been adequate punishment for any transgressions." During the nearly two decades since the representation, DeVier and Abrams have often lunched together, at the White House and elsewhere. In a 2009 interview, Abrams called DeVier, "the most honorable and upright man I have ever known."[22]

CHAPTER TWENTY-TWO

LEGAL WORK IN OKLAHOMA

When we first discussed our legal problems, DeVier's voice
was the clearest and most intelligent in the room.
I pledged to myself that I would form a relationship with him.
He was the expert we needed.

— Dale Laurance

DeVier's law firm, eventually known as Pierson Semmes and Bemis, developed a very broad national and international practice over the years. They represented many corporate clients before federal government agencies, handled several international arbitration proceedings, and tried or co-ordinated major litigation scattered around the country. There was no Oklahoma focus to the firm's work. That began to change when Occidental Petroleum Corporation (Occidental or Oxy) became a client.

Occidental was an interesting and highly successful in-ternational oil and gas producer. It began as a tiny California oil company owned and controlled by Dr. Armand Hammer, a flamboyant and controversial man whose roots went back to dealing with Vladimir Lenin, the first leader of the Soviet Union. Over the years, Occidental became a major oil and gas producer in the Middle East, Russia, South America, and Africa, as well as building up substantial domestic production in the United States through both exploration and acquisition.[1]

Occidental had a strong Oklahoma presence because

of its 1982 acquisition of Cities Service Company of Tulsa, Oklahoma, and its acquisition of MidCon in 1984. At that time, DeVier began working closely with Occidental's general counsel Jerry Stern and the eventual Occidental president, Dale Laurance. Both became good friends.[2]

As a result of the MidCon acquisition, Occidental was exposed to the travails of natural gas pipelines through the remnants of the curtailment damage litigation and the challenge of take-or-pay exposure. DeVier and his partners represented Occidental in the completion of the take-or-pay litigation, the sale of a gas pipeline, a dispute with the Department of the Interior over oil royalty payments, an internal investigation of the company's coal subsidiary, litigation involving a Kansas pipeline subsidiary, and advice on environmental Superfund liability. DeVier also advised the company's senior management on Foreign Corrupt Practices Act (FCPA) issues arising from relationships with foreign partners and consultants. In many ways, DeVier became an all-purpose legal fireman for the company.

After Occidental acquired Cities Service, the name was changed to OXY USA and company headquarters remained in Tulsa, Oklahoma. OXY USA had substantial oil and gas production throughout the continental United States, including Oklahoma, and operated related transportation facilities. Occidental acquired good people in Cities Service management, but also inherited serious legal problems. DeVier began spending a lot of time in Tulsa.

Dale Laurance was certain DeVier was the right man to lead the legal charge for Occidental. DeVier outlined the company's problems at a meeting in Houston, Texas. By the end of the meeting, Laurance focused on establishing a relationship with DeVier. "I was impressed with three things about DeVier," Laurance said. "He had tremendous intellectual ability, he possessed an enormous amount of experience and knowledge about our industry, and he had integrity. He made sense of a stifling and complicated problem."[3]

DeVier plays golf at the Los Angeles Country Club with Dale R. Laurance, president of Occidental Petroleum Corporation. DeVier was counsel to Occidental on a wide range of matters.

The first Oklahoma-based matter he handled was a dispute with a company called Columbian Chemicals Company (Columbian), a former Cities Service subsidiary that had been spun off as an independent company. Cities had retained much of the subsidiary's liabilities and passed them along to Occidental. The problems arose from environmental disputes at a number of Columbian plants in the United States and in several foreign countries. DeVier was asked to defend Occidental in several claims made by Columbian.[4]

At first, it appeared the matter could be resolved

quickly. Columbian agreed to binding arbitration before Judge Arlin Adams, a retired judge from the United States Third Circuit Court of Appeals. DeVier represented Occidental in the several week arbitration in Tulsa. The judge ruled for Occidental on virtually every issue. It looked as if only a nominal payment would be required to resolve all claims.[5]

Columbian surprised everyone by filing a state court action with a number of imaginative claims not covered by the arbitration, including an assertion that OXY USA had defamed Columbian by its statements of non-liability. DeVier removed the case to the United States District Court for the Northern District of Oklahoma and it was assigned to Judge Thomas R. Brett, DeVier's dear friend form high school and college.

One of DeVier's young partners asked him if Judge Brett would recuse himself from the case because of their friendship. DeVier laughed and responded, "Tom plays golf every Saturday with Jim Kincaid [who was representing Columbian], so personal friendships cut both ways." DeVier had no doubt that Brett would follow the law without regard to friendship.[6] After a spirited hearing, Judge Brett dismissed most of Columbian's claims. The remaining claims were remanded to state court and were ultimately dismissed. It was a complete victory.

In 1992, DeVier took on another problem Occidental had inherited from Cities Service. The Economic Regulatory Administration of the Department of Energy found that Cities had violated price regulations and was liable for payment, including interest, of more than $1 billion. DeVier was asked to take the lead in trying to coordinate the work of lawyers in three firms to resolve the matter. The Federal Energy Regulatory Commission ruled favorably for Cities, now OXY USA, on the issues before it, but left open the company's liability under pending alternative claims. Occidental's new general counsel, Donald deBrier, and DeVier met with the Deputy Secretary of Energy to discuss a possible settlement.

deBrier saw how DeVier was on top of the components that made up Occidental's problem. deBrier said, "Somehow he was able to be deeply engaged in the wide array of legal battles, but also was on top of all the interpersonal demands and internal and external politics in the company." deBrier said, "I quickly saw that he was an interesting combination of a clear legal thinker, scholar, tactician, and creative artist." deBrier later seriously questioned whether any senior attorney other than DeVier could have matched his performance in the landmark litigation that was to come.[7]

Because the potential liability was so large, DeVier worked with the financial management of Occidental to lay contingency plans in the event of a large final judgment. The payment of more than $1 billion would have been crippling for Occidental. DeVier and his staff prepared paperwork for an emergency filing in federal court to enjoin payment of any judgment pending appeal with waiver of the appeal bond. Fortunately, that plan never had to be used.[8]

To DeVier's surprise, the Department of Energy agreed to non-binding mediation before a retired federal judge. DeVier was counsel for OXY USA in the mediation and presented its case over a four-day period. At the close of mediation, a serious settlement discussion, the first in ten years, took place under deBrier's leadership. Occidental eventually agreed to a settlement payment spread over five years, and breathed a big sigh of relief.

DeVier worked closely with Occidental president Laurance in a number of settlement negotiations with senior management at companies antagonistic to Oxy. Laurance saw DeVier's "unique ability" to make adversaries comfortable during the discussions, even when negotiations were taken to the presidents of the opposing companies. Laurance said, "He took their fear away. He exuded a sense of being trustworthy. The other CEOs and lawyers may have had a different opinion on the law and facts, but they knew beyond the shadow of a doubt that DeVier knew what he was talking about, believed his position to be true, and was absolutely honest in his dealings." Laurance remembered, "At the end of a negotiation, DeVier had explained why the opponent needed to settle, and on what terms to be fair to all parties."[9]

Another interesting case had Oklahoma roots. OXY USA became involved in a contract dispute with a company called Continental Trend Resources, Inc., owned by Harold Hamm of Enid, Oklahoma. Continental Trend operated approximately 130 natural gas wells in western Oklahoma which were connected to a gathering system operated by OXY USA. Continental Trend sued OXY USA alleging a breach of contract and tortuous inference with contracts with third parties. In May, 1991, a federal court jury in Oklahoma City entered a verdict against OXY USA for $269,000 in actual damages and $30 million in punitive damages.[10]

The day after the verdict, DeVier was asked to take over

the case and handle the appeal. The big issue was whether the huge punitive damage award was excessive. It was six times the largest punitive damage award ever sustained in Oklahoma and 111 times the actual compensatory damages awarded by the jury. The law of punitive damages was being scrutinized by the United States Supreme Court at the time and DeVier was delighted to tackle the issue.

After Judge Wayne Alley refused to reduce the punitive damage award, DeVier appealed the verdict to the Tenth Circuit Court of Appeals, hoping that the appeals court would set aside the punitive damage award or at least reduce it to a reasonable sum. However, after filing briefs and arguing the case to three judges of the Tenth Circuit, the enormous punitive damage verdict was affirmed.

DeVier and his legal team filed a petition for *writ of certiorari* with the United States Supreme Court, arguing that the $30 million award was contrary to due process and was the largest punitive damage award ever approved by a federal appellate court. The Supreme Court granted certiorari, and without argument, reversed and remanded the punitive damages award to the Tenth Circuit for further consideration. Ultimately, the punitive damages award was reduced to $6 million and settled. The company was happy. DeVier remembered, "We had been stuck on a $30 million mountain for more than five years and a final $6 million resolution looked pretty sweet." [11]

By this time, DeVier was handling a number of major matters for Occidental and the company had a good deal of confidence in his legal skill. Donald deBrier said, "In representing Occidental's interest, DeVier was the master of them all. He managed several critical aspects of the crisis at one time, in a very commanding manner." But all this was a warm-up for the biggest legal project of DeVier's career.

CITIES V. GULF

*DeVier made sense of all the stacks of legal documents that
plagued Occidental in its fight with Gulf Oil.
In the end, he led a legal team that obtained the largest
civil judgment in Oklahoma history.*

— Dale Laurance

DeVier received a call from Occidental general counsel
Jerry Stern in early 1993. He had been reviewing Occidental's litigation contingencies and was puzzled by a case that
had been pending in state district court in Tulsa since 1982.
The case involved competing claims by Cities Service, now
owned by Occidental, and Gulf Oil Company, now owned
by Chevron, flowing from a 1982 merger agreement that
had been terminated by Gulf. DeVier was asked to make an
independent review and recommend how the company should
proceed.

The dispute was born in the "wild and wooly corporate
world" of the early 1980s. It was the heyday of corporate
mergers when many companies were acquired by both con-
sensual negotiations and unfriendly tenders. One technique
was for a corporate marauder to purchase a large block of
stock in a target company and then make a bid for control
through a tender offer and/or proxy contest. Sometimes
companies who found themselves "in play" would defuse the
unfriendly tender by paying "greenmail," a premium price to

reacquire their stock from the unwelcome suitor.

Oklahoma native T. Boone Pickens was prominent in the takeover atmosphere. To his fans, Pickens was a creator of shareholder value and to his enemies he was a "raider." Pickens had made a play for Phillips Petroleum Company and in 1982 set his sights on Cities Service. The company's management was very concerned and fought back with a competing tender offer to buy control of Pickens' Mesa Petroleum. To further frustrate Mesa's offer, Cities Service agreed to merge with Gulf Oil. Before the signed merger agreement was consummated, Cities bought back from Mesa the Cities stock Mesa had purchased.

Market reaction to the merger between Cities Service and Gulf was lukewarm and Gulf's board of directors began to grow cool on the deal. When the Federal Trade Commission issued a temporary restraining order stopping the merger unless Gulf divested a major refinery, Gulf terminated the merger.

Both sides sued. Cities brought suit against Gulf in Tulsa for breach of the merger agreement and fraudulent conduct by Gulf. Gulf counterclaimed for damages alleging that Cities had fraudulently misrepresented the size of its oil reserves. DeVier said, "It was clear that both companies had decided to make war rather than get married." Shortly after the aborted merger effort with Gulf, Cities Service began merger talks with Occidental and Oxy became the new owner in December, 1982.

The Cities-Gulf litigation in Oklahoma then entered a strange phase. Occidental retained the New York City firm of

Phillips Nizer to represent Cities. Seemingly endless discovery was sought and motions were filed monthly. DeVier said, "It was a phony war with no end in sight." Gulf preferred litigating in New York. Cities Service seemed to be in no hurry. Ten years after the suit was filed, there was still no trial date set in the Oklahoma lawsuit.[1]

DeVier and his team began the painstaking process of analyzing the pleadings, motions, and discovery in order to understand the facts and major legal issues. He met with lawyers at Phillips Nizer in New York City who obviously had no game plan to get the case ready for trial. They were mired in additional discovery and motion practice.[2]

After a four-month investigation, DeVier prepared a written report and met in Los Angeles with Jerry Stern and Dale Laurance. He told them that Cities had a decent case on the facts and that the company should begin acting like a plaintiff—that it was Gulf, not Cities, that should be making a settlement proposal. DeVier suggested that the case be taken away from Phillips Nizer and that primary trial responsibility be given to the Tulsa law firm of Gable & Gotwals that had been serving as local counsel. DeVier proposed that the case be aggressively pushed to trial.

It was a bold set of proposals that included several hurdles. Lou Nizer, a legendary lawyer and the senior partner of Phillips Nizer, had been a close confidante of Armand Hammer and was still a director of Occidental. DeVier was somewhat surprised when Stern called him and said the company would accept his recommendation on two conditions—that DeVier assume responsibility for the case and that he would go to New York to tell Lou Nizer.[3]

Over lunch in New York City, DeVier told Nizer who was "pretty gracious" under the circumstances. With that part of the job over, DeVier began assembling a trial team in his firm to assist him in the gargantuan litigation. Knox Bemis was a veteran litigator in energy matters. Peter Levin was a brilliant lawyer who was exceptionally strong in writing briefs and motions. David Hill was a tireless organizer of people and documents. Paul Ryberg had been active with DeVier in the curtailment damage litigation. It was a talented group of experienced litigators.

DeVier knew the lawyers at Gable & Gotwals, especially Oliver Howard whom he considered to be an extremely gifted litigator. He asked Howard to serve as co-lead counsel. In addition to Howard, Teresa Adwan, called "a beautiful writer" by DeVier, joined the team, along with David Bryant, a strong young litigator, and other Gable & Gotwals lawyers. DeVier added his law school classmate, Sam Daniel, to the team in view of his lengthy trial experience, including many appearances before Judge Deborah C. Shallcross, the judge assigned to the case.[4]

Howard and DeVier co-chaired a series of preparation sessions in Washington, D.C., and Tulsa. They reviewed all factual issues to determine if additional discovery was necessary. Cities' pleadings were amended to allege Gulf's willful and malicious breach of contract, a cause of action that would allow the potential award of punitive damages. Many pre-trial motions were filed, including a request for a discovery cutoff date and a trial date. DeVier said, "We wanted to make certain our opposing counsel and Chevron understand we meant business."[5]

Practicing his long-held belief that most disputed matters should be resolved by settlement rather than by trial, DeVier initiated settlement talks. Gulf and its successor Chevron was represented by the San Francisco law firm of Pillsbury, Madison & Sutro. The relationship with Pillsbury went back to the early part of the twentieth century when Chevron's predecessor, Standard Oil of California, was created as part of the breakup of John D. Rockefeller's Standard Oil Trust.

DeVier met with Pillsbury's lead counsel and several Chevron lawyers at settlement meetings in Washington, D.C., Los Angeles, and San Francisco. He pointed out Gulf's risks at trial, noting a number of rulings unfavorable to Gulf had taken place in New York and that Cities intended to use them in the Oklahoma trial. However, DeVier failed to persuade the Chevron lawyers. Their answer was always the same—Gulf had the legal right to withdraw from the merger, Cities' liability case was not supported by the facts, and Cities could not prove any damages. The recurring theme was that Cities should make a settlement payment, although at the last minute, Chevron suggested that perhaps both parties should just walk away. DeVier accepted the fact that the case was going to trial.[6]

During the year before trial, there was massive pre-trial preparation. Discovery had produced millions of documents and had left few secrets between the parties. Depositions were taken of the principal Gulf officials involved in the merger, especially Gulf Chairman James Lee and Vice Chairman

Harold Hammer. DeVier and Oliver Howard met many times with key Cities officials including Chairman Charles Waidlech and General Counsel Charlie Wheeler. Both had led the Cities' merger team in 1982.

In preparing for the presentation of evidence, the trial team prepared exhibits to be displayed on a large video screen, affectionately called "The Thing." The screen would be set up in the courtroom with a computer monitor at each counsel table. It was a state-of-the-art, high-tech production.

When the Judge gave parties a trial date, the litigation team set up shop in Tulsa in early 1996. A suite of rooms at the downtown Doubletree Hotel was rented and a litigation center was leased near the Gable & Gotwals office. The briefs generated "had already destroyed a small forest." DeVier's office looked out toward the Osage Hills of Pawhuska where he was born. He thought, "It is the return of the native." The rented space would be DeVier's home for the next six months with only occasional shuttles back and forth to Washington, D.C., on weekends.

Immediately before the trial was scheduled to begin on April 15, Gulf tried one more legal maneuver. A motion was filed in federal court in New York to enjoin the Tulsa trial permanently. Gulf's theory was that Cities was itself a member of the class of Cities' shareholders whose claims had already been settled in a class action. DeVier, Howard, and other lawyers flew to New York to argue the case. The same judge who had approved the class action settlement, Judge Michael Mukasey, later United States Attorney General, was hearing the new matter.

Judge Mukasey opened the hearing by saying, "Someone is playing games with this court and I intend to find out who it is." DeVier argued that Cities was certainly not playing games because the Tulsa lawsuit had been on file since 1982 and that there was no merit to the argument that Cities had become a member of a shareholder class of its own stock. Cities had not received any payment in the class action settlement because no one had suggested that the company was a part of the shareholder class. After a brief recess, Judge Mukasey denied Gulf's motion from the bench.[7]

Gulf sought an expedited appeal to the United States Court of Appeals for the Second Circuit. Shirley and Libby were in New York City and attended the very interesting hearing. DeVier was puzzled that the gallery in the Second Circuit hearing room was packed with a group of spectators that all wore "tight-fitting suits with broad pinstripes." Later he learned they were waiting for an appeal involving a major New York labor union.

The first question one of the Appeals Court judges asked DeVier was, "Did Cities receive any payment from the class action settlement?" DeVier was able to say, "Not one penny." From that point, he believed the panel to be friendly to Cities' position and was not surprised when the Second Circuit affirmed Judge Mukasey's ruling. The last barrier to trial of the matter in Tulsa had been removed.[8]

DeVier was not ashamed to make certain that the Tulsa jury understood that his client, Cities, was a hometown company. Cities had employed many Tulsans for decades. During his opening statement, Howard introduced DeVier as a native of Pawhuska and a graduate of the OU College of Law. At that moment, DeVier glanced to the opposing counsel table where a row of blue-suited Pillsbury lawyers from San Francisco prepared to represent Gulf.

Cities' case was presented in a straightforward and easy-to-understand manner. Cities had entered into a merger agreement with Gulf in good faith and had fully performed its end of the bargain. On the other hand, Gulf had gotten cold feet after executing the merger agreement and were, in the words of one Gulf document, looking for "a graceful way to back out." DeVier and Howard argued that Gulf's termination of the merger agreement because of possible objections from the Federal Trade Commission was an artifice—the company just wanted out. Cities had at Gulf's direction bought back its stock from Mesa at a cost of $225 million, stock that became worthless after Gulf reneged on the deal. Cities was entitled to damages for the cost of the Mesa purchase and punitive damages for Gulf's bad faith and fraud.[9]

DeVier believed Cities was off to a good start. He and Howard divided the direct and cross-examination of the major witnesses. They were pleased when Cities' officers made better witnesses than officials from Gulf. DeVier felt that Howard did a brilliant job of cross-examining Gulf's CEO and other key witnesses. Harold Hammer, who directed the merger activity for Gulf, became so confused in his response to DeVier's questions that he put key meetings in the wrong town, on the wrong dates, and with the wrong people in attendance.[10]

It was a grueling trial. There were so many battles over

the introduction of evidence, Judge Shallcross heard "night court" arguments for two hours or more after dinner. DeVier and Howard directed a briefing team back at the office to prepare memoranda on legal issues to be presented to the Judge during the trial day. There was also a night crew looking at the transcript of the trial testimony to mark items that Howard and DeVier might want to use the following day. Cities' motions were well received by the judge. Of special importance, she would not allow re-litigation of some of the issues that were decided by Judge Mukasey in New York.

Howard remembered, "During the trial, DeVier taught me the power of continuing to reflect and perfect my thinking about any aspect of the case. As a lawyer, he brought two admirable aspects together. He was a superlative, unparalleled orator in the courtroom, and an incredible organizer in preparing for the courtroom action. Few lawyers have both gifts." [11]

The key issue in the case became whether Gulf or Cities was responsible for the decision to repurchase the Cities stock from Mesa. If Gulf had directed the purchase in furtherance of the merger, Cities would be entitled to $230 million in damages. If Cities had made the decision, Cities would get nothing. Officials from both companies blamed the other.

DeVier thought the tie-breaker might be a videotaped deposition of Mesa owner T. Boone Pickens. As Cities' final evidence in the trial, Pickens' deposition was displayed on the large video screen. Pickens had called Gulf CEO Jimmy Lee to discuss the possibility of a buy-back of the Cities stock. In the deposition, Knox Bemis asked Pickens, "Why did you call Jimmy Lee about this matter rather that Chuck Waidlech at Cities?" Pickens' simple reply was, "I knew who was in charge." [12]

The closing arguments were high drama. Shirley joined DeVier in Tulsa for the last week of the trial. The courtroom was packed with local lawyers and reporters. Howard and DeVier divided the closing argument for Cities. Howard made the argument for punitive damages after DeVier presented the reasons why Cities was entitled to collect for the $230 million buy-back of its stock from Mesa. Howard said, "DeVier came across to the jury as candid and honest. The jurors knew he believed what he was saying. It is obvious they never questioned his integrity." [13]

Cities caught a break. After closing arguments were made by both sides, it was too late in the day for Cities' rebuttal argument. It was deferred to the following morning, giving DeVier and Howard the last word with a fresh and attentive group of jurors.

The jury deliberated for a day and a half. Late in the afternoon on July 18 they returned with their verdict. They unanimously found that Gulf had breached the merger agreement and awarded Cities $230 in actual damages and related fees. The jury did not award punitive damages, in retrospect a "good thing" because of the problems it would have created on appeal. DeVier remembered, "There was pandemonium at the litigation center." That night, DeVier, Howard, and Sam Daniel and their wives had a celebratory dinner and "toasted one another for being so wise and wonderful." [14]

DeVier and his team asked for an immediate hearing to enter judgment on the jury's decision and to add 14 years of pre-judgment interest. They were ready for the argument, having previously prepared a table showing the accrual of interest that was more than $500 million. As DeVier and Daniel were introducing documents to support the calculations, DeVier turned to his law school classmate and said, "When we were at the Law Barn studying contracts, did you ever think we would be in this position?"[15]

The court entered a judgment for $230 million in actual damages and $512 million pre-judgment interest. The total judgment of $742 million was the largest civil judgment in the history of the State of Oklahoma.

The fight was far from over because Gulf immediately announced plans for appeal. Gulf hired two additional law firms, including Crowe & Dunlevy in Oklahoma City, to help with the appeal. Gulf raised several legal issues, including not being able to re-litigate the issues decided in New York, and attacked Judge Shallcross as being biased in her handling of the case.

DeVier believed the Cities position on appeal was strong but a power outage at his firm while finishing touches were being added to the brief to the Oklahoma Supreme Court presented a last-minute problem. DeVier was afraid that all the weeks of work had been lost in a computer meltdown. However, the brief survived and was delivered on time to the Supreme Court in Oklahoma City.[16]

DeVier believed that the Oklahoma Supreme Court was an appellate court of very high quality. He was well acquainted with several of the justices. Chief Justice Hardy Summers was a law school classmate and fraternity brother. DeVier had known Justice Marian Opala when they were young lawyers in Oklahoma City in the late 1950s and Justice Opala had worked with DeVier's father as a Supreme Court referee before he became a member of the court. DeVier had a high opinion of Justice Alma Wilson, the first woman appointed to the high court, and had been at a number of professional meetings with Justice Robert Lavender and Justice Yvonne Kauger. He knew that the court would carefully follow the law in reaching its decision and thought the law was favorable to his client. But he understood that anything could happen on appeal.

After a long wait, the Oklahoma Supreme Court, on March 2, 1999, in an opinion written by Justice Lavender, affirmed the trial court judgment in all respects. Cities was only one step away from final victory.[17]

Chevron sought review in the United States Supreme Court even though post-judgment interest was accruing daily on the $742 million judgment. In its petition to the highest court in the land, Chevron referred to the "billion dollar final judgment in this action."

Occidental, to protect the large judgment, "pulled out all the stops" and funded a board of legal advisors to give counsel to DeVier and Howard's team of lawyers. The board was impressive and included Walter Dellinger, President Bill Clinton's Solicitor General, and Ted Olson, who argued *Bush v. Gore* before the United States Supreme Court and became Solicitor General in the administration of President George W. Bush. Both Dellinger and Olson were experienced Supreme Court practitioners.[18]

A group of constitutional scholars were asked to review the briefs for Occidental. The group included Lawrence Tribe and Arthur Miller of Harvard University, Geoffrey Hazard of Columbia University, and Judge Robert Bork, who had been unsuccessfully nominated to the Supreme Court.

The large collection of giant legal egos worked well together. A meeting in DeVier's law firm's conference room with Dellinger, Olson, Bork, Tribe, and Hazard was "surprisingly productive." Occidental's brief in opposition to Chevron's petition for the Supreme Court to the case was filed on October 22, 1999.

While the Supreme Court was considering whether or not to hear the case, Chevron finally tried to cut its losses. Chevron CEO Ken Derr called Ray Irani, Occidental's chairman and CEO, and offered to pay $200 million, more than it would have been required to pay to settle the case before the expensive trial. DeVier told Occidental that it was a ridiculous offer. He was asked if he could guarantee that the Supreme Court would not hear the case. He told them he thought Occidental would win, but he was not in the guarantee business.[19]

Occidental and Chevron ultimately agreed to settle the case for $775 million, more than the original judgment with pre-judgment interest, but less than the accrued post-judgment interest. On December 1, 1999, Chevron sent a wire transfer for $775 million to Occidental. The case was over.

To OXY USA vice president and general counsel Darrel Kelsey, winning the case was not as important as the "manner in which in which it was achieved." Kelsey said, "In a period when winning by whatever means unfortunately had become the norm, DeVier was invariably committed to bringing honor to our profession." Opposing counsel associated with many of the matters in which DeVier was involved went out of their way to express to Kelsey their great respect for him." [20]

DeVier's co-counsel at Gable & Gotwals echoed Kelsey's opinion. Joseph W. Morris, former federal judge and a wise adviser to the trial team throughout the proceeding, said, "He was the lead lawyer. His litigation plan was ingenious, detailed, and demanding. He was a delight to work with, and we won!" [21]

DeVier believed that the credit for the result should be shared with others. He said, "Oliver Howard is a brilliant litigator, as good in the courtroom as I have ever seen, and was a full partner in leading this enterprise. 'Ollie' and I had the support of a wonderful team of lawyers from both our firms and we could never have conducted this around-the-clock trial without them" [22]

DeVier was also grateful for the support he received from the Occidental legal department led by General Counsel Donald deBrier and from Occidental's president, Dale Laurance. DeVier appreciated the wise leadership of Dr. Ray Irani, Occidental's chairman and CEO, who made the final business decision to bring this matter to a close. DeVier said, "It was a team effort in every way." [23]

Handling *Cities v. Gulf* was the most satisfying event of DeVier's legal career. He reflected, "We were a band of brothers and sisters for six years from 1993 to 1999. It was a hell of a win, and it took place in Oklahoma." [24]

CHAPTER TWENTY-FOUR

HONORING HIS
MOTHER AND FATHER

Do not aspire to be the general's aide, you are the general.

— Frances Ratliff Pierson

As he looked back on his professional life, DeVier also reflected on his relationship with his parents. Both had been diligent in the duties of parenthood when he was a boy, including active participation in the Lincoln School Parent Teacher Association. He was ferried or carpooled as needed. His parents indulged his many boyhood whims—his two-man club and his obsession with mythology and radio heroes. While the family never had a substantial amount of money, DeVier never felt deprived.

Mr. and Mrs. Pierson were not bashful about punishing DeVier when they believed he needed it. When he made his mother unhappy, DeVier watched in horror as she went behind the house to get a switch from one of the bushes. The switching hurt, but the embarrassment was worse. His father infrequently used his belt on DeVier, always with the admonition, "This will hurt me more than it hurts you." DeVier categorically rejected that sentiment.

Mrs. Pierson was DeVier's Cub Scout den mother and his father was an assistant scoutmaster of Troop 29 when he became a Boy Scout. Best of all, his success in school was rewarded with the transfer of ownership in an old 1935

Oldsmobile for his use in his last year of high school.

DeVier's father was a stern man who headed toward First Methodist Church, later St. Luke's Methodist Church, each Sunday in a dark blue suit with a Bible under his arm. He loved to eat, especially his favorite meal of the week, Sunday breakfast, of eggs, bacon, and sausage all fried in the same skillet in what seemed like a mountain of grease.[1]

DeVier shares a happy moment with his mother, who thrived on his success in life, at the Phi Gam house at OU.

Welcome D. Pierson goes to church with his granddaughter, Libby, and grandson, Jeff. He always carried the same Bible under his arm.

Mr. Pierson was a dedicated lawyer. He had a sharp intellect and an effective courtroom manner. Even though he became chairman of the American Bar Association section on insurance, compensation, and negligence law, he never made enough money to accumulate any substantial savings. He and DeVier had a frank and painful discussion about the likelihood that DeVier would have to look elsewhere for a professional affiliation when he graduated from law school. Mr. Pierson practiced much of his life in a partnership with former Oklahoma Attorney General George Short in the old First National Building. After retirement, he was appointed a referee of the Oklahoma Supreme Court, helping write legal opinions for the state's highest court.

DeVier's sister, Carol, was born in 1940 when he was almost ten years old. After she left the crib, they shared the same bedroom for several years. The age gap was enormous. When she was in kindergarten, he was in high school. She was only nine when he left for college. Carol flourished although she did not follow her older brother in choice of schools. She attended Northeast Junior and Senior High Schools. Carol graduated from OU and was a member of her mother's sorority, Alpha Chi Omega. She surprised the family by running for a seat in the Oklahoma legislature as a feminist before it had become fashionable. She married Gerald Tucker, a successful insurance broker, had a fine daughter, Lorri, and two grandchildren.

Throughout his childhood, Mrs. Pierson was the unquestioned CEO of the household. DeVier remembered, "All of the Piersons, the aunts and uncles and all the children, knew she was the rock of the family." She was more socially conscious than her husband and was highly disciplined—she had a program for each day.

It is difficult for DeVier to adequately explain how important his mother was in his life. His future was her greatest project—she would do any and everything for him. She urged him to become a good speaker and to meet the right people in the right schools. DeVier's high school debate record and his successes in college and law school vindicated her efforts. When he was in the Army in Korea, she wrote him that he should aspire not to be a general's aide, but to be the general. DeVier said, "None of the things I have been able to accomplish in life would have happened without my mother." [2]

DeVier kept in close contact with his parents after he officially left the nest as a college student. He was only 20 miles away in Norman and frequently brought his friends home after social functions in Oklahoma City. DeVier said, "They endured the boisterous aspects of my college life, albeit with frequent concerns, as the necessary trade-off with their son receiving a college education."

Once Mr. and Mrs. Pierson were convinced that Shirley would not seduce him away from his law school studies, they embraced her fully and were enthusiastic participants in their wedding. Shirley became close to DeVier's mother as DeVier did to her mother. Both sets of grandparents were doting grandparents when Jeff and Libby came along.

Even after DeVier and Shirley moved to Washington, D.C., they returned home on a regular basis. For many years, Christmas was spent at either the Pierson or Frost home in

Oklahoma City. It was a job to pack the children's gifts for Braniff Airlines Flight 101 from Dulles Airport to Oklahoma City and then repack them after the children opened them at Christmas.

In their later years, the Piersons moved from the house on Northeast 20th Street to 1111 Huntington Drive on the edge of Nichols Hills. They were fortunate to have Ralph and Barbara Thompson as next door neighbors. The Thompsons provided daily support that DeVier and Shirley were often too far away to give.

On an October evening in 1970, DeVier was working on a submission to the Justice Department in connection with a steel merger when the telephone rang. It was DeVier's father who said, "Son, we have lost your mother." Mrs. Pierson had a heart attack and died before she could receive medical attention at a nearby hospital. She was only 67.

DeVier was stunned. His mother had appeared to be in good health—he believed she was immortal. He and Shirley flew to Oklahoma City as quickly as they could where they joined his sister Carol, her family, aunts and uncles, to pay their final respects at St. Luke's Methodist Church. DeVier felt a deep sense of loss.

DeVier was concerned about his father because he was highly dependent on his wife. There was a question whether he could live alone, but those fears were settled when Mr. Pierson did well, spending a lot of time in his job as a referee for the Oklahoma Supreme Court. He visited DeVier's family in Washington the following year.

In the spring of 1972, Mr. Pierson invited DeVier to

attend his law school class reunion. He had invited DeVier before, but this was the 50-year reunion of Mr. Pierson's 1922 law school class. DeVier and his father had a wonderful time visiting with old friends and associates. After the reunion, DeVier stayed over for two more days and the two Pierson men just talked. There were poignant conversations about DeVier's mother, other members of the family, and DeVier's work in the nation's capital.

DeVier never saw his father again. Two weeks after he returned to Washington, DeVier received a telephone call from his brother-in-law, Allie Reynolds, Jr., who had gone to Mr. Pierson's house to check on him when he failed to answer the telephone. He found Mr. Pierson dead from an apparent heart attack. He was 73 years old.

DeVier and Shirley and the children flew to Oklahoma City, helped arrange a funeral service at St. Luke's, and buried his father beside his mother. A few minutes before the service, Oklahoma Governor David Hall arrived at the family waiting area and took DeVier aside for a few private moments of conversation, a gesture DeVier has treasured as an act of friendship over the decades since, despite the legal problems subsequently encountered by Hall.

DeVier believed his parents died too young—it was un-fair for their lives to be cut short before they could enjoy their grandchildren fully and be a more constant part of his life in Washington, D.C. DeVier felt sadness, and some guilt, that he had been so preoccupied with his own career that he "was not always a dutiful son."[3]

Reflecting on the quick succession of life, DeVier's

parents' deaths made him conscious of his own mortality. He was the now the oldest living Pierson. On the long flight back to Washington, D.C., he closed his eyes, thanked God for such great parents, and admitted to himself that they often had given him more than he had returned.[4]

CHAPTER TWENTY-FIVE

KEEPING A HAND IN
PUBLIC POLICY

*After 1968, most of my time was spent in private law
practice, but I tried to stay active in public affairs,
an easy task in Washington, D.C.*

— DeVier Pierson

Practicing law in the nation's capital put DeVier in
position to continue some involvement with the White House
after the Johnson administration. He met with President Richard Nixon's top aide John Ehrlichman and other Nixon aides
several times to brief them on matters he had been handling,
especially the Trans-Pacific Route case. H.R. "Bob" Haldeman, Nixon's chief of staff, and his wife moved next door to
DeVier and Shirley in the Maryland suburbs. Shirley and Jo
Haldeman had an across-the-fence, neighborly relationship.

In addition, DeVier was an admirer of Nixon aide Bryce
Harlow, a fellow Oklahoma City native, who had been President Dwight Eisenhower's speech writer and advisor. DeVier
and Harlow had a number of lunches at the White House
mess and at nearby restaurants.[1]

DeVier continued to have regular contact with President
Johnson. C.R. Smith and DeVier traveled to the LBJ Ranch
in Texas in the fall of 1969 and spent several days with the
former President and First Lady. Most of the visit was spent
driving around the ranch with Johnson showing his guests his

land and livestock. One such trip took five hours.

DeVier was concerned about Johnson's appearance. He said, "He was overweight, ate everything in sight, was smoking and drinking more heavily, and had long hair that curled over his collar." To DeVier, it seemed that Johnson was "a man without a mission." However, he was working on his memoirs and spent two evenings discussing the sections on the initial escalation in Vietnam. For DeVier it was "a bittersweet trip."[2]

After the visit at the LBJ Ranch, DeVier kept in contact with Johnson by telephone, although the calls became more infrequent. The families exchanged gifts and cards at Christmas and Lady Bird often sent photographs of grandchildren and the ranch. DeVier and others close to the former President worried, with good cause, about Johnson's health.

In late 1971, DeVier became involved in the presidential campaign of Senator Edmund Muskie who had emerged as the leading candidate for the Democratic nomination for president after appearing on the 1968 ticket with Hubert Humphrey. Most of the Democratic establishment was behind Muskie. DeVier thought Muskie would make a good president. Berl Bernhard, DeVier's friend and fellow Washington lawyer, was Muskie's national campaign chairman. The campaign had a Maine flavor. At early meetings, DeVier met George Mitchell for the first time.

Before the 1972 primaries began, the Muskie campaign dispatched DeVier to Florida to make certain the Democratic leadership was behind Muskie. It was an easy task because all major Democratic state officials wanted on the Muskie bandwagon. DeVier met with Florida's governor, attorney general, secretary of state, and a number of state and local party officials.

Unfortunately, the early Muskie momentum never transferred to primary voters. DeVier said, "For reasons I have never fully understood, he lacked the required chemistry with voters." After a thin win in New Hampshire, and a poor showing in other primaries, Muskie eventually dropped out of the race. After the announcement, he wrote DeVier, "It is impossible for me to describe to you how deeply appreciative I am for the help you've given me these past months. In good times and bad, your support has been a source of great strength to me."[3]

With Muskie out of the race for the White House, the senator had more time for golf. When Shirley and DeVier hosted their friends from Oklahoma, Randy and Faith Mary Everest, DeVier took Randy to Burning Tree Club to play in the Sunday breakfast foursomes, a venerable event that paired teams of four players in competition for a small cash pot. Randy and DeVier were paired with Senator Muskie and John Charles Daly, the former host of "What's My Line?"

Randy was nervous about the excess of celebrity and hit his first drive off the end of his club into the woods. But, he rose to the occasion and birdied the final hole, sealing the win for their team. As they were counting their winnings, Muskie exclaimed, "You know, this is the first thing I've won this year!"[4]

In January, 1973, President Johnson died. DeVier was sad, but not surprised. The men in LBJ's family had a history of heart disease and a relatively short lifespan. Johnson was only 65. DeVier remembered, "Suddenly this giant who had dominated the Washington scene for many years was gone."[5]

C.R. Smith and DeVier flew to Texas for the funeral. The most moving part of the service for DeVier was the burial in the LBJ Ranch family cemetery. A large crowd of Washington public figures and LBJ's fellow Texans crowded the ranch as the former President was laid to rest.

On the return trip to Washington, D.C., DeVier reflected on his relationship with Johnson. He said, "He dominated my life for two years and had been very kind to me personally. I knew his flaws as well as his strengths. I valued the opportunity to serve him and to become his friend."[6]

DeVier also had great affection and admiration for Lady Bird Johnson, who was at President Johnson's side throughout his public career and was a dominant force in his life. DeVier remained in contact with her and the Johnson daughters, Lynda and Luci, through the years. When Mrs. Johnson died after a long period of failing health, DeVier felt her absence at a 2008 reunion of many of the Johnson team on the celebration of the centennial of the President's birth.

In early 1973, the nation's capital was consumed by Watergate, the "third rate" burglary of the Democratic campaign headquarters. The week before the controversy erupted, the Haldemans moved from next door to the Piersons to Georgetown. It was a fortuitous development because DeVier and Shirley were not subjected to the 24-hour-a-day presence of reporters and television cameras outside the Haldeman home from the initial stories in the *Washington Post* to Haldeman's eventual trial and conviction on charges of obstruction of justice in the wake of the cover up of the Watergate burglary.

DeVier and Shirley had become friends with *New York Times* Washington bureau chief Max Frankel and his wife, Toby. The couples had children the same age who attended the same school. While visiting the Frankels at their home outside New York City, DeVier and Frankel watched DeVier's successor as White House Counsel, John Dean, testify before the Senate Watergate Investigating Committee. Frankel, a veteran of many Washington scandals, said, "If Dean is telling the truth, Nixon is gone." [7]

Frankel was right. Soon, the Nixon presidency unraveled. "He became a tragic case, trapped in paranoia and insecurity," DeVier remembered, "He brought about his own demise by his irrational desire to punish his enemies, willing to use the levers of government power to conceal illegal actions." [8] When Nixon resigned, DeVier could not help but think about the incident eight years before when Nixon bumped into him and was unable to look him in the eyes.

After little exposure to the White House during the short presidency of Gerald Ford, DeVier became active in the 1976 campaign of Georgia Governor Jimmy Carter. DeVier was a member of Carter's Task Force on Energy Policy, wrote papers on energy issues, and provided comments on proposed energy speeches. DeVier was disappointed in the attention given the task force. "If we left any footprints in the campaign, I did not see it," he said. [9]

After Carter was elected, DeVier was asked to meet with members of his senior transition team staff. In the "highly informal and disorganized place, with many staffers in blue jeans," DeVier was asked if he was interested in returning to government service. He simply replied, "No." He was happy in his private practice that was becoming very successful.

While intermittently active in politics in the 1970s, DeVier retained close ties with the Oklahoma congressional delegation. In 1964, his law school classmate, Fred Harris, defeated former OU football coach Bud Wilkinson and arrived as Oklahoma's junior United States Senator. DeVier watched Harris become close to Robert and Ted Kennedy and take what he considered a "hard turn to the left." Harris was appointed Democratic National Chairman after failing to get a spot on the ticket with Humphrey in the 1968 presidential race.[10]

After losing support of conservative Oklahomans, Harris opted to not seek reelection in 1972 and instead ran for President of the United States. After a poor showing in New Hampshire, his effort plummeted. In what DeVier believed was the "line of the campaign," Harris told reporters covering the New Hampshire primary, "I knew my presidential campaign was about the little people. I just didn't understand that they were so little they couldn't reach the voting levers." [11]

DeVier admired Oklahoma's two United States Senators during the 1970s. Although disappointed by Henry Bellmon's defeat of his old friend, Mike Monroney, DeVier appreciated Bellmon as a "good and thoughtful man" and a fine senator.

DeVier and Shirley became very close friends with Senator Dewey Bartlett and his wife, Ann. "While Dewey was a staunch Republican," DeVier said, "he was an Oklahoman first." Bartlett led the effort to name the Federal Aviation Administration Center in Oklahoma City for Monroney, the champion of American aviation for decades.

DeVier's son, Jeff, was a summer intern in Bartlett's office. When Bartlett became ill with cancer, he spent many summer days beside the pool at DeVier and Shirley's home. During those times, DeVier and Bartlett read David McCullough's book, *Path Between the Seas*, and debated the pros and cons of the pending Panama Canal Treaty. When Bartlett died, DeVier flew with the official United States Senate delegation to Tulsa for the funeral.

DeVier visits with House Speaker Carl Albert and Oklahoma Congressman Ed Edmondson at a Washington event.

DeVier saw Oklahoma's substantial influence in the House of Representatives led by House Speaker Carl Albert from Oklahoma's third congressional district. DeVier regularly visited with Albert, Ed Edmondson, Tom Steed, Mickey Edwards, and Jim Jones, his fellow staff member in the Johnson White House.

In 1978, Oklahoma Governor David Boren was elected to replace Bartlett. From the beginning, DeVier saw greatness in Boren, "He became one of the most highly regarded members of the Senate with close friends on both sides of the aisle."

DeVier's mentor, Mike Monroney, died on February 13, 1980. There was a great sense of family loss for the Piersons. At the funeral service at the National Cathdral, DeVier delivered the eulogy as hundreds of former and present United States Senators and other Washington dignitaries listened. DeVier said:

It is a fitting part of this commemoration that we record Mike's remarkable achievements in public life. He represented his state in the House of Representatives and the Senate for over 30 years—longer than any Oklahoman... He was Mr. Aviation, the author of the Federal Aviation Act and the father of the federal government's role in modern civil aviation...He was a man whose wisdom and judgment was valued by five Presidents. History will record that Mike Monroney was a statesman of the first rank who made a lasting contribution...He was an articulate spokesman, but was far more interested in results than publicity.[12]

After hearing the eulogy, Senator Harry F. Byrd, Jr., of

Virginia wrote DeVier, "Your eulogy at Mike's funeral was so very fine that I have had it put into the *Congressional Record*." [13] On a lighter note, *The Daily Oklahoman's* longtime Washington reporter Allan Cromley was so impressed with the eulogy that he asked DeVier to prepare one for him. Cromley called DeVier's eulogy of Monroney a "rare performance that constricts one's chest, accelerates the pulse, and finally brings tears." [14]

DeVier with Mary Ellen Monroney, who was a dear friend and Washington mother to both DeVier and Shirley.

After the Washington funeral for Monroney, the family flew to Oklahoma City for a memorial service where DeVier and Mike Monroney, Jr., delivered tributes. Then they went to the Mike Monroney Aeronautical Center for the final event. Monroney's old friend and aide, Jay Perry, took off in an old open cockpit plane and scattered Monroney's ashes across the land he loved.

Fourteen years later, in 1994, Mary Ellen Monroney, the "Washington mother" for DeVier and Shirley, died. David Boren delivered a beautiful eulogy at the National Cathedral. Later, a group of Monroney friends raised funds to establish the Mary Ellen Monroney Garden at Boyd House, the OU presidential home.

After Mary Ellen's death, DeVier reflected on both their lives and how much the Monroneys meant to Shirley and him. He said, "He was a wonderful mentor. When he brought me to Washington, it was a fork in my life road and set the stage for a series of great opportunities. Mary Ellen was unique, a strong and loving person who influenced everyone around her. My life would have been very different without them." [15]

CHAPTER TWENTY-SIX

NATIONAL SECURITY AND FOREIGN POLICY

The first thing I want to do is to put to rest the ugly rumor that I was here for the final dinner of President Adams.

— President-Elect Ronald Reagan

The election of Ronald Reagan in 1980 was not a surprise to DeVier—he saw it as a victory for the conservative movement that had begun with Barry Goldwater's failed presidential effort in 1964. DeVier did not know Reagan at all, although his closest friends told him Reagan was everything Nixon was not—pleasant, witty, comfortable in his own skin.[1]

One of Reagan's closest friends and a member of his "kitchen cabinet" of advisors was Holmes Tuttle, a wealthy Californian who was born in Oklahoma. Holmes and Virginia Tuttle, his wife, became good friends with the Piersons and were understandably "ecstatic" over Reagan's election.

A month before the Reagan inauguration, Tuttle called DeVier with plans for a special luncheon for the President-Elect on the Saturday before Reagan would be sworn in the following Tuesday. Guests were to be limited to the Reagan family and Vice-President-Elect George H.W. Bush and his family. DeVier suggested the lunch be held at the City Tavern Club in Georgetown, an original structure used by President John Adams as a temporary home and office while the White

House was being completed. DeVier was a member of the private club and made the arrangements.[2]

Virginia Tuttle and Shirley helped prepare for the lunch. DeVier's mission was to work with "a very nervous" Secret Service detail that was concerned and unhappy with the old, small elevator in the club and the possibility that there was a line of sight from adjoining buildings through the windows of the room where the luncheon would be held. The Secret Service finally selected a spot, marked with a chalk "X," where the President-Elect should sit. DeVier understood the drill from his days in the Johnson White House.

The Piersons were invited to the lunch at which almost every other person was either a Reagan or a Bush. The President-Elect could not have been friendlier. When Reagan gave the response toast, he joked about his age, "The first thing I want to do is to put to rest the ugly rumor that I was here at the final dinner for President Adams."[3]

DeVier was seated with Vice President-Elect Bush at another table, located near the window. DeVier related the Secret Service selection of the special seat for Reagan. Bush told DeVier, "You don't have to tell me about the difference between the presidency and vice presidency." DeVier also had a pleasant conversation with Barbara Bush and each of the Bush sons. He had no idea one of them, George W. Bush, was a future President.[4]

As years passed, DeVier became more focused on national security and foreign politcy issues. He saw first-hand Reagan's success at foreign policy, as well as his singular failure in the Iran-Contra debacle. He agrees with historians who call Reagan one of the leading architects of the end of the Cold War.

In 1984, General Jack Merritt, commandant of the United States Army War College and DeVier's classmate at Classen High School and OU, invited him to participate in the annual National Security Seminar at the War College headquarters at Carlisle Barracks, Pennsylvania. General Merritt had been a Classen High School classmate of DeVier's and left OU for a brilliant military career that culminated in his reaching four-star rank. The conference allowed DeVier and Merritt to renew and revitalize their friendship which has continued through the years, including two trips together to China on national security issues. Merritt said, "DeVier is one of the

The Piersons are the guests of General and Mrs. Jack Merritt on the official train to the Army-Navy game. Left to right, Rosemary Merritt, General Merritt, DeVier, and Shirley. The Army banners were prepared as a joke to send to Admiral William J. Crowe, Jr., a close friend of both Merritt and DeVier.

smartest men I've ever known. He is always even-keeled. Even when presented a tough problem that others have spurned, he tackles it calmly." [5]

In 1988, after his initial representation of Elliott Abrams in the Iran-Contra investigation, DeVier became involved in other issues of Central American policy. Bob Tuttle, the son of Holmes Tuttle, was director of personnel at the White House and asked DeVier to be a member of the American delegation to monitor the elections in El Salvador. DeVier was delighted to accept. [6]

El Salvador had been deeply involved in the resupply program for the Contras in Nicaragua. Its Illepongo Airport was a major way station for delivery of supplies from both authorized and secret resupply programs. The government of El Salvador had been friendly to the Contras, making the trip to El Salvador interesting in any event.

The delegation was comprised of ten members of Congress and ten private citizens. It was co-chaired by Senator Richard Lugar, a leading Republican voice on foreign policy and soon to be chairman of the Senate Foreign Relations Committee, and Congressman Jack Murtha, a senior member of the House Appropriations Committee. Included among the congressional members was Congressman Mickey Edwards of Oklahoma. DeVier was sure he was the token Democrat among the ten citizen members of the delegation. [7]

The delegation was met at Illepongo by Ed Corr, another Oklahoman, who was United States Ambassador to El Salvador. The delegation was transported in an armored van accompanied by three vehicles filled with security forces. The first evening, members were briefed by the staff of the American embassy on the political situation prior to the elections, followed by dinner with Ambassador Corr.

After dinner, Corr, knowing of DeVier's representation of Abrams, asked for a private conversation in his study. Corr told DeVier that two years before, CIA Director William Casey came to El Salvador in "a black plane with no markings," and met with government officials, including President Duarte. Casey, "famous for his indecipherable mumbling," whispered in Corr's ear at dinner something about a secret activity. Corr later realized Casey was talking about the Iran-Contra resupply effort that in part was happening, under his nose, without his knowledge.[8]

The week before the El Salvador election, pro-Sandinista resistance forces, the FMLN, tried to intimidate potential voters in rural areas by killing one person in each hamlet and placing the body in the village square with his computerized voting card jammed in his mouth. It was unknown what kind of voter turnout to expect. However, as the delegation flew over roads and paths leading to the voting areas, there was a steady stream of people walking, sometimes for miles, down dusty and dangerous paths to cast their votes. The sight made DeVier realize how precious the right to vote was and the lesson this should teach many Americans.

On election day, the delegation broke into smaller groups to observe the voting. By the luck of the draw, DeVier was in a helicopter with Senator Lugar and Ambassador Corr that flew to various rural areas to observe the election in progress. When DeVier noticed how sluggish the helicopter was in lifting off from the ground, he was informed by Corr that the chopper had a lead shield installed to prevent sniper bullets from penetrating into the cockpit and passenger area.[9]

On election night, the delegation came together to swap notes and concluded that no major irregularities in the voting had been observed. Plans were made to return to the United States. DeVier was thankful because the FMLN had cut off the water supply to the hotel. Each night, maids put about two inches of water in each bathtub so the Americans could at least attempt to remove the dust from their bodies. "We were a pretty grubby lot," DeVier remembered, "when we boarded the plane for our return flight."[10]

As the delegation approached Washington, they were informed President Reagan wanted to meet with them immediately. They were transported from Andrews Air Force base to the White House and escorted to the Cabinet Room by Chief of Staff Howard Baker. The President entered and began making a formal statement from three-by-five cards, rather than asking members of the delegation about their observations. It was uncomfortable for a group who were expecting an informal discussion of the elections. DeVier thought they were getting a sneak preview of President Reagan's health condition that eventually ended his life.[11]

DeVier had a very high opinion of Republican President George H.W. Bush. When he was elected, DeVier recognized Bush was the most experienced President in foreign policy in a generation, coming to the presidency after serving as a member of Congress, Ambassador to the United Nations, CIA director, Ambassador to China, and eight years as Vice President.

President George H.W. Bush greets DeVier at a White House reception for the Johnson family and members of the Johnson administration. Left to right, Shirley (hidden), DeVier, Lady Bird Johnson, President Bush, and Barbara Bush.

DeVier said, "He is a warm and loyal human being." DeVier was impressed years before when Nixon was inaugurated but Bush chose to see his fellow Texan, Johnson, off to Texas following the inauguration rather than to celebrate with the new President. DeVier recognized Bush's genuine people qualities allowed him to maintain close friendships with many members of Congress, both Republicans and Democrats, during his term as President.[12]

Bush was especially gracious at a White House reception for the Johnson family and members of the Johnson administration on the 25th anniversary of the Great Society. DeVier and Shirley joined Lady Bird Johnson and other members of the family and former staff for the event. President Bush

United States Supreme Court Justice Sandra Day O'Connor with Shirley and DeVier at a Washington function.

made warm remarks praising LBJ's patriotism and efforts as President. The nicest touch for DeVier was when the Bushes took the Johnson family for a tour of the redecorated living quarters in the Executive Mansion, a place the Johnsons had not seen for many years. During the tour, First Lady Barbara Bush commented that she and her husband had not seen the living quarters during the eight years the Reagans lived in the White House.[13]

DeVier first met Bill Clinton in the spring of 1992 at a small dinner party in Los Angeles during the presidential primary season. DeVier said, "He had the capacity to look you in the eye and to engage you in conversation with a focus that, whatever the topic, you were briefly the most important person in his life." DeVier believed Clinton was the "best raw political talent" he ever saw.[14]

DeVier was not involved in the Clinton campaign, in part because of his respect for President Bush. However, former Occidental general counsel Jerry Stern was a fervent Clinton supporter and was in charge of preparing a proposed White House organization should Clinton win. DeVier made a number of suggestions to Stern. However, Stern's recommendations gave way to campaign staff ambitions when Clinton actually took office.

Although not active in the Clinton administration, DeVier kept in contact with several of its members, including Secretary of State Warren Christopher, with whom he had worked during the Johnson years, and his successor, Madeleine Albright, whom DeVier had first known when she worked for Senator Muskie. DeVier had more contact with a great man from another Washington era, Clark Clifford. The former Secretary of Defense and presidential advisor was in poor health and reeling from a damaged reputation because of his chairmanship of a foreign-owned bank that engaged in fraudulent banking practices. DeVier went to Clifford's home every two months or so and talked about policy issues they had faced in better times. When Clifford died, most of the political establishment from past administrations of both parties attended the services where he was eulogized by Richard Holbrooke, Ted Kennedy, and Vice President Al Gore.[15]

Because DeVier knew so many present and former government officials, it was not unusual to start up a conversation about the issue of the day over lunch, during a golf game, or entertaining friends. Being part of the social scene in Washington, D.C., allowed him to hear the latest official perspective and the juiciest backroom gossip about the nation's leaders.

In 2000, DeVier was an interested observer of the Bush-Gore presidential race, especially the post-election legal battle that involved a host of constitutional principles. While he thought that resolution of the contest was very important to the country, he was skeptical about the grounds of the United States Supreme Court intervention that ultimately decided the election. In 2001, he spoke on the subject at a meeting of an American Inns of Court chapter in Tulsa. He said:

> *So was the finality worth the price? Was judicial resolution of a presidential election better than letting the political process work its will through congressional resolution in the manner provided by the Constitution? And would the Supreme Court have divided in precisely the same way if the effect of the decision would have been to tip the election to Al Gore? We will never know the answer to those questions.*[16]

CHAPTER TWENTY-SEVEN

WRAPPING IT UP

I began some serious soul-searching about my future,
and how I wanted to spend the golden years.

— DeVier Pierson

Practicing law in the beehive of activity in the nation's capital for 30 years was an exciting experience for DeVier with few regrets as to the nature and scope of his practice. He felt blessed that his clients had been so interesting and that he had met and worked with hundreds of fine lawyers around the country. But DeVier thought it was time to take stock.

He was already involved in a number of matters for one of Washington's think tanks and was eager to continue his work at the University of Oklahoma and be in regular contact with his home state. In the back of his mind, he knew that any legal victories after *Cities v. Gulf* would be post-climatic. He said, "I would have been conflicted about taking on any other project of that magnitude so I concluded it was time to wrap things up."[1]

DeVier was also concerned about continuing his obligations to the people of his firm for an indefinite period. He was the principal "rainmaker" for the firm and wanted to be certain that his partners would be comfortable in continuing their practices after he left. He notified his partners that would continue as a full-time partner through 2000, but would then practice only part-time. He privately told each partner that he would assist them in finding another law firm if they did not want to continue in a group practice without him.

As a result of the discussions, the firm of Pierson Semmes and Bemis came to a formal close at the end of 2000. One group of lawyers in the firm continued to practice together and each of the other partners and associates, some with DeVier's assistance, landed positions with other law firms or organizations in Washington. DeVier said, "This was a compliment to their quality as lawyers and the reputations they had built over the years."[2]

Shirley and DeVier hosted a dinner in their home for everyone in the firm on December 7, 2000, and the firm had a farewell dinner at the City Tavern the following night. It was a bittersweet evening with the chance for story-telling and to celebrate 30 years of satisfying practice. It was not goodbye to them as individuals because DeVier still sees many of the firm's lawyers on a regular basis and has a luncheon with members of the "old gang" each quarter. But ringing down the curtain on the firm was certainly an end of an era.

It is gratifying to DeVier that each of his longtime partners have gone on to success in the next stage of their legal careers. Knox Bemis stayed with DeVier during some of his semi-retirement travels and they continued to work together. Peter Levin, Mark Greenwold, and Bill Lieblich became counsel for the National Association of Attorneys General (NAAG) to mastermind the nationwide litigation arising from the tobacco company settlements with the states. It did not hurt that the chairman of the NAAG tobacco task force was Oklahoma Attorney General Drew Edmondson.

David Hill and Jerry Clark became partners in the Washington office of Skadden Arps, a large and prestigious national law firm. Jay Costan continued as an energy guru in several Washington firms. Tom Warrick, one of DeVier's youngest partners, left private practice for a distinguished career at the State Department and became a footnote in history. He was the principal author of a State Department study at the beginning of the Iraq War outlining the organizational needs for the inevitable occupation of Iraq. Sadly, Defense Secretary Donald Rumsfeld, who had concluded Iraq would be a short war and that an elaborate occupation plan was unnecessary, rejected the plan.[3]

At the urging of his longtime friend, Harry McPherson, DeVier became Special Counsel to the firm of Verner, Liipfert, Bernhard, McPherson, and Hand, Chartered. The other Special Counsels at the firm were former United States Senators George Mitchell, Robert Dole, and Dan Coats. DeVier enjoyed renewing his friendship with Mitchell who he had first met during the Muskie presidential campaign. DeVier liked Dole's sardonic wit and became good friends with Coats, later appointed American ambassador to Germany, and visited Coats at the embassy in Berlin.

One of DeVier's favorite recollections during his time at Verner Liipfert was when Donald deBrier, Occidental's general counsel, came to Washington for a visit. DeVier set up meetings with Mitchell and Dole, a contrast in great American leadership. Mitchell described his recent return from a trip to the Middle East with a "very erudite" description of the political and economic situation in each country. Dole opened their meeting by asked deBrier if he had ever had any prostate problems. Dole was fresh from a national advertising campaign for a new prescription drug. DeVier said about the meetings, "Two great men with very different approaches!"[4]

After two pleasant years at Verner Liipfert, DeVier was caught up in the phenomenon of Washington firms consolidating with larger firms when Verner Liipfert merged with Piper Rudnick. After talks with some of the resulting firm's partners, DeVier agreed to continue as special counsel to Piper.   Piper has seen tremendous growth and is now DLA Piper with about 3,000 lawyers in offices scattered around the world. DeVier found himself officing with a legal giant.

In 2004, DeVier decided to move to the Washington office of Hunton & Williams. The firm had its origins as the premier firm in Virginia. It had gone from the largest firm in Virginia to become a national firm with nearly 1,000 lawyers with offices in Washington, New York, other cities up and down the Eastern Seaboard, Houston, and Los Angeles. It is a group of high-quality lawyers and has been a happy affiliation for DeVier.

During his 30 years of Washington practice, DeVier had handled several international matters for American corporations and traveled overseas to Europe and Asia in connection with those cases. However, he had little experience in public international law, the rules that govern disputes between sovereign nations ranging from arguments over international boundaries and controversies over nationalization of private investment to the international laws governing the conduct of war as embodied in the Geneva Convention and the Hague

Convention. It was a specialized field with a small cadre of prominent practitioners. Many of the disputes were resolved at The Hague in The Netherlands, the site of the International Court of Justice, international criminal courts, and special international tribunals established to arbitrate specific disputes.

While still at Verner Liipfert, DeVier was involved in one such international dispute at the request of Don Picard, a fine lawyer specializing in public international law and international arbitrations. The firm represented Ethiopia, the African country involved in the last war of the twentieth century with its neighbor in the Horn of Africa, Eritrea. A border dispute between the two nations escalated into open warfare over a two-year period with tens of thousands of casualties on both sides and a substantial number of displaced persons and prisoners of war. After the United Nations brokered a cease-fire, international tribunals were created at The Hague to resolve the boundary dispute, determine liability for the war, and decide if damages were proper for mistreatment of prisoners of war, crimes against civilians, and destruction of property.[5]

Don Picard asked DeVier if he would take the lead in presenting Ethiopia's position on the treatment of prisoners of war and on the causes of the war and its consequences. Although he was a "neophyte" in public international law, it was too interesting for DeVier to pass up.

He made two trips to The Hague to present Ethiopia's position. The tribunal conducted its proceedings at the Peace Palace, a building financed by American businessman Andrew Carnegie a century before. Carnegie believed nations should come to peaceful talks rather than go to war. DeVier said, "The building was filled with the ghosts of failed efforts to avoid warfare walking the corridors. It was instead the bloodiest century in history." The International Court of Justice held its hearings at one end of the main corridor and the special tribunal on the Ethiopia-Eritrea war was at the other.[6]

Each hearing lasted two weeks before a five-member panel of international experts. Live witnesses, affidavits, and exhibits were presented. Voluminous affidavits and legal argument, known as memorials and counter-memorials, were filed in advance of the hearing. DeVier led a team of ten lawyers and support staff working on a 24 hours-a-day basis.

The typical work day began with an early breakfast meeting in their litigation center for final witness preparation and a review of the issues likely to be presented that day. The hearing lasted from 9:00 a.m. to 4:00 p.m. Preparation for the following day continued through dinner and beyond. DeVier's system was to agree on assignments through the evening with a final work product delivered to DeVier's room at 3:00 a.m. when he arose to organize the materials and prepare his argument in time for the breakfast meeting.[7]

Despite the fatigue factor, DeVier loved the hearings at The Hague. His opponents were prominent members of the international law community, including a number of Oxford and Cambridge dons who had written treatises on many of the issues. DeVier presented the testimony of several Ethiopian officials and international law experts and cross-examined senior Eritrean officials.

They were dealing with horrendous war crimes. Eritrea had bombed a school in northern Ethiopia, killing 60 civilians, including many school children. Eritrea claimed it was an innocent mistake resulting from navigational error. However, DeVier was able to establish on cross-examination of the head of the Eritrean air force that his country's official position was decided without even examining computer or mechanical equipment first. DeVier was convinced the attack was deliberate. He also was able to establish significant differences in the treatment of prisoners of war and that Eritrea had begun the war.[8]

The tribunal eventually found that the war was commenced by Eritrea and that its conduct had violated several provisions of the Geneva Convention and the Hague Convention. It was a substantial legal victory although both nations were poor with limited ability to pay reparations. The boundary dispute was still being litigated in 2009.

While at The Hague, DeVier observed the International Criminal Court trial of Serbian President Slobodan Milosevic for genocide and other war crimes resulting from fighting in the former Yugoslavia. DeVier said, "It was a unique and sad spectacle. Milosevic was representing himself and railing against the judges of his fate. This bush league Hitler died of heart failure before the trial could be completed."[9]

As part of the Ethiopian representation, DeVier and his longtime partner, Knox Bemis, took the lead in litigation brought against Ethiopia and its state-owned bank in federal court in Washington, D.C., by a group of Eritrean depositors who claimed their funds had been seized during the war. They were successful in getting the case dismissed on the grounds that it was not a convenient forum because the international tribunal at The Hague was established for such purposes. However, the Court of Appeals for the District of Columbia reversed the decision because the judges were skeptical that the international tribunal would ever award damages. After the United States Supreme Court refused to hear the case, the matter continued.

Happily, the case was finally won. The federal court dismissed the case again, ruling that the case should have been filed in Ethiopia. This time, the dismissal was upheld by the appeals court and the litigation was over after eight years of sparring on paper. DeVier reflected, "As the old saying goes, the wheels of justice grind slowly, but exceedingly fine." [10]

DeVier has continued his relationship with Occidental Petroleum Corporation. He has counseled with Donald deBrier on a number of manners arising from the company's operations in the United States, the Middle East, South America, and Africa. He worked closely with his good friend, Dale Laurance, until Laurance retired from Occidental in 2004. He still meets periodically with Dr. Ray R. Irani, OXY's chairman and chief executive officer.

Following retirement, Laurance became a board member and eventually chairman of the board of Ingram Micro Inc., a public company initially formed by the remarkable and highly successful Ingram family of Nashville, Tennessee, which became the world's largest distributor of IT hardware and software. DeVier was asked to advise the Board of Directors of Ingram Micro on a number of matters of conern to the company.

As a result of the work with Ingram Micro and its Board

of Directors, DeVier has been able to maintain his close ties with Laurance and has established friendships with other members of the Ingram board. One such friend is Joe Wyatt, a "wise and experienced man," who was on the faculty at Harvard and the University of Texas before spending 20 years as chancellor of Vanderbilt University. DeVier, Laurance, and Wyatt are avid sports fans of their respective universities and maintain a good-natured rivalry during football season.

DeVier has also continued to pursue his interest in foreign policy and national security matters. He has served for more than a decade as a member of the board of directors of the Atlantic Council of the United States, a think tank created under the leadership of Dean Acheson as the umbrella group to support the post-World War II creation of the Atlantic community through the organization of the North Atlantic Treaty Organization (NATO) and the implementation of the Marshall Plan and the Truman Doctrine. DeVier is currently vice chairman and a member of the Council's executive committee.[11]

As a result of the Atlantic Council work, DeVier was invited to be a member of two Council-sponsored delegations to China and Taiwan to discuss national security issues. The delegations were half-military and half-civilian with four four-star officers participating. The delegations were chaired by DeVier's friend and fellow Oklahoman, General Jack Merritt. Another Oklahoma military leader, General Dennis Reimer, former Army Chief of Staff, also was part of the group that held a series of meetings with senior government, military, and communist party officials in China as well as two meetings with the President of Taiwan.

DeVier was impressed with the quality of the meetings and the sophistication of the Chinese officials. Most spoke English, although an interpreter was usually present to assure precise translations. The Chinese officials had been briefed on the backgrounds and positions of the delegation and were well prepared. It was clear that sorting out their relationship with the United States is still a central preoccupation of the Chinese government.

The subject matter at the meetings reflected the hot topics of the time in American-Chinese relations. The first trip in 2000 was made shortly after the accidental bombing of the Chinese Embassy in Belgrade by a United States missile during American military operations in Serbia. Every meeting began with a diatribe on this unhappy event. There was also a preliminary mantra at each meeting about Taiwan being a part of China and the need to eventually reunite the homeland. On the second trip in 2005, DeVier noted that China was far more concerned about economic issues and the preliminary lectures were held to a minimum.[12]

In China, DeVier and the delegation were treated to official dinners and side trips. In addition to formal meetings in the Great Hall of the People, a highlight for DeVier was a visit of several hours to the Chinese Communist Party compound tucked away in a suburb of Beijing. DeVier said, "It was like stepping back a thousand years to a series of pagoda-style buildings surrounded by beautiful trees and lakes." In the cloistered quarters, senior party officials, the real power center in China, conducted their business with the various cabinet ministers who are far better known to the Western world. It was a fascinating exposure to Chinese politics.

DeVier visited the Great Wall of China, the Summer Palace, the Forbidden City, his personal favorite, and public buildings around Tiananmen Square. In 2000, he was there on the eve of the official celebration of the 50th anniversary of the Peoples Republic of China. He and General Merritt had dinner in a restaurant overlooking the square and watched a dress rehearsal parade of tanks, troops, and thousands of young people organized by shirt color.

DeVier and Merritt made a side trip to Hong Kong and Shanghai. City government officials gave them a helicopter tour in Hong Kong and leaders in Shanghai showed off their new Pudong business area. In Shanghai, they stayed in the old Peace Hotel in the area where Lenin, Mao, and other fathers of communism met eight decades ago to plot the destruction of capitalism. They met with students at Fudan University through the courtesy of a faculty member who had spent a year at OU as an exchange professor.

While they were at Fudan University, DeVier was invited to speak to the law school. Language was not a problem because nearly all the students spoke English. After some bland remarks, DeVier received a number of questions about legal subjects ranging from international law governing use of force to the United States commercial legal framework and immigration laws. Then Merritt and DeVier participated in a seminar with the Foreign Affairs Institute at Fudan and found the well-informed students to be surprisingly skeptical about American intentions toward China. After the Belgrade embassy bombing had been discussed several times, DeVier finally asked the group, "How many of you really think the United States intended to bomb the Chinese embassy?" Most hands were raised.[13]

The delegation met with the president of Taiwan on both trips. Each man was fairly adamant about Taiwan being "an independent nation." It was the antithesis of the Chinese position which had been repeated over and over in Beijing. After the presidential meetings, national security officials would hasten to explain to the delegation that this did not mean that Taiwan would cross the red line of Chinese concerns and risk war. But DeVier left with the concern that the Taiwan Straits

General Jack Merritt, left, and DeVier discuss issues raised with Chinese government officials during two trips to China and Taiwan on national security matters.

continued to be one of the very dangerous areas of the world.[14]

General Merritt said, "On our trips to China, DeVier was incredibly analytical and saw the 'big picture' in relationships with the growing super power."[15]

In 2007, DeVier was reminded that "the clock never stops ticking." He received his 50-year service pin from the Oklahoma Bar Association. His law school class of 1957 held its 50-year reunion as stories of the past grew larger and larger with each re-telling.

DeVier believes his decision to cease the full-time practice of law in 2000 was a good one. Even with installing an office at home, amid some concerns from Shirley that he spends too much time there, he says, "Things have worked out pretty well."[16]

CHAPTER TWENTY-EIGHT

KEEPING THE OKLAHOMA TIES

DeVier is truly a role model for stewardship.
His devotion to OU has made it stronger and better.

— David Boren

When DeVier and Shirley decided in 1969 to stay in Washington, D.C., they were determined to keep their Oklahoma ties, and they have done so. For four decades, they have been frequent visitors to the state and DeVier has been one of the most active alumni of Classen High School and the University of Oklahoma. Seldom do DeVier and Shirley miss high school or college reunions. DeVier is a proud Oklahoman who has always considered Oklahoma his home and believes it to be a special place.

Through the years, DeVier has accepted many Oklahoma speaking engagements, a "great excuse" to see friends and family. He has spoken to the Oklahoma City Chamber of Commerce Friday Forum, twice delivered the commencement address at the OU College of Law, and has spoken, among other venues, at meetings of the Oklahoma Bar Association, Casady School in Oklahoma City, the National Conference of Christians and Jews, the University of Central Oklahoma, the American Inns of Court, and the Women's Club of Oklahoma City.

He has always had a message. In 1975, he told OU Law graduates that the legend of Washington lawyers as "rainmakers" was largely a myth and that "a good, well-prepared case is still better than a good, well-placed friend." He also reminded the future lawyers that attorneys were at the heart of the Watergate scandal and, while the rule of law brought the scandal to an end, "we still have some making up to do."[1]

In other speeches, DeVier talked about the need for a sane energy policy, his feeling that Vietnam had been a tragic error, and the challenges that America faced in a fragmented world at the end of the Cold War. A unifying theme in all speeches was his great affection for Oklahoma and his friends in the Sooner State.[2]

DeVier also dealt with legal issues and the responsibilities of the legal profession. Speech topics ranged from proper use of grants of immunity, an issue he faced in the Elliott Abrams case, to the most ethical ways for lawyers to bill their clients.

In 1990, he accepted an invitation from his good friend Dan Hogan, publisher of the *Journal Record* in Oklahoma City, to speak to the Corporate Women of the Year luncheon. DeVier chose the topic "The New World Order," one definition of the post-Cold War world, recognizing that women were rapidly becoming involved in every area of life and politics, including global affairs.

After the speech, Hogan asked DeVier to write a guest column in the *Journal Record*. For two years, DeVier "vented his spleen" and wrote about a variety of subjects, from foreign policy issues such as President George H.W. Bush's handling of Operation Desert Storm to his personal reflections of President John F. Kennedy on the anniversary of his assassination.[3]

Hogan, who has known DeVier since high school fraternity days, saw a great response to DeVier's columns. Hogan said, "Readers could tell he had great common sense and employed his intelligence to analytically look at the topics of the day and arrive at a reasonable conclusion."[4]

Hogan and DeVier are of different political party persuasions, but that has not hindered their lifetime friendship. Hogan said of DeVier, "He is the epitome of the old saying, 'you can agree to disagree.' He is decisive and organized in his thought process on any issue, but he also is generous in listening to the opinions of others."[5]

One of DeVier's strongest home ties is with the University of Oklahoma, particularly the OU College of Law. In 1990, he served on the OU Centennial Commission and came away with the feeling that he needed to be more active in university affairs, especially at the law school which had then fallen on hard times. To show his interest, he endowed the Welcome D. and W. DeVier Pierson Professorship as recognition of the two generations of Pierson graduates.

In May, 1994, he was the speaker at the annual dinner of the OU Associates, a prestigious group of university friends. However, he was upstaged by the last-minute appearance of United States Senator David Boren who had just been named the new president of OU. After Boren spoke, DeVier told his audience that he felt like Edward Everett, the principal speaker at the dedication of the Gettysburg Cemetery, who was certainly forgotten in history because President Abraham Lincoln had been added to the program to say a few words and delivered the Gettysburg Address.[6]

DeVier was excited about the potential for the university under Boren's leadership. He had become well acquainted with Boren in Washington and believed OU would soon become one of the preeminent public universities in the land. DeVier wanted to be part of what he called "the golden age of OU." DeVier said, "David is living proof of the old maxim that one man can make a difference. He was born for the job."[7]

DeVier soon became an integral part of the growth and development of OU. President Boren said, "He is one of the most generous graduates of the University in terms of gifts of his resources, time, and expertise." Boren praised DeVier's leadership at the law school as co-chair of the College of Law Board of Visitors, as a member of the governing board of the International Programs Center, and as a trustee of the OU Foundation.[8]

DeVier and President David Boren enjoy an OU football game together.

DeVier was the commencement speaker in 2003 for the OU College of Law, capping nearly a decade of intense support for the rebuilding of the law school.

DeVier has worked with Andy Coats, dean of the OU College of Law, since Coats became dean in 1995.

Paul Massad, who has worked for seven of OU's 13 presidents, said, "DeVier is one of the most 'take charge' people I have ever met. If he commits to direct or assist a project, that project will have his full attention. He has never forgotten his Oklahoma roots and has served this state and OU tirelessly."[9]

DeVier began spending a lot of his time in the mid-1990s helping the OU College of Law. Andrew "Andy" Coats, a highly successful lawyer, former mayor of Oklahoma City, and former district attorney of Oklahoma County, was named dean, signaling strong leadership ahead. Little change had been made in the physical facilities in the more than 20 years since construction, and, at that time, the law school's accreditation was in jeopardy.

DeVier was one of the first law school alumni who contacted Coats to offer his assistance. DeVier and Coats had a private dinner at the City Tavern in Washington to plot the future of the law school. Coats said, "DeVier told me that we had all the right people in place to move forward to make OU Law great again." In looking back on his first 12 years as dean, Coats said of DeVier, "No one has been more important to me or to the OU College of Law than DeVier." [10]

"When President Boren and Dean Coats began the mission of rebuilding the law school, DeVier played a major role in assuring its sound future," said Oklahoma Supreme Court Justice Steven Taylor. "Every OU Law graduate owes a great debt of gratitude to DeVier." [11] Former Oklahoma Attorney General G.T. Blankenship served with DeVier on commit-

DeVier, right, joins Robert Henry, Chief Judge of the United States Tenth Circuit Court of Appeals, in hosting United States Supreme Court Justice Steven Breyer, center, when Justice Breyer was a guest of the OU College of Law.

tees working to improve the law school. "DeVier brought his integrity and intellect to guide our effort," Blankenship said. "He perhaps is the smartest person I've ever known." [12]

Robert Henry, chief judge of the United States Tenth Circuit Court of Appeals, lauded DeVier for helping safeguard the law school. He said, "Every time the law school needed someone to step forward, DeVier was there. We could never have made such progress without his leadership." [13] DeVier was co-chair, with good friend Bill Ross, of the building

LEFT: DeVier joins prominent Washington lawyer and OU graduate Joel Jankowsky, left, Julian Rothbaum of Tulsa, a great friend of OU, and Jack Valenti, president of the Motion Picture Association of America, on a tour of new OU athletic facilities. DeVier presented Valenti for an honorary degree at OU.

In 1995, DeVier received the University of Oklahoma Regents Award. Making the presentation are OU President David Boren, left, and Regent Melvin Hall, right.

DeVier, right, and former Kerr-McGee Corporation President Lukè Corbett during a panel discussion on international economic issues as part of a foreign policy seminar at OU.

campaign that raised more than $7 million in private gifts to match government funds to build a new law school building. He also was co-chair with Ross of the OU College of Law Board of Visitors.

The dedication ceremony for the new law center took place in 2001. It was a special event with Justice Sandra Day O'Connor as the dedication speaker. DeVier accompanied Justice O'Connor and her husband, John, from Washington for the event. At the dinner following the dedication, President Boren read a resolution passed by the Board of Regents naming the new building the Andrew N. Coats Law Center, "a well-deserved tribute" to Coats. On the way back from dinner, DeVier told his old friend, Coats, "Now, Andy, you understand that we're going to wait awhile on a statue."[14]

DeVier's work for the College of Law continues. In 2009, the law school initiated a campaign for scholarships and other needed financial assistance to mark the law school's centennial. DeVier is serving as co-chair of that effort.

DeVier served on the board of trustees of the Univer-

DeVier and classmates from the OU College of Law Class of 1955 celebrated their 50th anniversary in 2005. DeVier began his legal studies with this class, although he graduated with the Class of 1957. With the group is OU Law Dean Andy Coats, second from right on the front row. *Courtesy University of Oklahoma.*

DeVier with law school classmates Judge Tom Brett, left, and Tony Massad, right, at a law school function.

sity of Oklahoma Foundation, the body that administers the university's endowment and participates in development activities of OU, for ten years from 1995 to 2004. During that time, he and a number of other trustees, including H.E. "Gene" Rainbolt, a man who DeVier greatly admires, led an effort to reform the board of trustees in a number of areas, including the institution of term limits and age limits to assure the presence of new blood on the board. Several years later, DeVier found himself on the senior side of both limits and left the board to become a trustee emeritus. He said, "I was 'hoist on my own petard.'"[15]

DeVier has made a difference in other areas of OU. He was a member of the President's Scholarship Circle and chair for national individual leadership in OU's Reach for Excellence campaign that raised more than $1 billion under Boren's leadership. For his service, the OU Regents presented him the Regents Award in 1995. He also received the College of Arts and Sciences 2009 Distinguished Alumni Award.

In 2007, DeVier was asked to chair of the Board of Visitors of the OU Honors College. The Honors College is comprised of National Merit Scholars and other undergraduate students of high academic standing and provides a special curriculum with a core faculty dedicated to these exceptional students. The Honors College is in effect a prestigious liberal arts college in the heart of a large state university. After talking over the matter with President Boren, DeVier agreed to take the position.

R.C. Davis-Undiano, dean of the Honors College, spoke to DeVier's leadership skills, saying, "DeVier brought a sense of dignity and purpose to the Board of Visitors that everyone respected and responded to."[16] DeVier is not just a "mere board member" who occasionally shows up for a meeting. Dean Davis-Undiano said, "He believes in the Honors College enough to give of his time. I take his advice very seriously and have come to view him as a valuable source of wisdom and guidance."[17]

DeVier enjoys interaction with the brilliant students who attend the Honors College. His dinner partner at a Board of Visitors dinner in 2008 was a young lady who had just been awarded a Rhodes Scholarship. Another time, DeVier was drafted into duty to conduct an evening-long dialogue on American foreign policy during the twentieth century with Dr. Rufus Fears, a nationally-prominent member of the OU faculty.

DeVier has been a frequent speaker to professional groups in Oklahoma. Several years ago, he spoke to the Tulsa chapter of the American Inns of Court. His subject was the interposition of politics and law with President Clinton's eleventh-hour pardons and the Supreme Court decision in *Bush v. Gore* as the case studies. DeVier remembered, "It was a room filled with 500 lawyers and two engineers, my old friend, Occidental President Dale Laurance, and David Hentschel, Occidental's head of domestic operations." After the dinner, while leaving the Southern Hills Country Club, DeVier met John Williams, founder of the Williams Companies, who asked what event DeVier had been speaking to. When DeVier said there were 500 lawyers and two engineers, Williams replied, "Sounds like an even fight to me."[18]

On several occasions, DeVier has been the guest speaker at the Fortune Club, a breakfast club of Oklahoma City business and professional men that includes many of his longtime friends. He has spoken on, among other topics, Iraq, the economy, judicial appointments, and ever-increasing political partisanship. At one appearance just before an election, Lee Allan Smith asked DeVier, "How will you vote in the fall?" DeVier replied, "Just as I always do, as a loyal American."[19]

In 2002, DeVier was awarded Oklahoma's highest honor—induction into the Oklahoma Hall of Fame. Shirley

Five members of the Oklahoma Hall of fame gather at a dinner in Tulsa. Left to right, James Hewgley, DeVier, G.T. Blankenship, Judge Tom Brett, and John Brock.

orchestrated a celebration with all three children present along with a large group of friends from Oklahoma, California, and Washington, D.C. Presenting DeVier for induction at the Hall of Fame ceremony was Admiral William J. Crowe, former chairman of the Joint Chiefs of Staff. DeVier called Crowe "one of the great men of our time and one of the great Oklahomans of all time" and was honored by his presence at the induction ceremony.[20]

DeVier is a proud Oklahoman and feels that the state has been very good to him throughout his life. In reflecting on his many friendships and activities in his native state, he said, "I hope I have been able to give something back, but I am still way ahead."[21]

CHAPTER TWENTY-NINE

FAMILY AND FRIENDS

*Many parts of my life have been important and satisfying.
But, at the end of the road, all we really have left
are family and friends.*

— DeVier Pierson

After education and marriage, DeVier and Shirley began their family on the requisite timetable. Jeff was born in 1959 and Libby in 1961, "standard spacing for a young Presbyterian couple." They were healthy and happy children who avoided any serious mishaps in early childhood except for Jeff's burns from fireworks at a July Fourth celebration with Stan Bevers and Libby's sitting for an extended period of time at the bottom of the swimming pool at Quail Creek Golf and Country Club.

When Jeff and Libby were young, the Piersons began traveling. DeVier and Shirley made a number of short trips to Oklahoma lakes with Fred and Nan Buxton, Dan and Sarah Hogan, and other young married friends. DeVier and Bill Bevers were Army JAG officers with a two-week summer camp obligation. Their best summer was when they were assigned to Fort Carson, Colorado, and spent the next two weeks with their wives and children at Green Mountain Falls at the base of Pike's Peak, including a visit to the nearby summer home of Stanley and Jerry Lee when the highlight was Stanley showing Jeff a good deal more fishing skill than Jeff's father possessed. Shirley and DeVier also took Jeff on

a vacation trip to Newport Beach, California, to spent two
weeks with Dick Zahm, DeVier's Korean War buddy, and his
wife Nancy, a sign of more California travel to come.[1]

The bigger challenges were at home. DeVier has been
"mechanically challenged" throughout his life and home
maintenance work posed problems. He rented a rototiller
to work on the Oklahoma red clay in the front lawn of their
home at 2521 Kings Way. When he fired it up, "it took on a
life of its own" and headed down the street with DeVier holding on "for dear life." For several weeks that hot Oklahoma
summer with the temperature hovering over 100 degrees,
DeVier and Shirley worked tirelessly to level the ground and
lay a kidney-shaped brick patio in their backyard. After their
marathon project was completed, their neighbor had a con-
crete patio installed in one afternoon, instilling in DeVier the
thought that he surely was an inefficient home management
expert and needed to delegate that work to others.[2]

Moving up, the Piersons lived for several years at 1401
Brighton on the edge of Nichols Hills. They especially
enjoyed living next door to Richie and Sherri Norville. The
couples and their children shared "many happy evenings"
with the women, who were very close, often sitting on Sherri's
front porch swing, waiting for DeVier and Richie to arrive
home. With more space in the new home, Shirley was able to
entertain their married friends and family on a regular basis.
When it became clear that they were staying in Washington,
DeVier and Shirley sold the Brighton house to another young
Oklahoma City couple, Jim and Christy Everest.[3]

While still living in Oklahoma City, DeVier briefly went

into the restaurant business with two close friends, Ed deCordova and Jack Catlett. They bought the Sooner Inn, a downtown Oklahoma City restaurant that was a popular luncheon spot for charcoal hamburgers and had a reasonable dinner trade. They bought the restaurant at "bargain basement" prices from two stock brokers at Merrill Lynch who had been ordered to divest their outside investments if they wanted to hold their jobs.[4]

The restaurant business was tough and demanded a great deal of personal attention from the owners. When they bought the business, DeVier gave an inspired speech to their eight employees in which he expressed hope that all eight would still be part of the enterprise at the end of the year. Unfortunately, at the end of the year, deCordova filled out 87 W-2 forms, reflecting the "mass of humanity" that had worked at the restaurant. DeCordova figured the business had nearly a 1,000-percent turnover that year.[5]

Later, urban renewal redeveloped the area and paid the owners a handsome sum for the Sooner Inn. DeCordova and Catlett wanted to borrow money from the Small Business Administration to finance a new location. Because DeVier had moved to Washington, D.C., and was now working for the government, he sold out to his partners. DeVier joked, "This turned out to be the right decision from a business as well as an ethical standpoint."[6]

The move to the nation's capital drastically changed the Pierson family way of life. Jeff had spent one year at Casady School and Libby was in pre-school. Fortunately, both were accepted by Sidwell Friends School, a well-known D.C. area private school initially run by the Quakers. The Sidwell lower school campus was only four blocks from the Pierson's first home on Edgemoor Lane in suburban Maryland. As a result, the Piersons saw "the sticker shock of private school tuition early in life."[7]

Jeff and Libby began with an "exalted view" of Washington because their first four years were spent while DeVier was working on Capitol Hill and in the Johnson White House. The children were on hand for private tours of the Capitol and the monuments, Easter Egg Rolls on the White House lawn, and visits to their father's office in the West Wing. On one memorable evening at home, Libby became flustered in answering the telephone and hung up on President Lyndon Johnson. Shirley picked up the phone and heard a booming voice with a Texas drawl say, "Well is anybody there?"[8]

Many of Shirley and DeVier's Oklahoma friends brought their families to Washington for the required tour of the nation's capital and were guests in the Pierson home. The Pierson family sometimes joined in junkets to the attractions of the area so that there were many Oklahoma visitors to the Civil War battlefields, Monticello, and Williamsburg. Dick and D'Arline McCubbin visited Shirley and DeVier on a driving tour of private schools before Dick assumed the post of headmaster of Casady School. DeVier commented, "They must be rich Okies because they had their wardrobe in well-organized compartments in the back seat of their car."

On another occasion, a busload of Oklahomans on a Chamber of Commerce trip arrived at the Piersons' front door. Shirley was always a gracious hostess for the Oklahoma guests and felt it was a special treat to have friends from home. In those days, it was easy for the Piersons to take their friends to the Capitol, the monuments, and other Washington landmarks free of security barriers and guards. Even access to the White House was more informal.[9]

The Piersons began making new friends in Washington, including their neighbors, Linda and Ed Sonnenblick, a brilliant cardiologist at the National Institutes of Health, and Janie and Wright Elliott, who became a senior executive at Chase Bank. Even so, the heart of their Washington social life still was the "Oklahoma Mafia" made up of Tom and Sally Finney, David and Mary Beth Busby, and Mike and Jocelyn Monroney. Joel Jankowsky, a close friend of Paul Frost, and his wife, Carol, and Max Berry and his wife, Heidi, also were Oklahoma friends in Washington. In 1970, Gene and Jan Morrell, longtime Oklahoma friends, moved to Washington when Gene took a job as a senior official at the Department of the Interior in the Nixon Administration. DeVier remembered, "Oklahomans were never very far away."[10]

In 1970, as DeVier's law practice was flourishing, he and Shirley purchased a three-story colonial white house with large white pillars in Chevy Chase, Maryland, in an area known as Kenwood. The house had been built in 1931 and the original owner had died in the living room. With two subsequent additions under Shirley's careful direction, the home in Kenwood has been the Pierson family headquarters for nearly four decades. DeVier said, "Shirley has always been the CEO of the home and I have been, at best, a junior vice president in the finance department."[11]

Shirley and DeVier acquired their home at 5326 Chamberlin Avenue in Chevy Chase, Maryland, in 1970. It has been the Pierson family headquarters for nearly four decades.

A third child, Stephen, was born in 1971. Jeff was 12 and Libby was 10. Stephen was not an accident—Shirley had one miscarriage and she and DeVier were anxious to add to the family. So, he was a very welcome addition. The only dispute was what his middle name would be. After a deadlock and the passage of time, they left it up to him.

Frequent trips to Oklahoma were part of the Piersons' lives. They continued to be close to Shirley's sister, Marta, who had married Allie Reynolds, Jr., the son of the famous Oklahoman who starred for the New York Yankees. Jeff and Libby were close to the Reynolds children, Michael, Debbie,

and David. DeVier and Shirley were particularly pleased
when Shirley's brother, Paul Frost, and his wife, Vicki,
remained in Washington for Paul's job with Union Carbide
Corporation. There was now a Pierson brood in Washington
as well as Oklahoma.

Left to right, Ed deCordova, Tom
Hughes, DeVier, and Dan Hogan
show off much younger legs, and
much shorter shorts, in a 1985 golf
tournament.

Shirley and DeVier
also developed
warm friendships
with many non-
Oklahomans in the
nation's capital.
Their closest new
friends were Bill and
Ann Morris, who
lived a few blocks away in Kenwood. Bill, a University of
Virginia graduate, was a "cave dweller," the local term for
persons born and raised in the Washington area. He was a fine
athlete and he and his son, Billy, won the national father-son
tennis tournament one year. Ann was a flamboyant beauty
from Houston and was the "centerpiece of every party." The
Morris family had three children about the same age as Jeff,
Libby, and Steve. DeVier said, "The Morris's were like our
Oklahoma buddies in the depth of our friendship." [12]

Shirley was very anxious to develop new friendships with permanent members of the Washington community. Through the Junior League, she made a large number of friends in the Chevy Chase community, including Sandy and David Berler and Carol and Allen Shiff, which blossomed into enduring family friendships. [13]

The Piersons' favorite vacation spot with the Oklahoma mafia and other Washington friends was the Ocean Club on Paradise Island near Nassau in the Bahamas. The small resort hotel was a 40-room facility built by Huntington Hartford during the time he owned Paradise Island as a place to entertain his friends. The rooms overlooked the Caribbean and a large tennis center adjoined the main building. The daily bill of fare was swimming, reading on the beach, playing tennis, eating, and visiting the casino down the street at night for blackjack or other games of chance.

Regulars on the Ocean Club trips were Tom and Sally Finney, David and Mary Beth Busby, Hal and Diane Mesirow, Tom and Priscilla McCoy, John and Diana Zentay, and their children. It was a strong tennis group. DeVier recalls one day when he and John Zentay played with actor Sidney Poitier and fugitive financier Robert Vesco on one side of them and Arthur Ashe and his wife on the other.

During the late 1970s, the older Pierson children moved on from Sidwell Friends to college. Jeff attended college at Emory University in Atlanta, Georgia, studied abroad in Paris, France, and did his graduate work at the Fletcher School of Law and Diplomacy on the Tufts University campus in Boston. A wound in DeVier's pride, but a decision he tolerated, was that Jeff chose Sigma Alpha Epsilon as his fraternity at Emory, rather than his father's beloved Phi Gamma Delta.

Early in his Emory career, Jeff suddenly decided he wanted to attend college in New England. He and DeVier looked at schools in Boston and traveled to Maine to visit the campus of Bowdoin College and Colby College. It was in the dead of winter and everywhere they went on campus they walked through mud and slush. While they were eating dinner at a Holiday Inn in Portland, Maine, it began to snow so heavily it covered the restaurant windows. Noting that it was 70 degrees in Atlanta, Jeff agreed that it was time to head back south and complete his education at Emory.[14]

Libby had different interests. She was a talented musician with a fine singing voice and, in the tradition of Grandmother Pierson, was an accomplished pianist. While at Sidwell she took home first place in the Maryland State Piano Competition.

After high school graduation, Libby headed west to Colorado College in Colorado Springs. The college was set in the foothills of Pike's Peak. Libby flourished under the school's block system, made good friends, and climbed and skied many nearby mountains before her graduation.

Shirley orchestrated DeVier's 50th birthday in 1981 with a party in Oklahoma City that included most of DeVier's friends of the past 30 years. Lee Allan Smith, who called DeVier "one of the smartest and socially graceful men I ever met,"[15] dreamed up a carton poster that placed DeVier's caricature into a setting that included the United States Capitol, the Scales of Justice, Burning Tree Club, and a Phi Gam pin on his shirt as he put the President on hold while he completed a round of golf. By the end of the evening, the Piersons felt they had never left Oklahoma.

One portion of a cartoon poster prepared by Lee Allan Smith as a part of DeVier's 50th birthday party in Oklahoma City in 1981. The poster depicts the various stages of DeVier's life, the Capitol, the White House, the practice of law, and his Phi Gamma Delta fraternity pin, as he puts the President on hold as he completes a round of golf at Burning Tree. Many of DeVier's friends attended the celebration.

A number of other friends turned 50 in 1981, including DeVier's college classmate and then-client, Hugh Roff, United chairman and CEO, United general counsel Bill Cassin, and Doyle Cotton of Tulsa, a major United shareholder. The Piersons joined the Roffs, Cassins, and Cottons on a combination business/pleasure trip to Italy for a natural gas conference followed by a gala 50th birthday party on an island in Lake Como. DeVier believed it was appropriate for United's outside counsel to be present to ensure that the trip was all business.[16]

DeVier and Shirley feel blessed by the many new friendships they have established since they made Washington their permanent home. Their next door neighbors for most of their time in Kenwood have been Bill and Ulla Fortune, both orthopedic surgeons who have operated on DeVier. They have built an especially warm relationship with Tom Leary, a leading Washington antitrust lawyer and later a member of the Federal Trade Commission, and his wife, Stephanie. Tom has been a wise counselor and advisor to DeVier. The Piersons and the Learys have spent many evenings together, including ushering in the new millennium at the Pierson home on the Eastern Shore of Maryland.[17]

Another pleasant aspect of Washington life has been the opportunity to establish friendships with a number of well-known journalists. Shirley and DeVier became friends with Jim Lehrer, the prominent public broadcasting news anchor, prolific author, and frequent moderator of presidential debates, and his wife, Kate, a very successful novelist in her own right. The Pierson and Lehrer children attended school together at Sidwell. DeVier and Jim often kidded each other about "trading places" one day with Jim going to DeVier's law office and DeVier appearing at the WETA studio prior to an evening broadcast. DeVier believes he "came out well ahead" in that mythical bargain.

The Piersons have a warm friendship with Diane Rehm, host of a nationally syndicated current affairs program on public broadcasting, and her husband, John, who DeVier worked with in the Johnson administration. A similar relationship exists with Roger Mudd, the legendary television commentator at CBS and elsewhere, and his wife, E.J., a noted poet. Along with David and Mary Beth Busby, the Piersons have had many wonderful evenings with the Lehrers, Rehms, and Mudds dissecting political events and delivering fearless forecasts of the future. Allan Cromley, dean of Oklahoma journalists in Washington, and his wife, Marian, have been Pierson family friends for years. DeVier has also maintained personal ties, especially on the golf course, with CBS commentator Bob Schieffer.[18]

DeVier, center, helps President David Boren, right, honor prominent PBS news anchor and author, Jim Lehrer, as the recipient of the first Gaylord Award at the Gaylord School of Journalism and Mass Communications at OU.

"DeVier has a great capacity for friendship," said David Busby. "No matter how busy he is, he is never too busy to help a friend. He will stop what he's doing if a friend is in crisis."[19] Busby and his wife, Mary Beth, are thankful for the Piersons' friendship and their support of efforts to make the Busbys' two mentally-challenged sons, Robert and Jack, feel part of the Pierson family. Mary Beth said, "They welcome our boys into their home and include them in family holidays and other events." DeVier has been a regular supporter of a foundation that helps further medical research for inherited mental and intellectual disabilities.[20]

Shirley also used her talents as a gracious hostess to assist DeVier in hosting special dinners for special occasions. When General Dick Burpee was Director of Operations for the Joint Chiefs of Staff, the Piersons hosted a dinner to honor top military leaders. General Burpee and other top brass enjoyed a formal dinner in full-dress uniform, "a very colorful affair." Burpee, formerly commander of Tinker Air Force Base in Oklahoma, said, "As you can imagine, it was a successful community relations effort to bring senior military people together with DeVier's friends in Washington."[21]

Another memorable evening was a farewell dinner for Virginia and Jack Weinmann when Jack left his post of Cheif of Protocol to become Ambassador to Finland. The Piersons invited all previous Chiefs of Protocol back to President Kennedy to honor Jack.

In the midst of their busy life, DeVier and Shirley were faced with a semi-empty nest. Jeff and Libby were adults and were seeing the world. Libby had lived in Florence and Rome, Italy, and studied in England. Jeff had lived in Paris and Belgium.

Only Steve was still at home. After he completed high school at Bethesda-Chevy Chase High School, in the family tradition, he then left the Washington area and enrolled at Chapman College in Orange County, California, the begin-

DeVier and his three children on a skiing trip to the Matterhorn in Switzerland in 1994. Left to right, Jeff, DeVier, and Libby. Steve is in front. The trip was not without incident. Despite some scares, they all lived to tell the tale.

ning of a larger California presence for the Piersons. When he graduated from Chapman, he had become a California kid and wanted to stay.[22]

Because the family had become so scattered, Shirley and DeVier looked for ways to bring them together on special trips. The most memorable was a ski trip to Zermatt, Switzerland. Their hotel balcony looked out at the Matterhorn. The trip was not without danger—Libby and Steve were lost in fog on the way down the main slope and ended up at the edge of a precipice. But all survived. DeVier had a family photograph printed on tee shirts for everyone to prove that the Piersons had skied at the Matterhorn and lived to tell about it.[23]

Libby was the first to make the move toward marriage. She brought Guy Sainty, a British old masters art dealer "of good reputation" to meet her parents. DeVier remembered, "He cheerfully submitted himself to parental inspection and passed with flying colors." A short time later, Guy called DeVier from a New York restaurant to say he had proposed to Libby but she had insisted he call her father to formally ask for her hand in marriage. Maintaining "the pretense that we had any real say in the matter," DeVier and Shirley happily agreed with Libby's decision.[23]

Libby and Guy were married on the Memorial Day weekend in 1995 at Christ Episcopal Church in Georgetown. The site was a compromise, reflecting the fact that Guy was Catholic and Libby was an Episcopalian-leaning Protestant. It was a white-tie affair with all the trimmings followed by a reception at the Cosmos Club. DeVier reflected that Libby was beautiful, it was the best party he and Shirley had ever thrown, it was surely the "largest collection of flowers under one roof in the Western world," and "it was the sharpest one-day reduction ever in my net worth," but "worth every penny of it."[25]

The Pierson men prepare for their sister's wedding in May, 1995. Left to right, Steve, Jeff, and DeVier.

The just-married Saintys with Guy's children at the altar of the Christ Episcopal Church. Left to right, Della, Charles, Libby, Guy, and Clementine.

Then it was Jeff's turn. Jeff had worked on Capitol Hill for Congressman Mickey Edwards and in the Office of Management and Budget in the first Bush administration, had gone through a brief first marriage, and had moved to Paris to work for the International Energy Agency. He met a beautiful young French doctor, Laurence Richard, at a costume party and fell in love. Shirley and DeVier flew to France in the fall of 1996 to meet Laurence's family and attend a civil ceremony so she and Jeff could return to America as husband and wife.

The following January all the Piersons went back to Paris

for the formal wedding in a Catholic church in a Paris suburb where Joan of Arc was the patron saint. The reception was held in a castle in the French countryside, complete with a moat and nightlong extravaganza. The formal dinner lasted nearly four hours. With some effort, DeVier had memorized a toast to the bride and groom in French, an effort well received by Laurence's French family and friends. After the triumph, however, DeVier could not speak another word in French to them, to the dismay of his new daughter-in-law.

Jeff and his new wife, Laurence, at their wedding reception outside Paris, France, in January, 1997.

Steve and Melinda McGraw were married in Santa Barbara, California, in the fall of 2000.

Because the Pierson family was becoming so international, DeVier thought it was important that everyone remain sensitive to their Oklahoma roots. He and Shirley arranged for a trip to Oklahoma for Libby and Guy, Jeff and Laurence, and Steve, who had yet to marry. They started in Oklahoma City with a tour of the city and a dinner party hosted by Dan and Sarah Hogan, with a large number of old friends in attendance. A day on the OU campus in Norman was highlighted by a visit with President Boren and First Lady Molly Boren at Boyd House and a tour of the campus, including the College of Law, the Fred Jones Museum of Art, and the expanding football stadium.

Next the Piersons toured Gilcrease Museum in Tulsa and attended a dinner hosted by Mary and Tom Brett with some of the Brett family and a number of Tulsa friends. On the final day of the Oklahoma trip, they paid homage to DeVier's birthplace of Pawhuska with a visit to his childhood home on Leahy Street, a tour of the Tall Grass Prairie, and barbecue at Black Bart's, one of DeVier's favorite Oklahoma eating establishments.[26]

Steve was the last of the Pierson children to tie the knot. He was "smitten" by movie and television actress Melinda McGraw, and no one wondered why. After a successful courtship, the Pierson family descended upon Santa Barbara, California, in the fall of 2000 for a memorable wedding. Steve and Melinda were married in the old Santa Barbara Mission, a mission church rich in California history. There were tense moments before the wedding. The limousine bringing Melinda to the mission did not show up on time at the hotel and

DeVier stands in front of his birth house on Leahy Avenue in Pawhuska, Oklahoma. The Pierson family visited Pawhuska as part of the Oklahoma tour put together by Shirley and DeVier in 1998.

was late getting to the mission. DeVier and Shirley's grandson and ringbearer, George Sainty, lost the wedding ring in the dust outside the mission. Fortunately, it was found one minute before Melinda arrived. DeVier noted, "Things are never dull in the Pierson family." [27]

In the 1990s, DeVier and Shirley established a bigger presence in California. After years of living out of hotel rooms on their trips there, they purchased a condominium in Newport Beach as their California base. This was good timing because close friends Dan and Sarah Hogan were buying a house there at the same time. In subsequent years, Ed and Nancy deCordova and Gordon and Anna Noel Williams, longtime Oklahoma friends, also bought in the area.

Bibba and Don Winn, DeVier's law school classmate, were down the road in their retirement home in Rancho Santa Fe. Libby and G.T. Blankenship spent a portion of each summer in La Jolla. John and Carolyn Mee made regular trips to Santa Barbara. Marylin and Sidney Upsher, George and Nancy Records, and Claude and Nancy Arnold were in "the desert" around Palm Springs. The group became the "West Coast Oklahoma Mafia."

Members of the "West Coast Oklahoma Mafia" together for a dinner in Newport Beach, California, in February, 2009. Left to right, Dan and Sarah Hogan, Shirley, in front, Gordon and Anna Noel Williams, Bibba and Don Winn, Nancy and Ed deCordova, and DeVier. They have been friends for more than a half century.

The home in California has been "a wonderful addition" to the Pierson lifestyle. They make two long trips each year to the Golden State, allowing them to stay in close touch with Steve and his family. The other children also visit their parents in California, a fact duly noted by friend Sarah Hogan, who said, "DeVier and Shirley are never happier than when they are with family and friends. He is a true family man, devoted to Shirley, their children, and grandchildren. At the same time, he makes us as friends always feel very special."[28]

DeVier and Steve on one of the many vacation trips to California. No ties allowed.

Many friends of the Piersons have been guests in Newport Beach. DeVier and Shirley are usually in California on DeVier's August 12 birthday and Shirley has orchestrated celebrations of a number of his significant birthday milestones.[29]

In addition to acquiring property on the West Coast, the Piersons bought a home on the Eastern Shore of Maryland midway between Easton and St. Michaels on a branch of the Tred Avon River. The property was part of the "King's thumbprint," land that King George granted to his favorites

John Drake, left, and DeVier catch up on old times during Drake's visit to Washington, D.C. John and DeVier have been friends since high school. John and his wife, Jeannie, have visited the Piersons several times.

among early Maryland aristocrats by putting his thumb on a map of the area to identify the location and size of the land being given. The original house had been expanded several times by previous owners and came complete with a swimming pool and dock. Under Shirley's supervision, a somewhat lackluster building became a beautiful second home.[30]

The Eastern Shore property is only 80 miles from the Pierson home in Chevy Chase. While he is not very nautical, DeVier bought his "flagship," an 18-foot Boston Whaler, to motor around Chesapeake Bay. The house and a guest house have been regularly used by the Pierson children and friends.

In addition to high school and college friends and their young married circle, Shirley has made some special friendships over the years. She became very close to Marylin Upsher when Marylin was living in Washington and that friendship has remained strong. Another close friend is Etel Valtasaari, the wife of Yukka Valtasaari, the longtime Finnish

Ambassador to the United States. The Piersons have hosted the Valtrasaaris on several visits to Newport Beach and they made their first trip to Oklahoma to see DeVier inducted into the Oklahoma hall of Fame. Shirley has never had a better friend than Colleen "Coke" Evans, who gave up a motion picture career to become the wife of Dr. Louis Evans, a Presbyterian minister, and who Shirley considers a soul mate. Another special tie is with Laurie Firestone, who the Piersons first knew when she was social secretary in the first Bush White House, and who is now a good friend in California.[31]

Now it was time for grandchildren. Libby and Guy had settled on the upper east side of Manhattan, within walking distance of Guy's gallery. Two years after marriage, the first Pierson grandchild, George Christopher DeVier Sainty was born. In January, 1998, Alexander Richard Pierson was born to Jeff and Laurence. In September, 2000, Libby gave birth to Julian Phelps Stair Sainty in Manhattan. Shirley and DeVier caught the last flight out of Washington for New York before the airport was closed by a hurricane scare in order to preserve their perfect record of attendance at the births of their grandchildren.

The next year, Clara Marina Pierson was born in Fairfax, Virginia. After three grandsons, Clara was the first Pierson granddaughter. It had been a long wait. Shirley was so excited when Jeff and Laurence said it was a girl that she refused to believe it until she was shown.[32]

The next grandchild was in every way a miracle. In the summer of 2002, Steve and Melinda announced that Melinda was pregnant. In mid-August, after attending a birthday dinner for DeVier, Melinda went into labor three months early and was rushed to the hospital. Lucy Grace McGraw-Pierson was born several days later "at her fighting weight" of only one and half pounds. "By God's grace and against all odds," DeVier remembered, Lucy survived after three months in the hospital and has flourished as a highly intelligent, creative, and verbal little girl.

ABOVE: The Sainty family on vacation. Left to right, Libby, Julian, Guy, and George. Arabella is in front.

LEFT: Lucy, Melinda, and Steve in a playful moment.

The Pierson family became even more scattered. After the attack on the World Trade Center on September 11, 2001, Guy and Libby moved to France and leased a home in Le Vesinet, a suburb of Paris. On December 7, 2004, Libby gave birth to Arabella Francesca Sainty, the sixth Pierson grandchild. Shirley and DeVier were just a few feet away. With six grandchildren, three boys and three girls, Shirley and DeVier had been present for all six births.[33]

All Pierson grandchildren are flourishing. In the Sainty family tradition, George and Julian are in English boarding school at Cothill near Oxford. Alex and Clara are second-generation Piersons at Sidwell Friends in Washington and have the children of President Barack Obama and First Lady Michelle Obama as classmates. Miracle grandaughter Lucy is an elementary school student in suburban Los Angeles. Young Arabella is a pre-schooler biding her time to get news of the Sainty's next adventure.[34]

By choice, the Pierson children have become widely scattered and pursuing different worlds. Jeff has remained in Washington, has held a number of government positions, including head of the Small Business Administration's Investment Division, and is now in the executive search world. Libby shuttles back and forth between Paris and London, where Guy's art gallery is located, to see her boys. Steve has remained in the music world with a blues band and now a children's band, Jambo. He writes musical scores and is running a large sound studio in Hollywood while Melinda's career in movies and television has continued to thrive.

All through these years, Shirley and DeVier have been

Estela Urquizu, right, a very important member of the Pierson family, at Steve's graduation from Chapman University in Orange County, California.

blessed by having Estela Urquizu as part of their family. Estela came to the Piersons from Guatemala in 1970 with her then-husband, Rolando. Shirley and Estela were pregnant at the same time with Steve and Estela's daughter, Jessica, who lived in the Pierson home and grew up with Steve as a sister. Estela has been an important member of the Pierson family ever since as keeper of the house, second mother to Steve, friend and helper to Jeff, Libby, and their families, a dependable babysitter for each of the grandchildren, faithful nurse to DeVier and others, and dear friend and confidant of all the Piersons for most of the past 40 years. DeVier said, "Every member of the family is important, but we all understand that Estela is indispensable."[35]

Because the family is so widely scattered, it has been a challenge for Shirley and DeVier to get them all together at the same time. There was a happy exception in the summer of 2007 when all the Piersons converged on Chevy Chase and the Eastern Shore of Maryland to celebrate Shirley and

The Piersons gather for Shirley and DeVier's 50th wedding anniversary at a party on the Eastern Shore of Maryland. Left to right, Libby, DeVier, Alexander, Shirley, Steve, Jeff, and Clara. The other four grandchildren were missing in action when this photograph was taken.

Shirley and DeVier on a trip to Rome in 2006.

DeVier's 50th wedding anniversary. Sometimes all wings of the family have been able to come home for Christmas. Otherwise, the travel is in opposite directions with Shirley and DeVier seeing Steve and his family on their trips to California and visiting Libby and her family in Paris with side trips to the Sainty boys at Cothill. In the age of cell phones and e-mail, everyone stays in frequent contact.

LEFT: Shirley and DeVier by the pool at their Chevy Chase home.

Shirley hosts a birthday dinner for DeVier on his 75th birthday in Newport Beach, California, in 2006.

Shirley and DeVier have wonderful memories of foreign travel with good friends. They made several trips to Europe with Hugh and Ann Roff and Gene and Jan Morrell. They joined an Oklahoma group on a raucous tour of the Greek Isles ending in Istanbul. Passengers included Ann Trost, Barbara Watson, Judy and Doc Jordan, D'Arline McCubbin, Dick Van Cleef, Geraldine Raupe, and Carol Drake. They toured Rome and Venice with Dale and Lynda Laurance. There have been countless vacation trips with Dan and Sarah Hogan. Shirley and DeVier have taken two extraordinary trips to the Mediterranean with George and Nancy Records on their boat which DeVier describes as "fairly adequate for a Pawhuska boy."[36]

As they look back on their life in Oklahoma and in Washington, DeVier and Shirley feel blessed by the quantity and quality of their friendships. DeVier said, "Many of my closest friendships are with people I grew up with in Oklahoma, classmates at OU, Army buddies, and then couples who were fellow young marrieds in Oklahoma City." Then the Piersons went to Washington as part of the Oklahoma Mafia and were able to make an additional circle of friends. They have now repeated that process with a group of new California friends. He said, "Other than my family, these friendships have been the most important blessing of my life."[37]

Shirley and DeVier in a not so private moment.

Shirley added, "I never dreamed that I would still have friends who were some of my closest friends all the way back to grade school. My Oklahoma friends are still my best friends, although wonderful friendships have emerged from our many years in Washington."[38]

Shirley and DeVier consider themselves very lucky.

CHAPTER THIRTY

UNTIL DEATH US DO PART

*I had encountered very little tragedy in my life
until 1978 when a series of horrible events
began to unfold with frequency.*

— DeVier Pierson

Until 1978, death had occurred in the Pierson family
and among DeVier's large circle of friends only as part of the
natural order of things. He thought his parents had died too
young, but they had lived long, worthwhile lives and their
deaths had not upset his assumption that people only die
when it is time. The year 1978 abruptly changed his thinking
and taught DeVier much about tragedy, mortality, and loss.

Tom Finney, one of DeVier's best personal and professional friends, died in January, 1978, of Lou Gehrig's disease.
He had told DeVier of his diagnosis two years before while
sitting in the quietness of the Pierson driveway. Shirley and
DeVier had spent many evenings at the Finney home during the next two years as he fought his fatal illness and were
at his bedside when he died. DeVier believed Finney to be
one of the smartest persons he had ever known. Finney was
a prominent Washington "mover and shaker" and was Clark
Clifford's law partner. He and DeVier were very close.[1]

It was the first time DeVier had lost a close friend. He
and Clark Clifford gave the eulogies at Finney's funeral. It
was the first of many eulogies for DeVier. He said he knew

why Finney was sought out by great national leaders such as Adlai Stevenson, John F. Kennedy, Lyndon Johnson, Ed Muskie, and Walter Mondale. DeVier said, "I understand why such men constantly turned to him. Tom always worked for the success of the enterprise. He sought a victory of men and ideals. He was not self-serving."[2]

Just three months after burying Finney, the Pierson family suffered a horrible tragedy. On May 5, 1978, a small airplane carrying four family members crashed in Wyoming. Shirley's brother, Paul Frost; her brother-in-law, Allie Reynolds, Jr.; Marta's son, Michael Reynolds; and Vicki's brother, Jack Love, all were killed. Shirley hurt so badly for her sister, Marta, who had lost her husband, oldest son, and brother in one instant. Vicki had lost her husband and brother. Shirley's parents had lost their only son, their son-in-law, and their grandson. They were numb with grief.[3]

Shirley and DeVier were informed of the news in a middle-of-the-night telephone call from Vicki who simply said, "They're all gone!" They immediately dressed and drove to Vicki's home in Virginia where they spent the remainder of the night praying and comforting one another. Then, they headed to Oklahoma.

"The services in Oklahoma City were surreal," DeVier remembered. There was a joint service for Paul, Allie, and Michael with three caskets at the front. DeVier was asked to give the eulogy on behalf of the family, a most difficult task. He said, "Life is after all a long chain of memories—some beautiful and some ugly, some bitter and some sweet. Because of the quality of the lives of Paul, Allie, and Michael, our memories will be warm, happy, and beautiful. These memories will support this brave family as they draw closer together to renew their own lives."[4]

The tragedy took a heavy emotional toll on the entire family. When DeVier returned to his Washington law office, he installed a "widow's line," a special telephone line from which he could direct dial Marta, Vicki, and Sally Finney. With the men gone in three families, he felt an ongoing responsibility to the women they had left behind.

In 2009, Marta gave witness that DeVier had successfully kept that promise for three decades. She said, "After Allie died, DeVier became more of a brother to me than a brother-in-law. He became the leader of the family. My children, David and Debbie, looked up to him. He was a role model for the children in patriotism and integrity."[5]

DeVier and Shirley have made certain they included Marta, Vicki, and their families at special occasions. Marta said, "When the time came for my children to further their education or get married, DeVier was always there for advice and help."[6]

The tragedies of 1978 were followed by the death of Mike Monroney in 1980. It was expected, but nevertheless a great personal loss for DeVier.

In 1982, the Piersons' close friend, Barbara Bevers, died of lung cancer. Barbara was the first of DeVier's Oklahoma contemporaries to die. She and DeVier had been college classmates. The Bevers and Pierson families had been constant companions and had often traveled together. At the funeral, DeVier spoke of Barbara dying young, "It is easy to feel bitterness at Barbara's death and even to believe the old adage that only the good die young. But perhaps we are wise enough by now to know that the fullness of life is measured by its quality rather than by its years."[7]

In May, 1983, Bill Morris died of cancer at the age of 50. For one year Morris had known his condition was terminal and often talked with DeVier about the past and the future. During that year, DeVier learned a "good deal" about personal courage. The Piersons joined other friends to celebrate holidays with Bill and Ann during that year. Before his death, Morris told DeVier that it was in some ways the best year of his life because "he stopped to smell the flowers" and "felt the full force of the love of family and friends."[8]

The year following Bill's death, DeVier and Shirley went to the Morris vacation home at Lake Winnepasaki in New Hampshire where Bill's son, Billy, invited DeVier to be his partner in the annual tennis tournament. "To fill in for his dad," DeVier said, "was very special."[9]

Six years later, Bill's wife, Ann, died of lung cancer, another great loss for the Piersons. She was only 53. The Morris children asked DeVier and Shirley to host an event in their home the night before the funeral. With Ann's casket in the living room, dozens of her friends from Washington and Connecticut gathered for an old-fashioned wake. They swapped favorite stories and remembered how "outrageous and irrepressible" she was. Ann had told all of her friends to wear red, her favorite color, instead of black. The church was full of red jackets at her services the next day.[10]

About the same time, Bill Bevers died of throat cancer in

Oklahoma City. He was the first of DeVier's male Oklahoma friends to die.

Longtime friend Randy Everest, also a close friend of Barbara and Bill Bevers, discovered many years ago why DeVier "always says the right things at the right time." Everest said, "It is because he really cared for the person he is eulogizing. They are not just a tribute. DeVier's words come from sincere and heartfelt loss." [11] Dr. John Drake said, "I don't know anyone who can convey our loss of friends and family better than DeVier. He says in eloquent language what we all feel at a time of great sorrow." [12]

DeVier has a gift of stopping in the midst of his busy schedule to comfort a friend who has suffered loss. Teresa Adwan will never forget receiving a telephone call from DeVier after her father's death. She said, "He is so attentive to people's rites of passage." [13]

In 1991, Shirley lost her father, Paul Karl Frost. Most of the family went to Oklahoma City for his services. Libby sang Paul's favorite German song, "Edelweiss," and brought tears to everyone's eyes. Of his father-in-law, DeVier said at the funeral, "Paul had an inquisitive mind, a fine memory, and a wide range of interests. He had a gourmet chef's love of food, a voracious reader's love of history, a keen observer's love of current events, a warm-hearted human being's love of his dogs, and the love of German music with the rich baritone voice needed to sing it." [14]

Just after Christmas in 1994, Allie Reynolds died. "Super Chief," as the New York sportswriters dubbed him after he was the first American League pitcher to hurl two no-hitters in a single season, was the patriarch of the Reynolds clan which Marta, Shirley's sister, had joined as young Allie's wife. His funeral service was a combination of a Christian funeral service and a Creek Indian burial ceremony. His casket was brought into the church by Creek singers in full tribal regalia. The funeral anthem, "Amazing Grace," was sung in Creek.

DeVier was asked to join Bobby Brown in giving the eulogy for Reynolds. Brown was Reynolds' roommate when they played for the Yankees. After he retired, he became president of the American League and was a highly successful surgeon in Dallas. Dr. Brown talked about Reynolds the baseball star. DeVier eulogized him as the family patriarch:

Allie's great legacy was his family. He loved his children... His daughter-in-law, Marta, who was like a daughter, nursed him and cared for him to the end. He was known as Pa-paw to his eight grandchildren and ten great grandchildren. He had a special, quiet love for each child, each grandchild, each great grandchild. He was never too busy to spent time with them. They were his legacy, his pride, and his central focus...

He wore the title "Super Chief" with great pride, but with some discomfort, because he knew that Chief was a sacred title, was not conferred lightly, and that he was not officially the chief of any Indian nation. But all American Indians were proud to call him Chief because he was the great ambassador of American Indian values who had the respect and admiration of all tribes and all nations.[15]

In March, 1996, Vicki Frost Martyak, the wife of

Shirley's late brother, Paul, died suddenly. It was a shock to the entire family. Vicki had remarried some years after Paul's death and, along with her husband, Joe, and their two adopted children, became members of the Pierson family. DeVier rushed back from a court hearing in New York City to the memorial service for Vicki and to say a few words of tribute. Since Vicki's death, Shirley has made a special effort to include Joe and the children in family gatherings. They still come to see "Aunt Shirley" and "Uncle DeVier."

The matriarch of Shirley and DeVier's family was Shirley's mother, Carrie Alice Phelps Frost, who was often called "Mimi." DeVier loved her dearly and, after he lost his own mother, Mimi took her place in his life. Four generations of Frosts, Reynolds, and Piersons gathered in Oklahoma City in 1999 to celebrate Mimi's 90th birthday.

A family gathering at the Pierson home. Left to right, Libby, Steve, Jeff, Shirley, DeVier, Alice Frost, Shirley's mother, Marta Reynolds, and Vicki Frost Martyak.

Mimi died two years later. At her funeral, DeVier asked, "Is there anyone out there who didn't love our Mimi?...Mimi was all about beauty. Not beauty parlor beauty, although she never was known to miss an appointment. Not a high-fashion beauty...but the beauty of her spirit and her capacity to appreciate all the beauty around her." [16]

Then DeVier spoke for the entire family:

We will never lose Mimi. The spirit of her beauty will hover around us and hold us close within her tenderness. We will hear her in the laughter of her great grandchildren. We will feel her when they inquire about the world around them, reach out for new challenges, and learn to accept with serenity those times when life treats them harshly. We will see her when they grow into adults and become loving parents with a strong faith and good values. [17]

With the passage of time, it was inevitable that the Piersons would continue to lose friends. DeVier's good friend and neighbor, John Kingdon, a well-known Washington lawyer, had died of cancer and his wife, Jo Ann, remains a close friend of Shirley and DeVier. DeVier was saddened at the death of George Christian, President Johnson's press secretary, who had been a good friend at the White House. Jack Valenti, one of LBJ's closest aides and the longtime president of the Motion Picture Association of America, died in 2006. His memorial service was a large and greatly expanded version of a full Catholic mass with a large turnout from both Hollywood and Washington. Two of DeVier's closest California friends, Sam Barnes and Dr. Bob Duey, died and DeVier gave tributes at each of their services in Newport Beach.

Shirley and DeVier were devastated at the 2006 death of Dougal Jeppe, their longtime friend from Classen High School and OU. Shirley and Dougal had grown up on the same street in Oklahoma City. They had kept in touch through the years and saw him and his family frequently after he and his German wife, Gaby, moved to Washington where Jeppe became head of the Washington office of *Newsweek* Magazine.

To DeVier, Dougal was always a breath of fresh Oklahoma air. He was one of DeVier's oldest friends from times together at Classen High School and in the Phi Gam house at OU. DeVier's eulogy for Dougal was heartfelt and stressed the "unquestionable fact that he was a cut above all of us on the social scene since we had been teenagers." After the service, Shirley and DeVier hosted a reception in their home for Dougal's family and his many friends from Washington, Chicago, New York, and California.

Lifetime friends Dougal Jeppe and DeVier reminisce over old times at the Pierson home on the Eastern Shore of Maryland. Dougal's 2006 death was devastating to the Pierson family.

In recent years, Shirley and DeVier have lost a number of other Oklahoma friends. They mourn the passage, among others, of Dick Van Cleef and Bill Rogers, who were groomsmen in their wedding, Dick McCubbin, Doc Jordan, Dave Raupe, Deak and Ford Price, and Ann Hoover. Gene Morrell, a good friend since college days and former Washington neighbor, died in Houston and Shirley and DeVier shared the grief of Jan and the Morrell children. DeVier observed, "It is sad but true that we can't slow down either Father Time or the Grim Reaper."

Another great loss for the Piersons was the death of Dr. Louis H. "Louie" Evans, Jr., who had been the chief pastor of the National Presbyterian Church in Washington when Shirley and DeVier joined the church. Shirley was close friends with Evans' wife, Coke. Dr. Evans and Coke were Shirley and DeVier's spiritual counselors.

Louie and Coke Evans came to Washington in 1994 to renew Shirley and DeVier's wedding vows. Left to right, John and Mary Jane Dellenback, close friends of the Piersons and Evans, DeVier, Shirley, Dr. Louis Evans, and Coke Evans.

Shirley was a member of a class at National Presbyterian called "The Wrestlers." Coke Evans was the moderator as they "wrestled" with global issues from a biblical perspective. Coke admits that she and her husband ministered to the Piersons, but, she said, "It went both ways. We ministered to them when a grandchild was sick or there was need in the family, but they were there for us to talk about problems or private circumstances. We shared life together as friends." [18]

Coke admires DeVier as a "global thinker," but believes DeVier's family life is even more interesting. She said, "During the years he was so busy, he made time for the everyday needs of his grandchildren. He applied it in every practical, down-home way, not just in holiday events. He has day-by-day involvement in the lives of his family. That is uncommon in this world." [19]

Shirley and DeVier continued to see the Evans on a regular basis after they moved back to California. Over the years, the Evans were guests of the Piersons in Washington, at the Eastern Shore of Maryland, and Newport Beach. Shirley and DeVier visited the Evans' vacation home at Bass Lake, California.

Dr. Evans' health began to decline and he was diagnosed with a rare strain of ALS. In the fall of 2008, DeVier and Shirley visited the Evans home in Fresno, California, and had "the strong feeling that we were telling Louie goodbye." Dr. Evans died several weeks later. A very moving service was held for him at the National Presbyterian Church to honor his life and to receive his ashes in the columbarium. Shirley and DeVier hosted a dinner for Coke, their family, and a group of close church friends in their home following the service.

DeVier believes the friendship with Louie and Coke Evans has been one of the great blessings of his and Shirley's life.   He said, "They have ministered to us during our most difficult times. Louie was a kindred spirit who inspired me and made me better. Coke is a saint on earth. Shirley and I will always be grateful to them."[20]

One of the great honors of DeVier's life was his close friendship with Admiral William J. Crowe, Jr. As Chairman of the Joint Chiefs of Staff in the Reagan administration and American Ambassador to Great Britain during the Clinton presidency, Crowe was always a proud and dedicated Oklahoman. DeVier believed him to be one of a small handful of American policy makers who were directly responsible for the end of the Cold War.[21]

On two occasions, DeVier and Shirley visited Admiral Crowe and his wife, Shirley, at the ambassador's estate at Winfield House in the London suburbs. When the Piersons arrived at the estate for the first time, Crowe took DeVier to overlook nearly a mile of manicured gardens and said, "Let me show you my backyard." DeVier never forgot Crowe's story of when he was heckled by a young man from Northern Ireland who said, "How would you feel if Texas tried to break away from the United States?" Crowe immediately responded, "You're talking to the wrong person. I'm from Oklahoma and we've been trying to get rid of Texas for more than 100 years."[22]

After Admiral Crowe returned to Washington following retirement as Ambassador to the Court of St. James, he and

Oklahomans gather for a meeting of the Board of Visitors of the OU International Programs Center in 2004. Left to right, General Jack Merritt, Admiral William J. Crowe, Jr., DeVier, and OU Vice President Dave Maloney. DeVier was proud that Admiral Crowe had presented him for induction into the Oklahoma Hall of Fame and returned the favor in 2006 when he presented Crowe for an honorary degree at OU.

DeVier maintained a close friendship. They had lunch together every week or so, often joined by David Busby, "to solve the problems of the world, to agonize over the great issues of our time—commitments of military forces, foreign policy, and the prospects for the OU football team."[23] In 2006, DeVier and Shirley accompanied the Crowes to Oklahoma and DeVier presented Admiral Crowe for an honorary degree at OU.

When Crowe's health began to fail in early 2007, he was often confined to the Bethesda Naval Hospital. The hospital had an inflexible policy for seriously ill patients of allowing only close family members to visit. Shirley Crowe helped DeVier pose as a nephew so that he could sneak into the hospital for regular visits.

Admiral Crowe died on October 18, 2007. His memorial service was held with full military honors in the Naval Academy chapel with President Clinton, Secretary of Defense Robert Gates, General Colin Powell, many senators and congressmen, and friends from Oklahoma and around the world were present. DeVier joined fellow Oklahomans David Busby, Sidney Upsher, and John Bozalis as honorary pallbearers. Eulogies were given by President Clinton and DeVier. Clinton spoke of Crowe's great service to his country. DeVier spoke of his close friend:

Regardless of our rank or station, each of us in this beautiful chapel today wears the same badge of honor— we are friends of Bill Crowe...He was the finest man I have ever known...Not just because of his lifetime of contributions to our country, although they were enormous. But because of the way he lived his life and the kind of person he was.

If you want to know Bill Crowe, you must understand first that he was from Oklahoma. He was a proud Oklahoman to the core...He was a great believer in...Oklahoma superiority. He took great pleasure in quoting Will Rogers' famous conclusion that when the Okies migrated to California during the Dust Bowl, it enhanced the intellectual level of both states.

To be sure, he was a sailor, a military strategist, a diplomat, an intellectual, and an outstanding national leader. But he was also a loving husband and father, raconteur, and warm and wonderful human being. In all of these arenas, he was simply the best.[24]

Since Admiral Crowe's death, DeVier has greatly missed the regular lunches and wide-ranging discussions. DeVier said, "Bill was a very wise man with a keen intellect who had the power to both analyze and implement. The magnitude of his contribution to the issues of our time is hard to overstate." To DeVier, Crowe was in many ways the greatest man he ever knew.[25]

CHAPTER THIRTY-ONE

A MESSAGE TO
MY GRANDCHILDREN

*Author's note: On Christmas Day, 2008, DeVier gave this
message to his children for delivery to his six grandchildren.
It is an appropriate way to conclude the story of his life.*

To George, Alexander, Julian, Clara, Lucy, and Arabella:
The six of you, my beloved grandchildren, are my posterity. My life began in 1931 and most of it has been lived during the very eventful twentieth century. Your life will be spent in a new century and in a very different world. So I thought it might be interesting to compare my world when I was your age with the world in which you will live.

When I was your age, my world was pretty small. It consisted of my home, the homes of friends in the same neighborhood, a small park two blocks away where we played football and baseball, and the one mile walk between home and my school. It was a great adventure to ride the streetcar to downtown Oklahoma City. My only road trips were to visit family in Pawhuska. Up to the time I entered college, I had been outside of Oklahoma only twice and had never flown in an airplane.

This does not mean that I had no knowledge of the larger world beyond my little square mile. But I learned about that world solely through newspapers, books and radio (no television), at home and in the library, and the newsreels at the lo-

A rare photograph capturing all six Pierson grandchildren at the Pierson home in Chevy Chase. Left to right, Julian Sainty, George Sainty, Arabella Sainty, Lucy McGraw-Pierson, Clara Pierson, and Alexander Pierson.

cal theater on Saturday afternoons, not by actual travel. I had vivid mental images of the world beyond, but had never seen it.

Communications with my friends were also simple and straightforward. We would make arrangements by phone or simply show up to play. We were together at home, at school, the movie theater, and, on occasion, on a downtown adventure by streetcar. I had a two-member club for several years. The relationships were all face-to-face, not augmented by technology.

When I was away at camp, I wrote some letters to my parents. But that was it. These were the only means of communication with other human beings when I was a boy.

It was also a much simpler era in terms of the "comforts of home." Refrigerators were in their infancy and I remember trips with my father to and from the ice plant to get ice for the "icebox" at home. We had plenty of fans since there was no air conditioning, either in the home or in a car. We had a full-fledged bathroom with tub and shower, but my grandparents' house in Pawhuska, like houses in many rural areas, did not have indoor plumbing. Water was pumped from a well for cooking and bathing and there was an outhouse in back for other bathroom needs. While we had no power problem, electricity itself was just making its way to many rural areas during the 1930s.

Think of the difference between my little world as a boy and your twenty-first century world. You can learn in an instant about any important event anywhere in the world. Through the magic of television and the internet, you can often see it happen in real time. You can talk to your friends—constantly if you wish—by cell phone or by e-mail and text message on your Blackberry. In this internet Facebook world, you may be linked, with or without your consent, to millions of others. Indeed, the biggest challenge of the twenty-first century for you may be to reserve time for the greatest treasure of all— the opportunity to curl up with a good book.

And you can see that world for yourself because the jet airplane, which did not exist in commercial form until I was an adult, has literally shrunk the globe. I rarely traveled outside Oklahoma when I was growing up because these were all such long trips. Your parents traveled considerably more as young people because jet airplanes made that feasible. And each of you is already a world traveler or will be very soon.

Think about the last few months. Over Thanksgiving, Alex and Clara's uncle stopped by to see us on a trip from Australia. During this Christmas of 2008, George, Julian and Arabella could come here from Paris and Lucy had no difficulty making the 3,000 mile trip from California to the East Coast. All of that would have been unthinkable in my boyhood.

These dramatic changes are a result of the march of science and technology in virtually every area of life, much of which occurred during my lifetime. It is hard to imagine in this jet age that the Wright brothers flew the first airplane less than 30 years before I was born. And that the basic creature comforts of the home—television, central heating and air conditioning, refrigerators, dishwashers, disposals, even flush toilets—either did not exist or were new products when I was a boy. Of course, no one had heard of cell phones, personal computers, the internet, Ipods, and the other miracles of the era of information technology until I was a middle-aged man. And what now? For one thing, you may even be entering an era where robotics will change the way many things are done at home as well as at the plant or office.

You are also going to be a part of the expansion of man's awareness of the universe beyond planet earth. After I was an adult, I watched via television the first man in space, John Glenn, who Alex and Clara have met at church, saw man step onto the moon for the first time, and witnessed the miracle of the space station and astronauts walking in space. In your lifetime, you will see exploration well beyond the moon and into the stars, and you may well witness a manned expedition to Mars. The relationship of speed, distance, and time will be reexamined. You will become part of a larger universe as well as a larger world.

I am also amazed when I think of the medical advances of the twentieth century that have taken place during my lifetime. When I was a boy, penicillin had not been discovered and was not available to me for my chronic ear infections. I was the first patient in Oklahoma City to receive this wonder drug, and my ear problems promptly went away. All of the common childhood diseases—measles, chicken pox, mumps, scarlet fever, even the common cold—posed serious health risks. I also remember how Oklahoma City was virtually shut down in the summer by polio epidemics—swimming pools and movies were closed, large areas quarantined, and some unfortunate friends were crippled for life or had to live in "iron lungs" in order to breathe. Indeed, at that time it would not have been possible for me to become a bionic man with an artificial knee because knee replacement surgery, along with the replacement of other orthopedic parts, did not exist.

Those risks seem unthinkable now in the medical world of penicillin, the Salk polio vaccine, MRIs, brain scans, and heart and other organ transplants. You can be sure that these medical advances will continue. All medical records will be computerized. I suspect that you will see safer and more long-lasting organ transplants and diagnostic tools beyond

The Pierson grandchildren gather at the Eastern Shore of Maryland to celebrate their grandparents' 50th wedding anniversary. Left to right, Alexander, Lucy, George, Julian, Arabella, and Clara.

our wildest imagination. In 2008, a woman had a face replacement. Hopefully, you will see a cure for cancer, that awful disease that has taken so many of my family and friends. In fact, you are very likely to experience the economic and social problems arising from longer life expectancies. This is a problem that, at this stage of my life, I'm very happy for you to have!

Another area that is likely to change dramatically in your lifetime is the manner in which we produce and consume energy. Think of how important energy is in your world. It provides the lighting, heating, and cooling for you at home, at school and, eventually, at work. It allows you to eat your meals, read your books, start your computers, drive to school, fly in a plane, or do anything else that requires moving from place to place on other than foot. Energy keeps our offices, factories, power plants and everything else going. Without energy in some form, our lives would simply come to a halt.

During my life in the twentieth century, most of this energy has been produced by what we call fossil fuel, the remains of dinosaurs and the decay of plants millions of years ago.

These fossil fuels are now in the form of oil, natural gas and coal that are embedded beneath the surface of our lands and oceans, I have been especially aware of the importance of the oil and gas industry since the biggest areas of oil and gas production in the United States were in Texas and Oklahoma when I was born in 1931. As a boy, I remember seeing natural gas flared from a well not too far from my bedroom. I worked two college summers in the oil fields in southern Oklahoma as a roustabout and as a roughneck. And I remember paying about twenty cents for a gallon of gas when I was a 16 year-old driving for the first time. When I was young, there was little thought that our dependence on oil and gas would change; indeed, when I was in the White House, our government's concern was simply to hold oil imports at a low level to protect the price received by domestic oil and gas producers.

Since World War II, the energy world has changed dramatically. Oil production in the Middle East, which had begun when I was a little boy, has become the largest single source of oil. After decades of bargain pricing, the rulers in the Middle East began to demand a larger share of oil revenues and eventually nationalized these resources. Large oil and gas reserves were also found in many other locations— Russia, Asia, Africa, South America—and began to compete in world markets. In the United States, foreign imports are well over 50 percent of United States oil consumption, and rising. The source and price of oil and gas is now both a national security and domestic political issue.

The economic challenge of your lifetime in the twenty-first century will be to eventually replace these fossil fuels with alternative sources of energy— wind, solar, hydroelectric, and biomass to name just a few. But most of these technologies are largely untested and will take many years to fully develop. Nuclear power is also a promising source of alternative energy, but it is very expensive and it may be easier to harness the atom than to deal with the problem of disposal of nuclear waste. The challenge is how to bring about this conversion to other energy sources over a reasonable time and at a price that you and other energy users will be able to afford.

The other twenty-first century energy problem is closely related. It is the problem of global warming. Most scientists now agree that it is a very real problem, although there is still a lively debate as to how severe its consequences will be. The fossil fuels, especially oil and coal, release so-called "greenhouse gas" into the atmosphere which are heat-trapping and will gradually raise the temperature of the planet. The leaders in most countries now agree that there must be limitations on the levels of these greenhouse gases, but they still disagree on the best way to get from here to there. An additional problem is that developing nations such as China are heavily dependent on coal for their energy production and the global warming problem cannnot be solved without global cooperation.

The biggest long-term issue is how to make this shift to clean non-fossil fuels on a schedule that will protect the planet and at a cost that will not destroy the economy. It will also be necessary to reduce the amount of energy that you and I consume; this may eventually require big changes in driving habits such as requiring car pools to work in certain areas, limits on highway use by trucks, and much more efficient use of energy in our homes, offices and factories. You are going to hear about this problem over and over again in your schools and on television. The solution is in many ways the biggest challenge of your time.

You and I do have one thing in common. We are living in a time of severe economic challenge. Whether you are living in the United States, as Alex, Clara and Lucy are, or in Europe, as George, Julian and Arabella are, you are living in a country with a market economy that favors private ownership of businesses. This should be a good thing; most economists would tell you that an economy based on entrepreneurship, the creation of new business, and innovation, the creation of new ways of making things, is likely to produce the best economic result over time. This does not mean that government does not need to participate; we call this a "mixed free enterprise" economy. Here in the United States during the nineteenth century and the early twentieth century—fueled by a network of railroads and canals and such inventions as the cotton gin, electric lights, telephones, and eventually cars and airplanes—that economy flourished. It provided profits for those owning the businesses, jobs for the rest of us, and the opportunity to become investors.

Just about the time I was born in 1931, that system almost fell apart. The stock market collapsed and the economy fell into what was known as the Great Depression. Throughout the country, many businesses failed, many workers lost their jobs and their homes, and there were long food lines. It looked as though our economic system might not survive. While I had no conception of it at the time, I was living in a very dangerous time as a young boy, and the country itself had an uncertain future.

Happily, the economy did survive. There were large infusions of capital and job creation from the federal government as a result of President Franklin Roosevelt's New Deal programs. Confidence was gradually restored, although unemployment was still high. Then the economy recovered through the stimulus of mobilization as the country entered World War II. At the end of the war, the United States provided funds to rebuild Europe under the Marshall Plan.

After that time, the global economy has largely flourished. While there have been several short recessions, economic growth has been constant and has been reflected, among other things, in higher stock market values. During the last decade of the twentieth century this growth continued, the stock market had its longest bull market run in history, and the general view was that the good times would continue indefinitely.

But that was not the case. The technology bubble burst in 2000 and growth began to slow. Beginning in early fall 2008, we have seen a meltdown in the economy in the United States and worldwide that is not only a recession, it is the worst economic crisis since the Great Depression. It has threatened the viability of the entire financial system — the commercial and investment banks, mortgage companies, insurance companies, and other financial institutions, and its ripple effect has reached from Wall Street to Main Street. I can only summarize the reasons for the crisis in this short message, but you can be sure that there are no heroes in this debacle.

When the collapse came, there was plenty of fault to go around. The financial industry had been greedy. The federal government—both the executive branch and Congress—had been inattentive to the need for regulation and instead egged on reckless mortgage practices in the name of broad home ownership, were indifferent to the need to regulate exotic new securities, and generally applauded the high leverage in financial institutions as a tool of healthy growth. And all Americans share in the blame when we bought homes we could not afford, incurred consumer debt we could not repay, and generally lived beyond our means. It is a day of reckoning for the American public as well as our economy.

As I write this message to you, the federal government has already committed $700 billion to attempt to prop up the financial system by buying "toxic assets." There are proposals to spend many billions more to try to keep the automobile industry alive. The incoming administration of President Barack Obama has proposed billions for an economic stimulus plan—fancy words for programs to create jobs and lift the economy. No one knows which of these programs will work and how much they will eventually cost. We do know that we will be borrowing the money to finance them and that most of that debt will be held by foreign nations rather than our own citizens.

I hope and believe that the economy will survive and that you will, as I did after the Great Depression, grow up and live your life in a time of relative economic prosperity. But I have to tell you that it may take awhile and that you may be facing some uneven economic times as a young adult. But wouldn't it be boring not to have any challenges!

Despite these challenges, you are blessed with the opportunity of living your lives in countries that are free and democratic. I say "countries" in the plural because I am very aware of the British and French wings of our family. I understand that some of you may spend large portions of your life outside of the United States in France, England, or elsewhere in Europe. While I am very proud to be an American, I recognize that the American story has its roots in Europe. Our political institutions were largely modeled on those of the British. Ties with France began with French assistance during the American Revolution and continue to this day. Wherever you live, you are likely to enjoy the many benefits of citizenry in a democratic country that values individual freedom.

I do not expect American political institutions to change dramatically, but they will no doubt evolve. The tussles between the three branches of government, and between federal and state governments, have continued for more than 200 years. I had a unique opportunity to witness some of these struggles at close proximity during my two years on Capitol Hill dealing with congressional reorganization and during the next two years in the Johnson White House watching one president trying, usually successfully, to impose his will on Congress. This struggle between the legislative branch and the President, umpired from time to time by the judiciary, will no doubt continue throughout your life. In our political system, the more things change, the more they stay the same.

But there has been significant change during the twentieth century in the way that the United States protects the rights of its citizens—what we call "civil rights." Sad to say, it took a long time to do so.

Some of you have already studied the Declaration of Independence with its famous proclamation that "all men are created equal." The founding fathers certainly meant "men" because there were no women among them. It would be another 150 years before women would even have the right to vote as full-fledged citizens. But the founders did not mean "all men" because they did not regard the American Indians who greeted their ancestors when they came to America as equals. And they certainly did not mean to include the Negroes who were their slaves, those involuntary immigrants who came to America in bondage.

The institution of slavery was a product of the American legacy as a British colony. But that did not justify the continuation of this immoral institution after the United States became an independent nation. Great Britain had never had slaves within its own territory and outlawed the slave trade in the early nineteenth century. France and other countries on the European continent did not have slaves. Our founding fathers considered whether to abolish slavery and instead recognized its existence under the Constitution and declined to provide any of the rights of citizenship to slaves. Here in the United States it took a terrible civil war almost a century after the creation of the nation, the only time that Americans have fought against and killed other Americans, to end legalized slavery and to confer some rights of citizenship on Negro Americans.

We did not do much better with the American Indian. While we never treated Indians as slaves, we did not respect their right to land or property and moved them from place to place to clear the way for the western migration. My state of Oklahoma had a special role in Indian policy. The so-called Five Civilized Tribes—Cherokee, Choctaw, Creek, Chickasaw, and Seminole—were moved forcibly from their homes in the southeastern United States along the infamous Trail of Tears to a new Indian Territory in part of what is now Oklahoma. And as you have no doubt heard, probably more times than you wanted, your grandfather was born in the capital of the Osage Nation in Pawhuska. Alex likes to tease me by calling me Pawhuska, which is Osage for "white hair."

While the constitutional amendments after the Civil War provided some political rights, Lincoln's Emancipation Proclamation did not eliminate racial discrimination. The Southern states, including Oklahoma after it was admitted as a state in 1907, had so called "Jim Crow" laws requiring segregation by race in virtually all areas. When I was a boy in Oklahoma City, I attended "lily-white" schools. Blacks had to attend their own schools. There was also residential segregation. I had no black neighbors, no neighborhood friends of other colors. Looking back, I am not very proud that I paid so little attention to the fact that African Americans could not go to stores, restaurants, hotels, or restrooms and had to sit in the back of the bus or the streetcar. I was not much of a civil rights pioneer.

I did not have any black friends. The first time that I worked or socialized with a black American was when I was in the Army at Fort Lee, although Virginia was still strictly segregated. I returned to the University of Oklahoma campus after the United States Supreme Court decision in Brown v. Board of Education had put into motion a desegregation of the school system. I'm proud to say that the first African American man to graduate from the OU College of Law was my classmate John Green –and embarrassed to recall that he was the only black man in a class of 80 graduates.

But change was coming and I was able to see some of it at close hand. I'm very proud of the fact that the President for whom I worked, Lyndon Johnson, pushed through the desegregation of public accommodations and the bill providing voting rights without regard to race. One of my colleagues in the White House Counsel's office was Cliff Alexander, an African American. But there were setbacks as well. I also watched parts of Washington, D.C., burn in the aftermath of Dr. Martin Luther King's assassination and participated in the response to race riots in Watts and Detroit. I came away from all of this with the strong feeling that the sooner our nation became truly colorblind, the better off we would all be.

I'm sure that much of this history sounds very strange to you. Your parents are products of the civil rights movement. They did not attend segregated schools. You certainly have the opportunity to be educated with, and to be friends with, young persons of all races. And that's the way it should be. In this shrinking world, racial barriers are as foolish as they are immoral.

Now, after more than two centuries of legalized slavery, civil war, Jim Crow laws, civil rights legislation and civil unrest, integration of educational institutions and public facilities, and, most significantly, the right to vote, the United States has taken the ultimate civil rights step. It has elected an African American President. The election of President Obama is an emphatic response to the long history of racial exclusion and, I think, signals a new day in the world in which all six of you will live. Indeed, Alex and Clara have the Obama daughters as classmates at Sidwell Friends.

If I could have one wish granted for your future, it would be that you grow up in a world more peaceful than my world of the twentieth century. It is a sad fact that throughout recorded history so-called civilizations have resolved their most serious disputes by military force—by going to war.

In the beginning of the twentieth century, there was an effort to provide a peaceful alternative to war by adjudication of international disputes. I presented two matters to an international tribunal at the location of that effort, the Peace Palace at The Hague. But that was not to be. The twentieth century was in fact the bloodiest century in recorded history—World War I, World War II, Korea, Vietnam, and numerous smaller conflicts. The old adage about man's inhumanity toward his fellow man was never more relevant.

Most of these twentieth century wars took place during my lifetime; I have seen the effects of some of them at close hand. World War II was the seminal event of my boyhood. It began when I was ten and ended when I was 14, only four years away from the draft. I spent a year in Korea just after the end of the Korean War and witnessed the devastation of war from Pusan to Seoul to the truce line. I struggled with the agony of Vietnam in the Johnson White House. I visited a Contra re-supply camp in El Salvador in the midst of the wars in Central America giving rise to the Iran-Contra scandal. My adult life was framed by the Cold War and, years later, I visited the remnants of the Berlin Wall and memorials established by both the Western Allies and the Soviet Union in Berlin and Moscow. I hate war and its consequences.

Now the world is even more dangerous. Since 1945 we have been living in the nuclear age where one bomb can cause hundreds of thousands, even millions, of fatalities. Availability of weapons of mass destruction (WMD) means that wars are no longer acts of individual combat or even mass infantry or artillery battles. They are giant acts of violence with enormous loss of life among both combatants and the surrounding civilian population. Twentieth century warfare has become increasingly lethal.

Now, in your lifetime, there is another dimension to warfare. Wars may begin through acts of violence by terrorist groups, shadowy non-state actors, so that it is often difficult to even determine the enemy. The so-called war on terrorism commencing on September 11, 2001, is the first major war of the twenty-first century; in response we have initiated military actions in both Afghanistan and Iraq, and have threatened other nations. The greatest fear remains that WMD may fall into the hands of terrorists who may be willing to proceed without the typical constraints of organized governments who must worry about their own future.

While you will always live in a dangerous world, I continue to hope that our leaders will have the wisdom to gradually reduce those risks during your lifetime. That we will adopt policies that will reduce tensions with other major powers—an emerging China, a resurgent Russia and a rapidly growing India--so that there will be more global cooperation among the great powers. That we will give priority to halting nuclear proliferation and to reducing, and eventually eliminating, nuclear stockpiles. That we find more creative ways of engaging in the Middle East, including an Israel-Palestine resolution, a better relationship with Iran and stabilization of a nuclear and very dangerous Pakistan That we will find the way to neutralize Al-Queda and the Taliban without a long term occupation of Afghanistan. And that slowly, with "soft power" rather than warfare, a new generation of young Muslims, those about your age, will come to believe that their life on this earth is preferable to martyrdom. Your parents will tell you that this is a very ambitious program, but that's what I would hope for during your lifetime.

So that's your world as I see it—modern and comfortable, high tech in communications and transportation, a shrunken planet amazing in its technological and scientific advances, highly dependent on energy and searching for the needed twenty-first century changes, a sound economy, but currently in crisis, the best political institutions in the world, and great progress in providing equal rights to all persons regardless of the color of their skin. But it will still be a very dangerous world with many challenges for our leaders.

As you prepare to deal with the world and its challenges, let me say a word or two about faith. It is a very personal matter. But I want you to know how important my personal faith has been to the quality and purpose of my life. It has supported me in tough times. It is fundamental to my relationship with your grandmother and we would be lost without it.

Like everyone, you will inevitably face some bad moments and personal difficulties. It is the human condition. These times will require all the support you can muster. It is very comforting to know that there is someone very powerful who loves you and is looking out for your interests. I hope that each of you find, nurture, and keep that faith.

It may surprise you that I don't intend to advise you on what you should do as you grow up in this world. I believe that any calling that gives you fulfillment and makes some contribution to a better life for others is just fine. You will find the right path to personal growth and happiness. Just remember to respect those around you and to love your family and friends. Most important of all, don't forget to have fun.

That's my message. Now it's up to you. By the way, this is not goodbye. I expect to be around for a long time as you mature and begin your own life journey. Even after that, you can bet I'll be watching.

With my love always, Your Grandfather

DeVier and Shirley with their grandchildren at Christmas of 2008. Left to right, DeVier, Lucy, Julian, George, Clara, Arabella, Alexander, and Shirley. For Shirley and DeVier, it does not get any better than that.

NOTES

CHAPTER ONE

1. Written recollections and interviews with Welcome DeVier Pierson, Jr., from June, 2008, to April, 2009, hereafter referred to as DeVier Pierson interview, Archives, Oklahoma Heritage Association, Oklahoma City, Oklahoma, hereafter referred to as Heritage Archives.

2. Letter from Frank Pierson to his family, 1938, Heritage Archives, hereafter referred to as Frank Pierson letter.

3. Ibid.

4. www.digital.library. okstate.edu/encyclopedia, "Cherokee Outlet Opening," Encyclopedia of Oklahoma History and Culture, hereafter referred to as Encyclopedia of Oklahoma History and Culture.

5. Ibid.

6. Frank Pierson letter.

7. Ibid.

8. *The Sooner* yearbook, 1922.

9. Ibid.

10. *The Daily Oklahoman,* June 28, 1925.

11. Encyclopedia of Oklahoma History and Culture, "Pawhuska."

12. Bob Burke and Von Russell Creel, *Lyle Boren: Rebel Congressman,* (Oklahoma City: Oklahoma Heritage Association, 1991), p. 30.

CHAPTER TWO

1. DeVier Pierson interview.

2. Ibid.

3. Ibid.

4. Ibid.

5. Ibid.

6. Ibid.

7. Ibid.

8. Ibid.

9. Ibid.

10. Ibid.

11. Ibid.

12. Letter from Terry Diacon to Bob Burke, September 27, 2008, Heritage Archives.

13. Rules of Sports Club, 1939, Heritage Archives.

14. Minutes of Sports Club, August 25, 1943, Heritage Archives.

15. DeVier Pierson interview.

16. Ibid.

17. Transcription of the induction ceremonies of the Oklahoma Hall of Fame, November 12, 2002, Heritage Archives.

18. DeVier Pierson interview.

19. Ibid.

20. Ibid.

21. Ibid.

CHAPTER THREE

1. DeVier Pierson interview.

2. Ibid.

3. Interview with Mary Brett, February 4, 2009, Heritage Archives, hereafter referred to as Mary Brett interview.

4. Letter from William J. Ross to Bob Burke, January 7, 2009, Heritage Archives.

5. Junior High School speech of W. DeVier Pierson, Heritage Archives.

6. DeVier Pierson interview.

7. Ibid.

8. Ibid.

9. Ibid.

10. Ibid.

11. Ibid.

CHAPTER FOUR

1. DeVier Pierson interview.

2. Ibid.

3. Ibid.

4. *The Daily Oklahoman,* November 15, 1946.

5. DeVier Pierson interview.

6. Ibid.

7. Ibid.

8. Ibid.

9. Ibid.

10. Ibid.

CHAPTER FIVE

1. DeVier Pierson interview.

2. Letter from Pat Williams to Classen High School students, Heritage Archives.

3. DeVier Pierson interview.

4. Interview with Bill Robinson, January 19, 2009, Heritage Archives.

5. Letter from John Brock to Bob Burke, December 16, 2008, Heritage Archives.

6. Interview with Lee Thompson, Jr., January 23, 2009, Heritage Archives.

7. Interview with Tom Brett, February 5, 2009, Heritage Archives.

8. Mary Brett interview.

9. DeVier Pierson interview.

10. Ibid.

11. Ibid.

12. Ibid.

13. *The Daily Oklahoman,* January 23, 2005.

14. DeVier Pierson interview.

15. En.wikipedia.org/wiki/ James Dean.

16. Letter from C.E. Grady to Mr. and Mrs. W.D. Pierson and DeVier Pierson, May 2, 1949, Heritage Archives.

17. DeVier Pierson interview.

18. Ibid.

19. Ibid.

20. Ibid.

CHAPTER SIX

1. DeVier Pierson interview.

2. Ibid.

3. Ibid.

4. Ibid.

5. Ibid.

6. Ibid.

7. Letter from William Paul to Bob Burke, April 1, 2009, Heritage Archives. See also *Willie of the Valley: The Life of Bill Paul* (Oklahoma City: Oklahoma Heritage Association, 2006) by Bob Burke and Eric Dabney.

8. DeVier Pierson interview.

9. Ibid.

10. Ibid.

11. Ibid.

12. Ibid.

13. Ibid.

14. Ibid.

15. Ibid.

16. Ibid.

17. Ibid.

18. Ibid.

CHAPTER SEVEN

1. DeVier Pierson interview.

2. Ibid.

3. Ibid.

4. Ibid.

5. Ibid.

6. Ibid.

7. Ibid.

8. *The Daily Oklahoman,* March 4, 1955.

9. DeVier Pierson interview.

10. www.paulnoll.com/Korea/War/

11. DeVier Pierson interview.

12. Ibid.

13. Ibid.

14. Ibid.

15. Ibid.

16. Ibid.

17. Ibid.

18. Ibid.

19. Ibid.

CHAPTER EIGHT

1. Bob Burke, *Courage Counts: The Life of Larry Derryberry* (Oklahoma City: Oklahoma Heritage Association, 2003), p. 71. See also *The University of Oklahoma College of Law: A Centennial History* (Oklahoma City: Oklahoma Heritage Association, 2009) by Bob Burke and Steven Taylor.

2. DeVier Pierson interview.

3. Ibid.

4. Ibid.

5. Ibid.

6. Interview with Duke Logan, January 19, 2009, Heritage Archives, hereafter referred to as Duke Logan interview.

7. DeVier Pierson interview.

8. Ibid.

9. Letter from Lee West to Bob Burke, November 15, 2008, Heritage Archives.

10. Ibid.

11. Ibid.

12. Ibid.

13. Ibid.

14. Ibid., *Oklahoma City Times*, December 21, 1956.

15. Letter from William J. Holloway, Jr., to W.D. Pierson, January 3, 1957, Heritage Archives.

16. Letter from Lewis Ryan to W.D. Pierson, December 26, 1956, Heritage Archives.

17. Letter from Caradine Hooton to DeVier Pierson, January 10, 1957, Heritage Archives.

18. Letter from Ben Cameron to DeVier Pierson, February 14, 1957, Heritage Archives.

19. DeVier Pierson interview.

20. Ibid.

21. Ibid.

22. Ibid.

23. Ibid.

24. Ibid.

CHAPTER NINE

1. Interview with Shirley Pierson, February 2, 2009, Heritage Archives, hereafter referred to as Shirley Pierson interview.

2. DeVier Pierson interview.

3. Shirley Pierson interview.

4. DeVier Pierson interview.

5. Ibid.

6. Shirley Pierson interview.

7. Ibid.

8. DeVier Pierson interview.

9. Ibid.

10. Ibid.

11. Ibid.

12. Letter from Marian Opala to Bob Burke, December 18, 2008, Heritage Archives.

13. DeVier Pierson interview.

14. Ibid.

15. Ibid.

16. Ibid.

17. Ibid.

18. Ibid.

19. Ibid.

CHAPTER TEN

1. DeVier Pierson interview.

2. Ibid.

3. Ibid.

4. Ibid.

5. *The Journal Record*, November 20, 1993.

6. DeVier Pierson interview.

7. Ibid.

8. Ibid.

9. Ibid.

10. *The Daily Oklahoman*, November 4, 1960.

11. DeVier Pierson interview.

12. Ibid.

13. Ibid.

14. Ibid.

15. Ibid.

16. Ibid.

17. *The Daily Oklahoman*, February 6, 1964.

18. Ibid.

CHAPTER ELEVEN

1. DeVier Pierson interview.

2. Ibid.

3. Shirley Pierson interview.

4. Ibid.

5. Ibid.

6. *Oklahoma City Times*, May 31, 1965.

7. DeVier Pierson interview.

8. Ibid.

9. Ibid.

10. Ibid.

11. Ibid.

12. Ibid.

13. Ibid.

14. Ibid.

15. Ibid.

16. Final Report of the Joint Committee on the Organization of the Congress, U.S. Government Printing Office, 1966, p. 89, hereafter referred to as Joint Committee Final Report.

17. Ibid.

CHAPTER TWELVE

1. DeVier Pierson interview.

2. Ibid.

3. Ibid.

4. *The Daily Oklahoman*, February 10, 1967.

5. *The Daily Oklahoman*, February 17, 1967.

6. *Congressional Record*, March 7, 1967, p. S3289.

7. DeVier Pierson interview.

8. *Congressional Record*, p. S3294.

9. Ibid.

10. Shirley Pierson interview.

11. DeVier Pierson interview.

13. Letter from Mike Monroney, Jr., to Bob Burke, December 22, 2008, Heritage Archives.

14. DeVier Pierson interview.

CHAPTER THIRTEEN

1. DeVier Pierson interview.

2. Ibid.

3. Ibid.

4. Ibid.

5. Interview with Harry McPherson, February 9, 2009, Heritage Archives, hereafter referred to as Harry McPherson interview.

6. DeVier Pierson interview.

7. Harry McPherson interview.

8. DeVier Pierson interview.

9. Ibid.

10. Ibid.

11. Memorandum from DeVier Pierson to President Lyndon Johnson, December 1, 1967, Heritage Archives.

12. Memorandum from DeVier Pierson to President Lyndon Johnson, May 1, 1968, Heritage Archives.

13. Memorandum from DeVier Pierson to President Lyndon Johnson, July 27, 1968, Heritage Archives.

14. DeVier Pierson interview.

15. Ibid.

16. Ibid.

17. Ibid.

18. Ibid.

19. Ibid.

20. Ibid.

21. Ibid.

22. Ibid.

23. Ibid.

CHAPTER FOURTEEN

1. DeVier Pierson interview.

2. Ibid.

3. Ibid.

4. Ibid.

5. Ibid.

6. Ibid.

7. Ibid.

8. Ibid.

9. Ibid.

10. Ibid.

11. *Time Magazine*, January 12, 1968.

12. DeVier Pierson interview.

13. Ibid.

14. Ibid.

15. Memorandum from DeVier Pierson to President Lyndon B. Johnson, March 4, 1968, Heritage Archives.

16. Memorandum from DeVier Pierson to President Lyndon B. Johnson, March 9, 1968, Heritage Archives.

17. DeVier Pierson interview.

18. Memorandum from DeVier Pierson to President Lyndon B. Johnson, March 14, 1968, Heritage Archives.

18. Ibid.

19. DeVier Pierson interview.

20. Ibid.

21. Ibid.

22. Ibid.

23. Ibid.

24. Ibid.

25. Ibid.

CHAPTER FIFTEEN

1. DeVier Pierson interview.

2. Ibid.

3. Ibid.

4. Ibid.

5. Ibid.

6. White House log of presidential activity, June 5, 1968, National Archives.

7. DeVier Pierson interview.

8. White House log of presidential activity, June 5, 1968, National Archives.

9. Interview with DeVier Pierson by Dorothy McSweeny, March 27, 1969, Library of Congress.

10. DeVier Pierson interview.

11. Ibid.

12. Ibid.

13. Ibid.

14. *Tulsa Tribune*, September 27, 1968.

15. DeVier Pierson interview.

16. Memorandum from DeVier Pierson to President Lyndon Johnson, November 7, 1968, Heritage Archives.

CHAPTER SIXTEEN

1. DeVier Pierson interview.

2. Ibid.

3. Letter from James B. White to DeVier Pierson, January 19, 1968, Heritage Archives.

4. Duke Logan interview.

5. Marian Opala letter.

6. Letter from Larry Nichols to Bob Burke, December 15, 2008, Heritage Archives.

7. DeVier Pierson interview.

8. Ibid.

9. Ibid.

10. Ibid.

11. Ibid.

12. Ibid.

13. Shirley Pierson interview.

14. Ibid.

15. Ibid.

16. Ibid.

17. George Christian, *The President Steps Down*, New York: The Macmillan Company, 1970, p. 273.

18. DeVier Pierson interview.

19. Ibid.

20. Ibid.

21. Lyndon B. Johnson, *The Vantage Point*, New York: Holt, Rinehart, and Winston, 1971, p. 563.

22. DeVier Pierson interview.

CHAPTER SEVENTEEN

1. DeVier Pierson interview.

2. Ibid.

3. Ibid.

4. *Newsweek*, February 3, 1969.

5. DeVier Pierson interview.

6. *The Daily Oklahoman*, January 23, 1969.

7. *Newsweek*, February 3, 1969.

8. DeVier Pierson interview.

9. Ibid.

10. Ibid.

11. Ibid.

12. Letter from David Semmes to Bob Burke, December 16, 2009, Heritage Archives.

13. Interview with Knox Bemis, January 16, 2009, Heritage Archives, hereafter referred to as Knox Bemis interview.

14. DeVier Pierson interview.

15. Ibid.

16. Ibid.

17. Ibid.

18. Ibid.

19. Ibid.

20. Ibid.

21. Ibid.

22. Ibid.

23. Ibid.

CHAPTER EIGHTEEN

1. DeVier Pierson interview.

2. Ibid.

3. *Congressional Record*, October 14, 1970.

4. Ibid.

5. DeVier Pierson interview.

CHAPTER NINETEEN

1. DeVier Pierson interview.

2. Ibid.

3. Ibid.

4. Ibid.

5. Ibid.

6. Ibid.

7. Ibid.

8. Ibid.

9. Ibid.

10. Ibid.

11. Ibid.

12. Ibid.

13. Interview with Peter Levin, February 3, 2009, Heritage Archives, hereafter referred to as Peter Levin interview.

14. DeVier Pierson interview.

15. Ibid.

16. DeVier Pierson interview.

17. Ibid.

18. Ibid.

CHAPTER TWENTY

1. Peter Levin interview.

2. DeVier Pierson interview.

3. Ibid.

4. Ibid.

5. Interview with Hugh Roff, February 5, 2009, Heritage Archives, hereafter referred to as Hugh Roff interview.

6. DeVier Pierson interview.

7. Ibid.

8. Hugh Roff interview.

9. *Legal Times*, September 10, 1984.

10. Hugh Roff interview.

11. Ibid.

12. DeVier Pierson interview.

13. Ibid.

14. Ibid.

15. Ibid.

CHAPTER TWENTY-ONE

1. Interview with Harry McPherson, February 9, 2009, Heritage Archives, hereafter referred to as Harry McPherson interview.

2. DeVier Pierson interview.

3. Interview with Elliott Abrams, February 4, 2009, Heritage Archives, hereafter referred to as Elliott Abrams interview.

4. Elliott Abrams, *Undue Process, A Story of How Political Differences Are Turned Into Crimes*. New York: Free Press, 1992, p. 21, hereafter referred to as *Undue Process*.

5. DeVier Pierson interview.

6. Ibid.

7. *The Legal Times*, June 8, 1987.

8. Ibid.

9. DeVier Pierson interview.

10. *The Daily Oklahoman*, June 4, 1987.

11. DeVier Pierson interview.

12. Ibid.

13. *Undue Process*, p. 16-17.

14. DeVier Pierson interview.

15. Ibid.

16. *Undue Process*, p. 61.

17. DeVier Pierson interview.

18. *Undue Process*, p. 203.

19. DeVier Pierson interview.

20. Ibid.

21. Ibid.

22. Elliott Abrams interview.

CHAPTER TWENTY-TWO

1. DeVier Pierson interview.

2. Interview with Dale Laurance, February 27, 2009, Heritage Archives, hereafter referred to as Dale Laurance interview.

3. Ibid.

4. DeVier Pierson interview.

5. Ibid.

6. Ibid.

7. Interview with Donald deBrier, January 16, 2009, Heritage Archives, hereafter referred to as Donald deBrier interview.

8. DeVier Pierson interview.

9. Dale Laurance interview.

10. DeVier Pierson interview.

11. Ibid.

CHAPTER TWENTY-THREE

1. Ibid.

2. DeVier Pierson interview.

3. Ibid.

4. Ibid.

5. Ibid.

6. Ibid.

7. Ibid.

8. Ibid.

9. Ibid.

10. Ibid.

11. Interview with Oliver Howard, January 5, 2009, Heritage Archives, hereafter referred to as Oliver Howard interview.

12. DeVier Pierson interview.

13. Oliver Howard interview.

14. DeVier Pierson interview.

15. Ibid.

16. Ibid.

17. The Oklahoma Supreme Court decision was handed down in Case Number 87,979, from the District Court of Tulsa, County, Oklahoma, C-82-1998.

18. DeVier Pierson interview.

19. Ibid.

20. Letter from Darrel Kelsey to Bob Burke, January 9, 2009, Heritage Archives.

21. Letter from Joseph W. Morris to Bob Burke, January 19, 2009, Heritage Archives.

22. DeVier Pierson interview.

23. Ibid.

24. Ibid.

CHAPTER TWENTY-FOUR

1. DeVier Pierson interview.

2. Ibid.

3. Ibid.

4. Ibid.

CHAPTER TWENTY-FIVE

1. DeVier Pierson.

2. *Tulsa World*, June 15, 1969., DeVier Pierson interview.

3. Letter from Edmund Muskie to DeVier Pierson, May 4, 1972, Heritage Archives.

4. DeVier Pierson interview.

5. Ibid.

6. Ibid.

7. Ibid.

8. Ibid.

9. Ibid.

10. Ibid.

11. Ibid.

12. Eulogy delivered at funeral of Mike Monroney, February 16, 1980, Heritage Archives.

13. Letter from Harry Byrd, Jr., to DeVier Pierson, February 19, 1980, Heritage Archives.

14. Letter from Allan Cromley to DeVier Pierson, Feburary 19, 1980, Heritage Archives.

15. Ibid.

CHAPTER TWENTY-SIX

1. DeVier Pierson.

2. Ibid.

3. Ibid.

4. Ibid.

5. Interview with Jack Merritt, February 25, 2009, Heritage Archives.

6. DeVier Pierson interview.

7. Ibid.

8. Ibid.

9. Ibid.

10. Ibid.

11. Ibid.

12. Ibid.

13. Ibid.

14. Ibid.

15. Ibid.

16. DeVier Pierson speech to The American Inns of Court, Tulsa, Oklahoma, chapter, May 11, 2001, Heritage Archives.

CHAPTER TWENTY-SEVEN

1. DeVier Pierson interview.

2. Ibid.

3. Ibid.

4. Ibid.

5. Ibid.

6. Ibid.

7. Ibid.

8. Ibid.

9. Ibid.

10. Ibid.

11. Ibid.

12. DeVier Pierson interview.

13. Ibid.

14. Ibid.

15. Jack Merritt interview.

16. DeVier Pierson interview.

CHAPTER TWENTY-EIGHT

1. DeVier Pierson speech to graduating class of OU College of Law, 1975, Heritage Archives.

2. DeVier Pierson interview.

3. Ibid.

4. Interview with Dan Hogan, February 20, 2009, Heritage Archives, hereafter referred to as Dan Hogan interview.

5. Ibid.

6. DeVier Pierson speech to OU Associates, May 14, 1994, Heritage Archives.

7. DeVier Pierson interview.

8. Letter from David Boren to Bob Burke, January 15, 2009, Heritage Archives.

9. Letter from Paul Massad to Bob Burke, January 21, 2009, Heritage Archives.

10. Letter from Andy Coats to Bob Burke, December 10, 2008, Heritage Archives.

11. Letter from Steven Taylor to Bob Burke, December 14, 2008, Heritage Archives.

12. Interview with G.T. Blankenship, December 22, 2008, Heritage Archives.

13. Letter from Robert Henry to Bob Burke, December 1, 2009, Heritage Archives.

14. DeVier Pierson interview.

15. Ibid.

16. Letter from R.C. Davis-Undiano to Bob Burke, January 6, 2009, Heritage Archives.

17. Ibid.

18. DeVier Pierson interview.

19. Ibid.

20. Ibid.

21. Ibid.

CHAPTER TWENTY-NINE

1. DeVier Pierson interview.

2. Ibid.

3. Shirley Pierson interview.

4. Interview with Ed de-Cordova, January 16, 2009, Heritage Archives.

5. Ibid.

6. DeVier Pierson interview.

7. Shirley Pierson interview.

8. Ibid.

9. Ibid.

10. DeVier Pierson interview.

11. Ibid.

12. Ibid.

13. Shirley Pierson interview.

14. DeVier Pierson interview.

15. Interview with Lee Allan Smith, January 6, 2008, Heritage Archives, hereafter referred to as the Lee Allan Smith interview.

16. DeVier Pierson interview.

17. Shirley Pierson interview.

18. Shirley Pierson interview.

19. Interview with David and Mary Beth Busby, January 16, 2009, Heritage Archives.

20. Ibid.

21. Letter from Richard Burpee to Bob Burke, December 15, 2008, Heritage Archives.

22. Shirley Pierson interview.

23. DeVier Pierson interview.

24. Ibid.

25. Ibid.

26. Ibid.

27. Ibid.

28. Interview with Sarah Hogan, February 20, 2009, Heritage Archives.

29. Shirley Pierson interview.

30. Ibid.

31. Ibid.

32. Ibid.

33. Ibid.

34. Ibid.

35. DeVier Pierson interview.

36. Ibid.

37. Ibid.

38. Shirley Pierson interview.

CHAPTER THIRTY

1. DeVier Pierson interview.

2. DeVier Pierson eulogy of Tom Finney, February 2, 1978, Heritage Archives.

3. Shirley Pierson interview.

4. DeVier Pierson eulogy at funeral of Paul Frost, Allie Reynolds, Jr., and Michael Reynolds, May 9, 1978, Heritage Archives.

5. Marta McGee interview.

6. Ibid.

7. DeVier Pierson at funeral of Barbara Bevers, September 23, 1982, Heritage Archives.

8. DeVier Pierson interview.

9. Ibid.

10. Shirley Pierson interview.

11. Letter from Randy Everest to Bob Burke, January 15, 2009, Heritage Archives.

12. Letter from John Drake to Bob Burke, January 6, 2009, Heritage Archives.

13. Teresa Adwan interview.

14. DeVier Pierson eulogy at funeral of Paul Karl Frost, October 22, 1991, Heritage Archives.

15. DeVier Pierson eulogy at funeral of Allie Reynolds, December 30, 1994, Heritage Archives.

16. DeVier Pierson eulogy at funeral of Carrie Alice Phelps Frost, July 5, 2001, Heritage Archives.

17. Ibid.

18. Interview with Coleen Evans, March 16, 2009, Heritage Archives.

19. Ibid.

20. DeVier Pierson interview.

21. Ibid.

22. Ibid.

23. Ibid.

24. DeVier Pierson eulogy at funeral of Admiral William J. Crowe, Jr., October 31, 2007, Heritage Archives.

25. DeVier Pierson interview.

INDEX

A

Abel, I.W. 191-192
Abrams, Elliott 211-219, 262
Abrams, Rachel 217-218
Acheson, Dean 277
Adams, Arlin 223
Adams, John 259-260
Adwan, Teresa 327
Albert, Carl 255-256
Albright, Madeline 267
Alcott, Louisa May 21
Alexander, Cliff 131
Alley, Wayne 226
Alpha Chi Omega 13, 244
Alpha Omegas 35
American Airlines 166
American Bar Association 52, 211, 244
American Gas Association 185, 207
American Inns of Court 282, 292
Amundsen, Earl 48, 88
Andrews Air Force Base 174, 264
Anthony, C.R. 26
Anti-Dumping Act 194
Arnold, Claude 54, 313
Arnold, Nancy 313
Ashe, Arthur 301
Atlantic Council 277
Auvergne Demolays 35-36

B

Baker & Botts 185, 195-196
Baker, Howard 264
Baker, James 118
Barnes, Sam 330
Barr, Joe 157
Bartlett, Ann 254-255
Bartlett, Dewey 254-255
Bartlett, Ely 185
Barton, Jerry 73
Bauer, Gary 219
Baylor University 40
Bayonet Bowl 69-70
Beacon Club 86

Bellmon, Henry 162, 188, 254
Bemis, Knox 179-180, 195, 231, 236, 270, 275
Bernhard, Berl 250
Berry, Jim 88
Bethesda Naval Hospital 335
Bevers, Barbara 96, 325-326
Bevers, Bill 54, 56, 73, 96, 98, 294, 326-327
Bevers, Stan 294
Black Bart's 311
Blankenship, G.T. 73, 287-288, 293, 311, 313
Blankenship, Libby 313
Blue Jackets 41
Boggs, J. Caleb 112, 124
Boggs, Tommy 175
Boren, David L. 170, 215, 256, 258, 284-288, 305
Boren, Molly 311
Bork, Robert 219
Boyd, Alan 167
Boyd House 258, 311
Boyd, Alan 127, 137
Bozalis, John 336
Braniff Airlines 107
Brett, Mary James 24, 30, 42, 311
Brett, Mrs. John 35-36
Brett, Thomas R. 24, 36, 42, 73, 223, 290, 293, 311
Breyer, Stephen 287
Brock, John 36, 42, 293
Brown v. Board of Education 34
Brown, Bobby 328
Browne, Henry 74
Browne, Kelsey 47, 74
Browne, Virgil 26
Bryant, David 231
Bureau of the Budget 136
Burning Tree Club 251, 303
Burns, John 126
Burpee, Richard 306
Burzio, John 127
Busby, David 101, 126-127, 176, 298, 301, 335
Busby, Jack 306

Busby, Mary Beth 127, 298, 301
Busby, Robert 306
Bush v. Gore 292
Bush, Barbara 265-266
Bush, George H.W. 174, 219, 259-260, 264-266, 283
Bush, George W. 117, 219
Buttram Oratorical Contest 30-31
Buttram, Frank 26
Buxton, Fred 86, 294
Buxton, Nan 86, 294
Byrd High School 40
Byrd, Harry, Jr. 256-257

C

Califano, Joseph 128, 130, 157, 166
Cameron, Ben 81
Camp Classen 25, 30
Camp Kickapoo 30
Camp Little Wolf 30
Canal Square Building 180
Carlisle Barracks 261
Carnegie, Andrew 273-274
Carter, Doug 135
Carter, Jimmy 253-254
Casady School 282
Case, Clifford 112
Casey, William 263
Cassin, Bill 202, 303
Catlett, Jack 49, 96, 296
Catlett, Joanie 96
Central High School 34, 36
Central Intelligence Agency 210
Chandler, Stephen 93
Chase Bank 298
Cheatham Furniture Manufacturing Company 98-99
Cheney, Dick 219
Cherokee Outlet 9-11
Chevron 228, 323, 240
Christ Episcopal Church 308
Christian, George 330
Christopher, Warren 118, 267
Churchill, Winston 27

Cities Service Company 221-241
Cities v. Gulf 228-241, 269
City Tavern Club 259-260, 270, 287
Civil Aeronautics Board 73, 166
Clark, Jerry 271
Clark, Joseph 115-116
Clark, Ramsey 160
Clarkson, Harry 67
Classen High School 34-48, 85, 282, 331
Clay, Roger Bob 19-20, 30, 35
Clements, Dick 49
Cleveland, James 112
Clifford, Clark 146-151, 161-162, 165, 176, 179, 267, 323
Clift, Montgomery 64
Clinton, Bill 131, 142, 219, 239, 266-269, 292, 336
Coats, Andy 286-287, 290
Coats, Dan 271
Cold War 210
Cole, Nat King 64
Coleman, Barbara 96
Coleman, Jack 96
Collier Award 109
Collins, Everett 105
Colorado College 302
Columbian Chemicals Company 222
Congressional Record 257
Connally's Men's Wear 74-76
Continental Trend Resources, Inc. 224
Corbett, Jack 289
Corr, Ed 262-263
Cosmos Club 308
Costan, Jay 271
Cotton, Doyle 202, 303
Cox, John 37-38, 40-43, 48, 50, 88
Crocker, John 166-167
Crolius, Theodore 179
Cromley, Allan 257, 305
Cromley, Marian 305
Cross, Dr. George L. 57-58, 81
Crowder, Eddie 49, 51, 54